WORKING-CLASS LIVES
IN EDWARDIAN HARROGATE

WORKING-CLASS LIVES IN
Edwardian
HARROGATE

Paul Jennings

First published in 2021
by Palatine Books,
Carnegie House,
Chatsworth Road
Lancaster LA1 4SL
www.palatinebooks.com

British Library Cataloguing-in-Publication data
A catalogue record for this book is available from the British Library

Paperback ISBN 13: 978-1-910837-37-5

Designed and typeset by Carnegie Book Production
www.carnegiebookproduction.com

Printed and bound by Halstan

To my mum and dad

Contents

List of Illustrations

Preface and Acknowledgements

THE ORIGINS of this book are twofold. First, I wanted to return to a detailed local study after books which took a broad view of their subject: *The Local: A History of the English Pub* (2007) and *A History of Drink and the English, 1500–2000* (2016). That first local study had looked at *The Public House in Bradford, 1770–1970* (1995), the city where I was born, in which I grew up and where I later again worked in university adult education. So too in this book I wanted to look at the town, Harrogate, in which we have lived now for some twenty-three years. Second, its subject matter was suggested to me from sympathy as a historian with the history of so-called ordinary men and women and the realization that those of the famous spa of Harrogate had hitherto been neglected in writing on the town. More prosaically, I had always been amused by the common reaction to the information on where we lived that we must be 'posh' to do so.

During the years of research, I have incurred many debts which I should like to acknowledge here. I thank the staff of Harrogate Library; Leeds General Reference Library; Cambridge University Library; and the Marshall Economics Library, Cambridge. I thank also staff at North Yorkshire County Council Record Office, Northallerton; West Yorkshire Archive Service at Leeds; and Hull History Centre. For access to records held by them and hospitality during my visits I thank the Chief Solicitor of Harrogate Borough Council; the heads of Grove Road Community Primary School, Oatlands Infant School, St Robert's Catholic Primary School, Starbeck Community Primary School and Western Primary School; and the following churches: Harlow Hill Free Methodist; St Wilfrid's Parochial Church Council; Trinity Wesleyan; and the Wesley Centre. I thank also the Registrar at the North Yorkshire County Register Office, Harrogate for research assistance. For information, discussion and hospitality I thank Bilton Historical Society, Malcolm Neesam and Terry Williams of the New Park Heritage Centre. Help and information along the way were also given by Valerie Chadwick, Enid Rispin and the late Mike Hine. For photographic assistance I thank James Smith and my sons Albert and Frank and for the map of Edwardian Harrogate, William Sutherland.

For reading and commenting on work in progress I thank Stephen Caunce, Ray Greenough, John Jackson, Felicity Jennings, Donna Melia, Malcolm Neesam, Dave Russell, George Sheeran, Zoe Thomas and Geoff Timmins. Of course, only I am responsible for any errors or shortcomings the book contains. Above all, I thank my family for their love and support.

Paul Jennings
Harrogate, June 2020.

Abbreviations used in references and bibliography

HA	*Harrogate Advertiser*
HH	*Harrogate Herald*
NYCCRO	North Yorkshire County Council Record Office
PP	Parliamentary Papers

As prices and wages are given in pre-decimal currency, it may be helpful to give decimal currency equivalents:

6*d*.	=	2½p
12*d*. (1*s*.)	=	5p
2*s*.	=	10p
10*s*.	=	50p
15*s*.	=	75p
20*s*.	=	£1
One guinea	=	£1.05

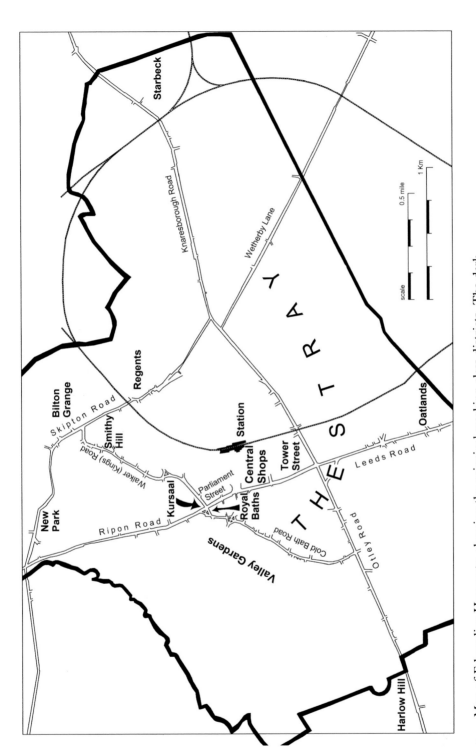

1.   Map of Edwardian Harrogate, showing the principal working-class districts. The dark line is the borough boundary. (Drawn by William Sutherland RIAS RIBA for the author.)

Introduction

EDWARDIAN HARROGATE enjoyed both a national and international reputation as an exclusive health and leisure resort. As one English newspaper reported in June of 1913, 'there are many thousands of people in England who regularly at this time of year turn their eyes to Harrogate'. Over in Europe, the readers of Berlin's leading newspaper were told that it was 'probably unassailable in its position as the leading Spa'. Across the Atlantic, the *New York Times* similarly advised those planning a European tour in the spring of 1914 that, along with the newly refurbished Tower of London, Harrogate was the place to visit.[1] The town itself had no doubts about its prestige. Its two newspapers, the *Harrogate Advertiser* and *Harrogate Herald*, were always keen to laud its success, regularly noting the breaking of records for the numbers of those arriving for its celebrated waters: in August 1910, for example, ending a report with this prophecy: 'Harrogate has a fine past, but the future promises not only to be brilliant, but unbounded.'[2]

The town's workers were an essential part of that success, yet many contemporaries seem not to have noticed them. According to an editorial in the *Advertiser* in January 1906, visitors had 'frequently remarked upon the absence of any signs of poverty and the apparent dearth of the working-class element'. Writer A. A. Thomson, who grew up in the town and fictionalized it as Nidvale, from the river which flows to the north, in his 1935 novel *The Exquisite Burden*, could characterize it as containing 'a bare minimum of "working" inhabitants'. But that *Advertiser* editorial, under the heading 'Harrogate's Unemployed', offered a corrective to such views, for 'if those classes do not flaunt their misfortune or existence before the world at large, yet they are present all the same'.[3] A similar situation inspired a contemporary study of another place not usually associated with its working men and women – Cambridge. In 1906, Eglantyne Jebb, an Oxford-educated woman from a well-to-do background who went on to found the Save the Children Fund, published a study of the university town, where she then lived, which declared that whereas previous histories and guides had focused on its colleges, churches and eminent men, she wished to know 'something of the lives of the many as well as the few'.[4]

This book seeks to do the same for the working class in Harrogate. A modern history described them as those without whose labour the town's 'middle-class world' could not function and identified five main elements which comprised it. These were the hotel servants and those employed in ancillary enterprises ranging from livery stables to laundries; shop assistants and the craft workers employed in tailoring, dressmaking or millinery; domestic servants; railway workers; and those in the building trades, together with the men in sawmills, brickworks and quarries.[5] But the book goes on to provide only a brief discussion of some one-and-a-half pages. This neglect of working people in resorts is true generally. A rare study, of the Welsh spa town of Llandrindod Wells, noted 'a significant gap in the historiography in regard to the workers in these towns'.[6] Another, of Bath, commented how the working class there 'have been so discreetly camouflaged into becoming mere appendages of the genteel class that it is akin to discovering new territory'.[7] There have been more studies of seaside towns but, with the exception of John K. Walton's study of *The Blackpool Landlady*, they share this neglect, with workers appearing rather as visitors.[8]

It is to fiction that we must turn for the most famous depiction of workers in a resort town. This is Robert Tressell's *The Ragged Trousered Philanthropists*, completed in 1909 and published in 1914. His Mugsborough, although not itself a seaside town, was based on the genteel coastal resort of Hastings and his experience there of the building trade. At various points in my research on Harrogate I was reminded irresistibly of his town: the close links between employers and the town council, for example, or the charitable efforts of the well-to-do at times of economic distress. His work is, of course, a novel, whose 'main object was to write a readable story full of human interest', but one whose portrait of a town and its working class, for all its limitations of characterization and plot, provided a further inspiration for this history.[9]

As a historian I was influenced by the efforts of those who, since the 1960s and 1970s, have sought to explore 'history from below', the worlds of so-called ordinary men and women rather than the wealthy and powerful. An enormous amount of work has indeed been done towards that aim since then, covering many aspects of people's lives, from work and family to leisure and religion. But much remains to be explored, including their lives in the kind of town I have chosen. It rests too in a belief in the value of detailed local study. This allows a more in-depth examination of the subject, which may be used either to confirm or contest existing generalizations. It may also reveal new themes or questions, which may not always be discernible at a more general level.[10] It recognizes, as Asa Briggs asserted in relation to Victorian cities, the individuality of places.[11] The local context was vital in shaping developments and in turn helps us to understand how society worked. Indeed, the need for more attention to local and regional variation in workers' lives has been called for in a recent survey of twentieth-century labour histories.[12]

For the necessary detail I have used a range of sources. Principal among them were the censuses of 1901 and 1911, both the published reports and the returns, which provide details of all of Harrogate's inhabitants on census night. These enabled me to create a working-class population and permitted analysis, for example, of patterns of employment, household structure, migration and residence. It was also possible to trace individuals to earlier censuses, and to other sources, using the facility offered commercially by Ancestry. I also used newspapers, trade directories, school and church and chapel records, the registers of baptisms and marriages and the records of the borough council. One source, however, that was lacking for my Edwardians was the oral testimony used in several works on the period, notably Paul Thompson's *The Edwardians*.[13] I have drawn upon those works, together with some published memories of childhood and school days in Harrogate and the recollections of descendants of several residents.

The book then seeks to present a portrait of working-class life in a certain type of town and to say something more broadly about working-class people and their place in Edwardian society. Why, finally, is the focus on those years before the First World War? First, the period, generally taken to be the years from Edward VII's accession to the throne in 1901 and beyond his death in 1910 to the outbreak of war in 1914, has been viewed as Harrogate's heyday. For Thomson, his Nidvale 'basked in the Autumn of its perfection'. To a modern local historian, Malcolm Neesam, this was its 'Edwardian High Summer'. He cited, for example, the 'exceptionally brilliant year of 1911' and some of the British and foreign royalty who visited, together with the 'usual smattering of cabinet ministers, archdukes and maharajas'. As he expressed it: 'Never had the town been so rich and elegant ... never had the future looked so bright.'[14] Certainly there is much to support that glowing picture. Several of its most notable buildings had been, or were, completed at this time. The Royal Baths had been opened in 1897, 'the last word in scientific hydrotherapy and luxury'.[15] A Kursaal, or 'cure hall', deriving its name from continental practice, was opened in 1902. Two years earlier an opera house had been completed. Several existing hotels were remodelled and two huge new ones opened: appropriately the Majestic and the Grand. The town had shared in the great national building boom of the 1890s and, in recognition, its boundaries were substantially enlarged in 1900. Beyond Harrogate those years have also been viewed as a golden age before the horrors of war. But they were also difficult ones: of labour unrest, to which Harrogate was not immune; the bitter struggle over the powers of the House of Lords; a militant women's suffrage campaign; the threat of civil war in Ireland; and a darkening international scene.

The book is structured as follows. Chapter 1 surveys how Harrogate had developed as a spa from the first published discovery of its waters in the late sixteenth century up to that Edwardian heyday. It outlines too how it became a residential town, an important retail centre and home to a range of private schools and other institutions. Since this is a book about the working class, Chapter 2 examines the question of class and how it has been studied by historians and explains how I created a working-class population from the census, before outlining some of the general features of working life in the town and key working-class institutions. Chapters 3 and 4 then look in detail at those workers: who they were, the jobs they performed, for what pay and under what conditions. The next four chapters go on to examine several aspects of working-class life. Chapter 5 looks at their neighbourhoods, homes and health. Chapter 6 examines the family and household, including the then common practice of taking in lodgers, ending with those on the margins of society in common lodging houses or sleeping rough. The domestic economy – who earned what and what they needed to spend to live - is detailed and some assessment made of living standards, ending with those periods of unemployment which caused real distress in the town. Chapter 7 focuses on the children, particularly their experience of school and immediate futures on leaving. Finally, Chapter 8 looks at children's play, including that which fell foul of the law, before examining how adults found amusement. It then assesses the part organized religion in the town's many churches and chapels played in working-class lives.

Notes to Introduction

1 M. Neesam, *History & Guide Harrogate: A history of the English Spa from earliest times to the present* (2001), pp. 68 and 77.

2 *HA*, 13 August 1910, p. 2.

3 *HA*, 27 January 1906, p. 2; A. A. Thomson, *The Exquisite Burden* (2003), p. 24.

4 E. Jebb, *Cambridge: A brief study in social questions* (1906), p. 2.

5 B. Jennings (ed.), *A History of Harrogate & Knaresborough* (1970), pp. 425–6.

6 S. Lewis, '"A Resort of the Common People in Great Troops" – Llandrindod Wells Spa and its workers in the late nineteenth and twentieth centuries', *Transactions of the Radnorshire Society*, 76 (2006), pp. 144–67.

7 G. Davis, '"The Scum of Bath": The Victorian poor', in B. Stapleton (ed.), *Conflict and Continuity in Southern England: Essays in the social history of rural and urban labour from medieval to modern times* (1992), pp. 183–98.

8 J. Walton, *The Blackpool Landlady* (1978).

9 R. Tressell, *The Ragged Trousered Philanthropists* (2004), and 'Introduction' by T. Hunt, p. xi. Tressell was the pseudonym of Robert Noonan or Croker, it is uncertain which.

10 J. K. Walton and J. Walvin (eds), *Leisure in Britain, 1780–1939* (1983), p. 2; P. J. Waller, *Town, City and Nation: England, 1850–1914* (1983), pp. 10–11.

11 A. Briggs, *Victorian Cities* (1968), p. 34.

12 M. Chase, 'Twentieth-century labour histories', in C. Dyer *et al.*, *New Directions in Local History Since Hoskins* (2011), pp. 54–65.

13 P. Thompson, *The Edwardians: The remaking of British society* (1975).

14 Thomson, *Exquisite Burden*, p. 24; Neesam, *History*, Ch. 5 and M. Neesam, *Exclusively Harrogate* (1989), p. 82.

15 Neesam, *Exclusively Harrogate*, p. 60.

CHAPTER ONE

The Creation of Edwardian Harrogate

*A*RX *CELEBRIS* *FONTIBUS* was the motto registered for the newly created Borough of Harrogate in 1884. It signified, in the words of Richard Carter, brother of the first mayor, Nicholas, as they presented to the Corporation a gold municipal chain and badge of office: 'an elevated plateau, celebrated for its springs'.[1] Usually translated as 'a citadel famous for its springs', it was to their presence, according to the nineteenth-century historian of the town, William Grainge, that 'the origin, progress, and present state of Harrogate' were 'entirely owing'.[2] Their mere presence, however, was not the reason for Harrogate's growth. They had to be successfully publicized and exploited and a paying public attracted to 'take' them. The infrastructure of a spa town needed to be developed: the pump rooms, baths, entertainment facilities and accommodations. This chapter outlines that process before setting out how, later in the nineteenth century, on the basis of the successful spa, the town also became a residential and commuter hub, an important regional retail centre and a base for a range of institutions such as private schools, hospitals, convalescent homes and orphanages.

It is with the waters that we must begin. They were many and varied. Within a radius of two miles of the town centre some eighty-eight springs came to the surface, although fewer were used medicinally. They fell into two main groups: chalybeate, or iron, and sulphur waters. Of the former were two springs in particular – the Tewit and St John's Wells – both at High Harrogate. Of the latter in Low Harrogate, originally a separate

7

settlement, the qualities of the Old Sulphur Well, or 'Stincking Spaw', were vividly described by the gentlewoman traveller Celia Fiennes as having a 'Smell ... so strong and offensive that I could not force my horse near ...'[3] Beginning with that Tewit Well, they were publicized from the turn of the seventeenth century, from when the modern spa dates. Indeed, the term English Spa was first applied to Harrogate, after the town of Spa in the then Spanish Netherlands, present-day Belgium. Although waters had been utilized since Roman times, notably of course the thermal ones at Bath, the therapeutic value of mineral waters was now set out in a growing number of publications.[4] This value was claimed to be considerable. Edmund Deane in his *Spadacrene Anglica or the English Spa Fountain* of 1626, the first such work on the local waters, covered everything from cancers, skin complaints, epilepsy, or the 'falling sickness' as it was known, ringworms, headaches and migraines, melancholia to infertility, among many ailments.[5]

Since the waters were the source of Harrogate's success it was of course crucial that their exploitation be secured. When the Royal Forest of Knaresborough, which included the Harrogate area, was enclosed by an act of parliament of 1770, the Duchy of Lancaster agreed that those areas where the springs were found be protected so as not to harm the interests of the innkeepers, and the farmers who supplied them, who derived 'great advantage' from the 'great variety of genteel company' coming for the benefit of their waters. In this way was created the 200-acre Stray, which in a great arc of open grassland took in the springs of both High and Low Harrogate. In the words of the final Award following the enclosure act:

> ... the said two hundred acres of land shall forever hereafter remain open and unenclosed and all persons whomsoever shall and may have free access at all times to the said springs and be at liberty to use and drink the waters there arising and take the benefit thereof without being subject to the payment of any acknowledgement whatsoever ...[6]

The wells were provided with suitable and attractive facilities from public subscriptions. Those at High Harrogate had been protected with stone basins, the St John's Well also having a pump room built over it. Then a meeting in 1807 of 'Gentlemen, innholders and inhabitants' concerned to protect the Sulphur Well at Low Harrogate, led to the erection the following year of a new pump room consisting of a dome supported by twelve stone columns. In addition to those public places, wells also were developed on private land. Two chalybeate wells were now discovered, also in Low Harrogate close to the road to Ripon, the second named the Cheltenham Spring from the similarity of its water. In 1822, Joseph Thackwray, the owner of the Crown Hotel, which was adjacent to the Sulphur Well, discovered another source of this water, erected over it a pump room in Chinese style and laid out pleasure gardens. It was Thackwray too who further developed provision for the long-established practice of bathing in the waters with the building in those gardens of the Crown or Montpellier Baths in the mid-1830s. These had been preceded by another private development, of the Victoria Baths behind the Crescent Hotel, also nearby in Low Harrogate.[7]

It was the threat posed by a private development to the public supply, by Thackwray digging a new well on his Crown property, which set in train further moves by the innkeepers and others whose livelihood depended on the public wells to protect them. This became linked to a concern to drain and improve the Stray, also for the wider benefit of the town and visitors. The resulting Improvement Act of 1841, emerging from discussions between the inhabitants and the Duchy of Lancaster, which owned the freehold of the Stray and much of the town, in the event went beyond this protection to create a new local government body. Twenty-one Improvement Commissioners now had powers not only to protect the mineral wells and to make and enforce bylaws for the Stray but also over roads and footpaths, sewerage, law and order and such matters as the licensing of hackney carriages.[8] This body then erected over the public Sulphur Well a much more substantial Royal Pump Room, which opened in 1842. (2) This building, which could hold 150 people, offered the water by sale or subscription but a free pump was also set up on its outside wall. In the same year the two wells at High Harrogate were also provided with new covers but it was the Royal Pump Room which by now was much the more important source.[9]

The Improvement Commission was at first dominated by the town's innkeepers, who remained content with this provision for taking the sulphur water. Further moves to improve facilities were prompted by

2.   The Royal Pump Room, built over the Old Sulphur Well in
1842, photographed in 1911. To the right is the Crown Hotel.
(Courtesy the Francis Frith Collection)

a shift in the dominance of that body to the town's shopkeepers and
builders. A New Victoria Baths was opened in 1871, the Commissioners
having bought the old baths, with eighteen bathrooms together with
facilities for shower and vapour baths. Underground reservoirs could
hold 200,000 gallons of sulphur water drawn from springs on the site
and from the aptly named Bogs Field, where more springs rose to the
surface, situated a short distance to the south-west. But it was the new
Harrogate Corporation, established in 1884, which took the step of
creating a new, larger baths which would be able to accommodate the
much wider range of bathing facilities and treatments by then available.
It was by so doing that Harrogate was able to maintain its position as a
leading international spa, where other hydros like Ilkley, for example, also

3. The Royal Baths, opened in 1897, 'the last word in scientific hydrotherapy and luxury', photographed in 1911. Parliament Street can be seen to the left. (Courtesy the Francis Frith Collection)

in Yorkshire, experienced decline.[10] These Royal Baths were opened in 1897. (3) The building contained four large suites of baths, accessed from a central hall, where for drinkers a choice of mineral waters was offered. Nearly forty different kinds of baths were provided, using a variety of waters, peat and electricity, for a wide range of cases, notably gout, rheumatism, arthritis, sciatica, lumbago, skin diseases and neurasthenia. There was also a glass-roofed Winter Gardens.[11] At the same time, it was proposed to rebuild the original Pump Room but disagreement among councillors over a perceived threat to the waters by development and the desirability of demolishing such a historic structure ended instead with the construction of a light-weight annexe of iron and glass which opened in 1913.[12]

Whilst the 'health imperative' was crucial to the development of spas, there were other attractions. They also offered, in the words of a study of European spas generally, 'the pleasurable fruits of civilization': of food, drink, dancing, sociability and shopping in a fashionable location.[13] From the first, Harrogate also catered for those desires. In the earlier years of the spa social diversions were centred on inns like the Granby, Queen or Dragon at High Harrogate or the Crown at Low Harrogate: tea and dining, public balls and gambling. In 1806 a purpose-built Promenade Room was opened close to the Sulphur Well, a venue also for balls, musical recitals, lectures and card parties. Temporary theatres were succeeded by a permanent building at High Harrogate in 1788. Subscription libraries catered for quieter moments. Outdoors, a racecourse was laid out on the Stray in 1793 and archery competitions were also held. Hunting was pursued in the surrounding countryside, which also offered opportunities for sightseeing, including the famous Dropping Well at nearby Knaresborough, the romantic ruins of Fountains Abbey and the striking forms of Brimham Rocks.[14]

Those pleasures continued but over the course of the nineteenth century were considerably expanded. The Royal Cheltenham Spa and Concert Room was opened in 1835 with a ballroom and pleasure gardens. There were further developments there in the mid-1860s with a new terrace and improvements to the grounds and then the original pump room was replaced by a glass and iron wing with pump rooms and a covered promenade. The former Promenade Room was converted to a theatre. There were three other halls, offering a variety of entertainments, and in 1911 the Empire Music Hall opened in a former chapel off Cheltenham Parade, now boasting a magnificent proscenium arch. Nevertheless, by the close of the century the perceived inadequacy of existing provision prompted two major developments. In 1900 the Grand Opera House was opened by a private company at the junction of Chapel (from 1908 Oxford) Street and Cheltenham Parade with seating for nearly 1,300 people who were treated to plush upholstery and all modern conveniences. Then in May 1903 the Corporation opened a Kursaal, adjoining the Spa Rooms estate, which it had also bought, following the visit of a local deputation to several European resorts, in a deliberate emulation of continental developments. Although reduced in scale and cost from its original conception, the completed building, designed by the noted theatre architect Frank Matcham, also seated nearly 1,300 people in its glorious main hall in stalls, grand circle, upper circle and boxes. Above them the ceiling of its dome was decorated with thousands of gold-leaf stars. The hall was encircled by a 360-degree ambulatory, or promenade, whose eastern section led onto a raised veranda overlooking the gardens. The seating in the stalls could be rolled back to provide a ballroom or even space for equestrian events. The southern promenade also opened into the northern glazed extension of the Spa Rooms; the intervening space being used as a café for both buildings.[15]

Open space for leisure and recreation was, as we have seen, provided in private pleasure gardens but the public amenities were more important. In 1858 the Improvement Commissioners had built a small pump room, the Magnesia Well, in the Bogs Field. The land fringing the path thence from the main Pump Room was planted and by 1886 was known as the Valley Pleasure Gardens. Further parcels of land were added and the whole area landscaped for the Queen's Golden Jubilee year. The acquisition of another large field in 1902 completed the creation of the Valley Gardens, which with a further purchase, of part of Harlow Moor, created a large and beautiful open space for both townspeople and visitors. The Stray also was now brought under the Corporation's control, which was important as it included the Bogs Field with its many springs. The 1841 Improvement Act had given the so-called Stray Owners, who 'owned' pasture rights over imaginary four-acre 'gates', or sections, the power but not an obligation to maintain and improve it. Criticism of their failure to exercise that power adequately and concern over the increased and unregulated use of the Stray by what were deemed undesirable entertainments and 'unseemly gatherings', prompted the Corporation to seek greater control. Accordingly, a special act of parliament was secured which allowed it to take over the Stray for a payment of £11,780 and granted it powers over its use. The Harrogate Corporation Act of 1893 also ensured, in the words of one alderman, 'that there could be no circuses, no wild beast shows, no niggers holding their entertainments within 75 yards of any house'. In other words, nothing should be permitted which threatened the town's image as a select resort.[16] **(4, 5, 6)**

OPPOSITE

4. The Stray looking towards the Crown Hotel at centre, showing the major redevelopment of 1900. To the left is Royal Parade and to the right the lower part of Montpellier Hill. The writer of the postcard asked what father thought about the sinking of the *Lusitania*. (Author's postcard)

ABOVE

6. The Stray looking towards the rebuilt White Hart Hotel of 1847, showing the entrance to the mews. Royal Parade and the Crown Hotel are to the right. Photographed late 1890s. (Used with permission from Harrogate Library, North Yorkshire County Council.)

LEFT

5. The Stray looking towards the Prospect- (centre) and Alexandra (to right) Hotels. To the left Montpellier Hill leads up towards Prospect Crescent. Note the cabmen's shelter at the centre. Photographed in 1902. (Courtesy the Francis Frith Collection)

In addition to the pleasures afforded visitors by all those entertainments and attractions, provision was also made for their spiritual needs. An Anglican chapel of St John had been erected on land given by the Duchy of Lancaster at High Harrogate in 1749. Subsequently enlarged, a new Christ Church was then consecrated in 1831. Reflecting the growing importance of Low Harrogate, St Mary's was opened there in 1825. Nonconformity also had a presence in the town but was associated at first more with its working people than the visitors.[17] The growth both of visitor numbers and a permanent population from mid-century saw a huge expansion in the number of places of worship, including some of the most imposing buildings in the town, like the Wesley Chapel of 1862 or St Peter's of 1870–71.

The visitors had to be accommodated. The earliest stayed at local farms or cottages but hotels and lodging houses were opened from the later seventeenth century. The first custom-built inn was 'almost certainly' the Queen's Head at High Harrogate, joined before the close of the seventeenth century by the Granby, Dragon, Salutation and two smaller establishments: the World's End and Bay Horse. At Low Harrogate were opened the Crown, Bell, Promenade and White Hart Inns, with the Globe, or Half Moon (later known as the Crescent), the Blacksmith's Arms (later the Swan) and The Chequers (later the George) following in the eighteenth century. Over the course of the nineteenth century existing hotels were rebuilt or extended and several new ones opened. The old White Hart was replaced with a beautiful new building in 1847. The Crown was reconstructed and extended, as were too the Swan and George, with similar developments at the Queen and Granby Hotels. Opposite the new station a North Eastern Railway Hotel was opened. Other examples included on Victoria Avenue the Claremont and Avenue Hotels and on West Park the Prospect, Alexandra, Commercial, Clarendon and Brunswick (later the Prince of Wales). Along Cold Bath Road, which led, as its name suggests, to another spring, were opened the Wellington (originally as the Robin Hood), Binns' (later the Lancaster) and the Adelphi and Beechwood Hotels.[18]

The Swan Hotel was one of several 'hydros' established in the final quarter of the nineteenth century in response to the fashion for self-contained curative establishments incorporating a range of baths.

7.   The Swan Hydro, photographed in 1911, showing the
extensions of 1892. (Courtesy the Francis Frith Collection)

The hotel had been bought by the Harrogate Hydropathic Company
in 1878, was overseen by a medical superintendent and fitted out with
bathing facilities, including a Turkish Bath. Extensions begun in 1892
provided seventy-five additional bedrooms, a new dining room and
Winter Gardens. (7) Smaller hydros included the Connaught on Cold
Bath Road and the Imperial on Royal Parade, opposite the Pump Room.
Two more large establishments were then opened in 1892 and 1893: the
Cairn Hydro on Ripon Road and Harlow Manor Hydro on Cold Bath
Road, which were joined in the new century by the Spa Hydro.[19]

The beginning of the Edwardian period saw the culmination of
this process of hotel development, with, for example, the opening of
Southlands on Ripon Road, major redevelopment of the Crown in 1900,
further enlargement of the George, the rebuilding of the Wellington

17

in 1900–1 and additions to both the Adelphi and Prospect Hotels. In addition, two huge new hotels were now opened. The first was the Majestic in 1900. It was indeed built on a majestic scale overlooking the town, providing accommodation for over 400 guests, with spectacular public rooms and a Winter Gardens with 8,000 square feet of floor space: 'the biggest glazed interior in Yorkshire'. (8) The Grand, overlooking the Valley Gardens, opened in 1903. It too had impressive public rooms. Whilst the Majestic's grand lounge was fitted with painted murals of life at old English spas, that of the Grand was hung with expensive tapestries depicting old Harrogate.[20] In total then, listed in a trade directory published in 1912, there were nearly forty hotels. They varied greatly in scale from the likes of the Majestic, Grand or Crown to smaller

-8. The Majestic Hotel photographed in 1901, not long after its opening in July the previous year. (Courtesy the Francis Frith Collection)

establishments like the Esplanade Private Hotel facing the Stray or the Kensington and Belvedere Private Hotels at the bottom of Valley Drive. There were also in the town centre two temperance hotels. In addition, there were twenty-eight boarding houses, with several also located on Valley Drive, and including a number catering for Jewish visitors like the Strathmore on Cold Bath Road.[21]

The greater number of visitors, however, were accommodated in lodging houses. In the early years of the spa, whole families with their servants would take lodgings for all or part of the season. It became the norm for innkeepers to run one or more such houses, like those of the Crown, for example, on Bath Terrace, built in about 1791 overlooking the hotel's baths and gardens.[22] Over the nineteenth century this became the typical means of staying in Harrogate. Already by 1849 over half of the visitors named in the weekly lists printed in the local papers were in lodgings.[23] By the Edwardian period there were several hundred houses letting apartments, as the arrangement had come to be known and was so described in trade directories. Numerous streets in the town, like Cheltenham- and Mount Parade, Walker (from 1910 King's) Road or Valley Drive and Harlow Moor Drive above it, were full of such houses. Typical advertisements from 1900 included one for apartments to let comprising sitting room with one or two bedrooms, piano, bath etc. at West Lea Avenue off Otley Road, in a 'healthy position' near Harlow Moor, or another for comfortable apartments with good cooking. They were also available without board and could be let on a permanent basis. Those letting apartments also advertised in regional newspapers, for example in the *Eastern Mercury*, the 'leading mid-weekly for suburban London and Essex.[24] Taken together, by the Edwardian period this variety of accommodation was catering annually for an estimated minimum of 75,000 visitors.[25]

The town's accommodation sector clearly catered for a range of budgets. But those budgets had to extend to the cost of a stay of varying lengths of time. Harrogate's success was therefore dependent on the growth in the number of those with the financial means to enjoy its attractions. The long-term growth of the economy, particularly following the Restoration and over the course of the eighteenth and nineteenth centuries, created ever-growing numbers of the upper and middle classes with disposable income and the desire to spend it on their health and leisure. Especially important to its early success were those of Yorkshire, comprising the landed gentry of the Vale of York and professional families from York itself or towns like Beverley and Richmond, but also, and increasingly important, the commercial and industrial middle class of its West Riding, particularly of the great industrial cities of Leeds and Bradford. By the Edwardian period, however, the number of visitors from further afield had grown considerably. By 1910 the share of those from the West Riding had decreased and there were increasing numbers from south-east England. More than one in eight were then coming from London itself, a reflection of the northern spa's acceptance in metropolitan society.[26] The number from overseas had also grown.

Harrogate was geographically ideally placed to receive them. The town was close to the Great North Road and on the trans-Pennine route from York to Liverpool. From the mid-eighteenth century those two were supplemented with a network of improved turnpike roads: from Leeds through Harrogate to Ripon; from Wakefield through Bradford to Killinghall to the north of Harrogate and thence also to Ripon; together with more local connections. These helped to establish the resort before the railway provided a crucial boost. Already from 1835 coaches connected Harrogate to the developing new lines but then in 1848 a branch of the York and North Midland Railway from Church Fenton and Wetherby was opened, terminating at Brunswick Station on the edge of the town. The Leeds and Thirsk also opened a line from Thirsk through Ripon and Starbeck, then separate from Harrogate a mile-and-a-half to the east, connecting to Leeds in the following year. Then in 1862 the North Eastern Railway provided a link into Harrogate itself and a station was opened on its modern central site. A further important link provided a through line to Bradford in 1865. Subsequent improvements both to the levels of service and journey times further facilitated local travel and made the journey easier for those more distant visitors. Connections to London were originally through Leeds or York but the Edwardian traveller enjoyed several daily direct connections to the capital.[27]

From the turn of the century, the arrival of the motor car and motor bus made a further addition to transport provision and led quickly to the creation of a local infrastructure of garages, body makers and dealers.

20

Hotels converted all or part of former stables to accommodate them, like the Prince of Wales at West Park, hiring out both carriages and motor cars.[28]

These transport links also made possible the growth of a permanent middle-class residential population. The censuses of 1901 and 1911 contain numerous individuals, often widowed or single women, described as living on 'private means'. There were also many businessmen, particularly in the textile trades. To take examples from 1911: living at twenty-roomed Willaston, overlooking the Stray, was William Benn, a worsted spinner and manufacturer from Queenshead (later Queensbury) between Bradford and Halifax, the two centres of worsted manufacture. Although dominant, textiles were not the only business. Benn's neighbour, at The Briary, was Harold Pope, a colliery proprietor.[29] Its attraction to those seeking a place of retirement or semi-retirement had been evident for some years and from the early 1850s seasonal commuting had developed, as businessmen took their families to Harrogate for part of the summer but could still travel to their place of work when necessary. The improved rail access after 1862 from central Harrogate to Leeds and Bradford then made it as convenient for business and professional men to live in as those towns' outer suburbs.

Several developments now met the growing demand for housing. In 1860, in anticipation of the new railway link, the Victoria Park Company was formed to develop a large area of land in the central part of the town between the original settlements of High and Low Harrogate. Wide roads were laid out, including Victoria Avenue connecting West Park Stray with Queen Parade, and building plots offered for sale on which were erected a range of villas, semi-detached houses and superior terraces. Other developments included West End Park on land between Leeds and Otley Roads; Beech Grove facing West Park Stray; new streets off Cold Bath Road; the Alexandra Park and Franklin estates north of the town centre; and East Parade and North Park Road to the east of the railway station. (9) Towards the close of the century the Dragon estate on the site of the former hotel and its grounds was begun and also Valley and Harlow Moor Drives on the east and the Duchy estate on the west sides respectively of the Valley Gardens.[30] Development on the latter estate continued through the Edwardian period and there was also further building on both sides of Leeds Road, between the Stray and Leadhall Lane on its west side and on its east the working-class district of Oatlands. In this way, much of central Harrogate and particularly its western side took on the character of a middle-class residential district.

In contrast, the largest working-class districts were, like Oatlands, located on the town's periphery. They had, however, been preceded by some smaller, more central, developments, where no restrictions were

9. Middle-class housing on Lancaster Road, between Beech Grove overlooking the Stray and Cold Bath Road, photographed in 2020. (Author's photograph)

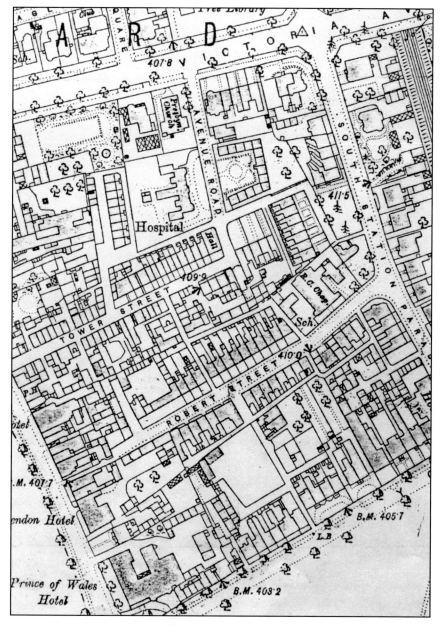

10. Tower Street is at centre, with to the left West Park. The district's central location is clear. Parts of the Stray can be seen also to the left and at the foot of the map. At the top, Victoria Avenue had been laid out from 1862. The railway from Leeds can be seen to the right. (Ordnance Survey, 25″ to the mile, published 1891, reproduced with the permission of Ordnance Survey.)

placed on the type of housing to be constructed, as was the case on land owned, for example, by the Duchy of Lancaster. One such was Tower Street, which branched off West Park, and was developed from the 1830s with a range of smaller properties on land owned by Thomas Thackwray. (10) Other developments were Union Street, a narrow thoroughfare behind Parliament Street and, along Chapel Street: Chapel-, School- and Northumberland Courts.[31] To the north, off Otley Road at Harlow Hill, was another small development of workers' housing. More extensive was that north of the central area at Smithy Hill, off Skipton Road. This area was considerably extended later in the century along Denmark Street towards Walker Road and around Grove Road, where a municipal cemetery had been opened, to the railway line and the town centre. Streets there, like Mayfield Grove, had a more mixed working- and lower middle-class character, as was the case too with those built on the west side of Walker Road. Another small development led off Westmoreland Street, which branched off Skipton Road, into Mowbray and Myrtle Squares. A much larger one, of chiefly working-class houses, was the Regents, as it was known from the name of several of its streets, off the east side of Skipton Road between its junction with Westmoreland Street and the railway.

Three other working-class districts were each over a mile from the centre of the town and all beyond the boundary of the Improvement Commission, where land was cheaper and rates lower.[32] New Park to the north grew along Ripon and Skipton Roads above the gas works, which was developed from the mid-1840s. There were also several quarries in the area and its industrial character was completed by the later electricity works at Oakdale and a large commercial laundry on Euclid Street, one of two new streets built just beyond the borough boundary.[33] To the south Oatlands was developed on land at the corner of Leeds- and Hookstone Roads. By 1892 it was reported that over 250 houses had been completed there with a further 30 being built. The developer, builder William Walker, who described himself as the 'founder of the village', also owned the adjoining brickworks which, with another commercial laundry off Leeds Road, gave this district too an industrial character. (11, 12) As at New Park, more housing was built in the Edwardian period beyond the borough boundary on the south side of Hookstone Road.[34] Starbeck, on

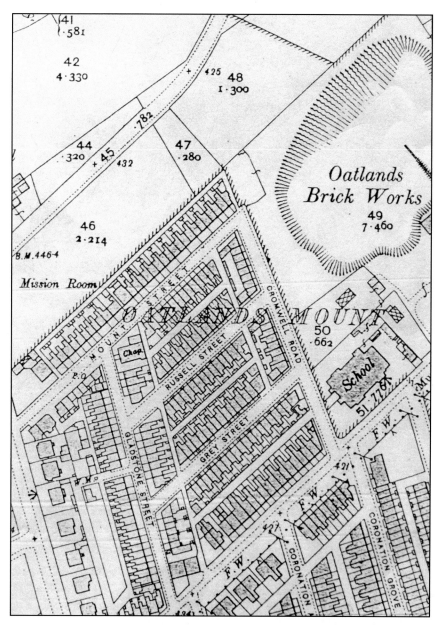

11.   Oatlands. To the left is Leeds Road and at bottom Hookstone
Road. The brickworks of the district's builder is to the right. Note
the naming of the streets after heroes of Liberalism and the new
post-1900 streets at bottom right. (Ordnance Survey, 25″ to the
mile, revised edition of 1907, reproduced with the permission of
Ordnance Survey.)

12. House in Gladstone Street, Oatlands. Photographed in 2018. (Author's photograph)

the road and railway to Knaresborough, was the most important such industrial suburb. In addition to extensive railway works and sidings, there were also brickworks, saw mill, moulding works, maltings, a steam-powered corn mill (later the site of an ice manufacturer), mineral water works and two commercial laundries.[35] To accommodate their workers, from the 1880s there were extensive housing developments on both sides of the railway. (13, 14, 15) During the Edwardian period one new district was completed, building having begun in the mid-1890s, between Skipton Road and Bilton Lane, called Bilton Grange. It was not, however, exclusively working-class but contained a mix of housing types: smaller dwellings but also more substantial properties and villas.[36]

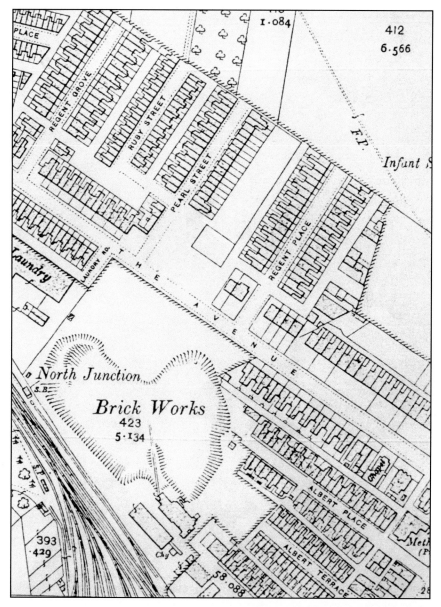

13. The industrial suburb of Starbeck, showing the railway to the left, the Provincial Laundry and brickworks. The Avenue at centre had a more middle-class character. (Ordnance Survey, 25″ to the mile, revised edition of 1907, reproduced with the permission of Ordnance Survey.)

14. The maltings at Starbeck, run for many years by William Tattersall and Company, supplying breweries in Leeds and Tadcaster. It was closed in 1969 and demolished. Drawn here shortly before then by George Walker. (Courtesy of Harrogate Museums and Arts, Harrogate Borough Council.)

15. Albert Place, Starbeck, showing clearly on this building photographed in 2018 the onset of major development from the 1880s. (Author's photograph)

Overall, the housing stock more than trebled in the thirty years from 1861 to 1891, from 931 houses to 2,857 and the population rose from 4,737 to 9,482. The pace of growth then accelerated markedly from the late 1880s, doubling the size of the town in little more than a decade. This growth stimulated calls for the extension of the borough boundary, which when it was created in 1884 was the same as that of the original Improvement Commission. As Alderman Fortune, himself a builder, argued in 1896, the development of New Park, Oatlands and Starbeck would not have happened 'if it had not been for the progress made by Harrogate'.[37] When the extension took effect in November 1900 the size of the town was increased from 1,287 to 9,423 acres and its rateable value rose from £125,954 to £166,864. This enlarged borough had 6,228 houses in 1901 and the population now reached 28,423. It continued to increase over the next decade, although not at the previous rate, and stood at 33,703 in 1911.[38]

The growth of Harrogate as a residential town as well as resort greatly stimulated its development as an important retail centre. In addition, its rail links up Nidderdale to Pateley Bridge and to Ripon and Knaresborough led to its replacement of the latter town as the local market and shopping centre. From the late 1860s the area bounded by Chapel-, Parliament- and James Streets was developed as the main shopping area. Earlier in the history of the spa, High Harrogate had been an important commercial centre but this now moved to the new developing centre. Significantly, the main post office was moved from High Harrogate to James Street in 1865. Houses in Parliament Street, which at first had a residential character, were converted into shops, whilst in High Harrogate the opposite process took place. The character of retailing also changed. Whereas retailers had come for the season, some now settled in the town and were joined by others.

Parliament- and James Streets, particularly the latter, became shopping streets of some exclusivity. (16) In the former, for example, was Fattorini's jewellers. The original Antonio Fattorini, born in Italy in 1797, had moved to Leeds after the Napoleonic wars. He and his wife had first come to Harrogate for the season with their Oriental Lounge on Regent Parade at High Harrogate, returning to Leeds for the winter. Permanent settlement came later with one of the sons, also Antonio, opening premises first

16.   Parliament Street, which forms a section of the main Leeds to Ripon road. Formerly residential, its buildings were adapted to retail use to make it one of the town's main shopping streets. Photographed here in 1905, the tower of the Royal Arcade can be seen to the right. (Courtesy the Francis Frith Collection)

on Royal Parade then in 1884 in Parliament Street.[39] Another jewellery business, that of James Ogden, was founded in 1893 with premises in Cambridge Street. For a time, it traded in Parliament Street and further shops were opened on Cambridge Crescent and in Station Square. The latter was closed when Ogden acquired their premises in James Street in 1910, which was provided with a new interior and its frontage graced with an elegant canopy. Before 1914, branches had also been opened in the resorts of Bath, Llandrindod Wells and Scarborough.[40] The James Street property had been vacated by Marshall and Snelgrove, which had opened in the town in 1906. It now acquired property further along James Street and opened a new store strikingly faced with white tiles and similarly graced with a wrought iron veranda to the street. This firm, which had made its name in London specializing in silks, furs, carpets and drapery goods, helped give James Street its cachet.[41]

In addition to shops such as these, there were three arcades: the King's in James Street, the Lowther between Cambridge- and Oxford Streets and the Royal in Parliament Street. The latter was provided with the Arcade Tea Rooms, one of several cafés, refreshment- and dining-rooms and restaurants serving the shopper during the Edwardian period in addition to the catering offered by hotels and the Kursaal. Another one in Parliament Street was the Café Imperial. In Station Square, Standing's, which had opened in 1883, contained a basement smoke room lined with oak panels, a ground-floor grocery, an 'oriental' café on the first floor with a Moorish vaults and stained-glass windows and a second-floor bakery.[42]

The needs of residents and visitors were also met by, among other shops in 1911, fourteen antique dealers, seventeen fancy goods shops, thirty-two tobacconists, fifty-six confectioners, fifty-three drapers and seventy-five dressmakers and costumiers. There were now also branches of national chains, part of an emerging trend, like bookseller, newsagent and stationer W. H. Smith & Son at the station and other locations, chemist Boots in Parliament Street, or Home and Colonial Stores in Beulah Street.[43] In addition, a public Market Hall had been opened by the Improvement Commissioners in 1874, and embellished with a clock tower three years later, in which traders such as butchers, poulterers, provision dealers, greengrocers and fruiterers rented permanent stalls. To this were later added outside shops in Cambridge Street and Station Square.[44]

The market had been erected in part to stop trading by hawkers, but their occasional appearance before the local bench suggests it was not wholly successful. In 1905, for example, four local women selling flowers were fined for obstructing the highway in James Street, the chairman assuring them that he was quite sure that the authorities did not wish to harass them in their work, but they must not cause an obstruction. Five years later, more flower sellers, again in James Street, one, Marie Donovan from Harrogate, with a 'basket' a yard long and two feet wide, were now told that such obstructions must cease, as it happened all too often and in future would be more severely dealt with. The second of them, Sarah Hare from Bradford, was fined again the following year.[45]

Street traders also worked the working-class districts of the town, like an 'old offender' given a month's hard labour for selling old clothes without a pedlar's certificate in Denmark Street in March 1911.[46] But it was the small shops in those and lower-middle-class areas that constituted the largest group of retailers, making up most of the one hundred grocers trading in 1911, for example, or the forty-seven fruiterers and greengrocers and thirty-seven butchers. (17) The eighteen fried fish dealers, or fish and chip shops as we know them, were almost exclusively in those districts. One other important development finally was the Cooperative Society. Formed in 1887 with a shop in Beulah Street, by its twenty-first anniversary it had central departments in Albert Street plus a further six branches.[47]

Harrogate also offered an attractive base for a range of institutions. The growing demand from the burgeoning resident middle class for day-school

17.   Lupton's grocer, general supply store and Post Office at the junction of Skipton- and Ripon Roads, New Park, c. 1900. (Courtesy Terry Williams, the New Park Heritage Centre.)

places, plus from parents elsewhere for boarding their offspring in a town with both a healthy situation and reputation as a genteel resort, led to the establishment of private schools. Where they were not purpose-built, the town possessed premises suitable for conversion. Their advertisements reveal their consciousness both of that middle-class market and the town's attractions, as in these examples from 1900. For boys, Walter Kaye, the proprietor of Pembroke College on Queen Parade, provided preparation for commercial life, accountancy, medical and law exams or for public schools and universities. In a common flourish, he boasted that 350 certificates had been gained in fifteen years. Health, however, was the first consideration, special attention being given to younger pupils and leisure hour pursuits. Trinity College on Park Avenue was offering 'Thorough training for Professional and Mercantile Pursuits' and boasted of its cricket and football fields, tennis courts, gymnasium and large swimming bath. For girls, Highfield on East Parade, where Misses Wilson and Tomlinson were assisted by four resident mistresses and a visiting master, offered a 'Sound modern education based on high-school principles, seconded by individual teaching, together with careful mental and physical training'. It also stressed its 'home comforts' and 'the greatest care taken of delicate girls'. This last reassurance was not unusual: Trinity College also promised that 'young and delicate boys' were 'especially catered for'. Specialist markets were also addressed, for example, 'Arrangements for Indian and Colonial Boys' at Clifton College, also on Queen Parade.[48] (18)

The census of 1901 recorded details of thirty-six private schools within the borough plus three large schools just beyond its boundary in more open country to the south: New College off Leadhall Lane, Pannal Ash- and Ashville Colleges. A total of 682 children were boarded at those schools, of whom just over a third were girls. In 1911 the total schools had fallen slightly to twenty-nine plus four outside the borough: the three of 1901 and Convent High School for girls off Hookstone Road. New College and Ashville each now boarded seventy-seven boys, with another sixty at Pannal Ash, which also had three girls. Overall, however, girls now outnumbered boys in the private-school boarding population: 346 to 325. The largest girls' school and much the largest school overall was now Harrogate Ladies' College, with 135 boarders housed in its new premises

18.   Dunorlan School, Park Road. In 1901 it was under the
personal supervision of Miss Stocker, late headmistress of Bradford
Girls Grammar School, and Miss Sharpe of Newnham College,
Cambridge and accommodated twenty-nine girls aged thirteen to
eighteen. Building photographed in 2018. (Author's photograph)

off Duchy Road or accommodated in neighbouring hostels. Most schools
were much smaller. The only other large boys' school was Oatlands with
thirty-six boarders. More typical were Western College off Cold Bath
Road with thirteen boys or Bilton Grange on Skipton Road, which was

home to just six, down from thirty-four ten years earlier, although it was now styling itself 'a boarding and day school', rather than the boarding school for boys 'of the upper classes' of its 1868 foundation. For girls, middle-range schools were Elmwood on Willaston Road with thirty-eight boarders; Birklands on Kent Road with thirty-three; and Waldernheath on Cornwall Road with thirty-two. Most of those hundreds of children were from homes in the north of England, particularly Yorkshire, with a smaller number from elsewhere in the country and just a few born in the colonies.[49]

The town's healthy situation, and of course its spa facilities, also made it a natural home for a variety of medical institutions. By the beginning of the Edwardian period there were the Royal Bath Hospital and Convalescent Home in Cornwall Road; the Infirmary on Avenue (later Belford) Road; the Yorkshire Home for Chronic and Incurable Diseases in Montpellier Parade; the Northern Police Convalescent Home on Harlow Moor Road; the Convalescent Home of the Sunderland Infirmary – Heatherdene – on Wetherby Lane (now Road); and two smaller convalescent homes respectively on Harlow Moor Drive and, for the mentally ill, on Station Parade. At Starbeck, there was Hill House Home for Inebriate Women. Ten years later in 1911, to those had been added the Durham County Hospital Convalescent Home on Cornwall Road; Dr Barnardo's Home for Crippled Children on Tewit Well Road; and further small nursing homes.

The town also was home to two orphanages: the Northern Police Orphanage on Otley Road and the Primitive Methodist Orphan Homes, which occupied several houses on Pannal Ash Road. Much smaller were a YWCA home on the Esplanade with four boarders on census night in 1911, engaged in dressmaking, needlework or millinery, and St Monica's Home on Harlow Terrace, which was a so-called prevention and rescue home for young women either at risk of falling into prostitution or immorality, or who needed help, often having become pregnant. There were two young women there on census night. There were, finally, a District Nursing Society Home in Robert Street with two nurses present and the Theosophical Trust Student Centre on East Parade with a lone boarder.

By the Edwardian period then Harrogate's celebrity and prosperity rested on the spa. At the beginning of those years, the *Advertiser* was reporting a new record in the number of water drinkers and bathers: 1,300 of the former at the Royal Pump Room one Tuesday in late July and another 315 at the Royal Baths Pump Room. At the Royal Baths too there had been 480 bathers with another 300 at the Victoria Baths. A decade later a week in August had 'smashed all records' with more than a thousand bathers daily. By then, at the height of the season, some 2,000 people were using the Royal Pump Room every morning.[50] The town was provided with a range of accommodations catering to upwards of 75,000 visitors annually, including in some of the most impressive buildings in the town. They enjoyed not only the waters but a range of indoor entertainments and beautiful open spaces. It had become also a residential town for the professional, commercial and industrial middle classes, chiefly of the West Riding, those with private incomes and the wealthy retired. Its central district had been developed as an attractive shopping centre to cater to them and the wider district. Further, it provided a congenial home for a range of private schools and other institutions. But all this in the end depended upon the labours of its working class. It is to those men and women that we now turn.

Notes to Chapter 1:
The Creation of Edwardian Harrogate

1   H. H. Walker, *History of Harrogate under the Improvement Commissioners, 1841–1884* (1986), p. 460.

2   W. Grainge, *The History and Topography of Harrogate and the Forest of Knaresborough* (1988), p. 127.

3   J. A. Patmore, *An Atlas of Harrogate* (1963), pp. 9–11; C. Morris (ed.), *The Journeys of Celia Fiennes* (1947), p. 80.

4   Patmore, *Atlas*, pp. 3–4.

5   E. Deane, *Spadacrene Anglica or the English Spa Fountain* (1922).

6   M. Neesam, *Harrogate Great Chronicle, 1332–1841* (2005), pp. 124–46.

7   Neesam, *Chronicle*, pp. 162–71 and 177–84.

8   Neesam, *Chronicle*, pp. 383–94.

9   Jennings, *Harrogate*, pp. 295–6.

10 D. Carpenter, *Ilkley: The Victorian Era* (1986), pp. 53–6.

11 Neesam, *History*, pp. 50–5; Jennings, *Harrogate*, pp. 409 and 417–18.

12 Neesam, *History*, pp. 67–8.

13 D. Blackbourn, 'Fashionable spa towns in nineteenth-century Europe', in S. C. Anderson and B. H. Tabb (eds), *Water, Leisure and Culture: European historical perspectives* (2002), pp. 9–21.

14 Neesam. *Chronicle*, pp. 149–51, 195–223 and 349–51; for a detailed contemporary description see A. B. Granville, *Spas of England and Principal Sea-Bathing Places: The North* (1971), pp. 36–127.

15 Neesam, *History*, pp. 60–1; M. Neesam, *The Archive Photograph Series: Harrogate* (1995), p. 110; M. Neesam *et al.*, *Kursaal: A History of Harrogate's Royal Hall* (2008).

16 Jennings, *Harrogate*, p. 423.

17 Neesam, *Chronicle*, pp. 239–58.

18 Neesam, *Chronicle*, pp. 100–8, 301–10 and 322–64; *History*, 61–2.

19 Jennings, *Harrogate*, pp. 415–16.

20 *HA*, 21 July 1900, supp; M. Neesam, *Hotel Majestic* (2000); *History*, pp. 63–4.

21 *Robinson's Harrogate, Knaresboro', Wetherby and District Directory 1912* (1911); R. D. Livshin, *The History of the Harrogate Jewish Community* (1995), p. 7.

22 M. Neesam, 'Lodgings fit for ladies and gentlemen at Bath Terrace', in *HA*, 3 March 2000.

23 Patmore, *Atlas*, p. 31.

24 *HA*, 7 July 1900, p. 1.

25 Patmore, *Atlas*, p. 31.

26 Patmore, *Atlas*, pp. 31–2.

27 Jennings, *Harrogate*, pp. 233–4 and 303–12; J. Rogers, *The Railways of Harrogate and District* (2000).

28 *Robinson's Directory, 1912.*

29 For reasons of space, I have not provided references to individual details from the census returns.

30 Jennings, *Harrogate*, pp. 311–14.

31 Neesam, *Chronicle*, p. 316–27; deeds to Tower Street properties, Harrogate Borough Council.

32 Jennings, *Harrogate*, p. 426.

33 T. Williams, *A Pictorial History of New Park Harrogate* (1984).

34 *HA*, 8 August 1891, p. 2; 11 June 1892, p. 8; and 29 August 1896, p. 3.

35 *Robinson's Directory 1912*; Jennings, *Harrogate*, p. 314; S. G. Abbott, *Starbeck: A journey through the past* (n.d.), pp. 59–60.

36 P. Broadbank, *Twentieth Century Housing Development in Harrogate: A study of development in the town* (2003).

37 *HA*, 16 May 1896, p. 5.

38 Jennings, *Harrogate*, pp. 314–15; Neesam, *History*, p. 64.

39 P. Beaver, *A Pedlar's Legacy: The origins and history of Empire Stores* (1981), pp. 16–26.

40 M. Neesam, *Ogden Harrogate: 120 years – a history of a family business* (2013).

41 M. Neesam, *Harrogate in 50 Buildings* (2018), pp. 41–2; E. D. Rappaport, *Shopping for Pleasure: Women in the making of London's West End* (2000), p. 150.

42 M. Neesam, *A-Z of Harrogate: People - places – history* (2019), pp. 69–71; *Robinson's Harrogate, Knaresborough, Wetherby and District Directory, 1914* (1913).

43 *Robinson's Directory 1912*; J. B. Jefferys, *Retail Trading in Britain, 1850–1950* (1954), pp. 21–5.

44 Walker, *Improvement Commissioners*, pp. 328–41.

45 *HA*, 19 August 1905, supp., 3 September 1910, p. 6; and 13 May 1911, p. 5.

46 *HA*, 25 March 1911, p. 5.

47 Anon, *1887 to 1908: 21 Years of Progress: The Harrogate & District Co-operative Society, Ltd* (1908).

48 Jennings, *Harrogate*, p. 399; *HA*, 24 January 1900, p. 1; *Robinson's Harrogate, Knaresborough, Ripon, Pateley Bridge and District Directory 1902* (1901), pp. 20–21.

49 Jennings, *Harrogate*, p. 399.

50 *HA*, 3 August 1901, p. 2 and 13 August 1910, p.2; Neesam, *History*, p. 67.

CHAPTER TWO

The Working Class

I N THIS CHAPTER there are four key points I wish to make. The first
is to stress the importance of class, both in the minds of Edwardians
and as a central influence on the courses which their lives took. I will
also look at how historians have dealt with class, from those who share
this belief in its importance to those who have qualified it or asserted
the contrary. The second is to define the working class and explain how
I created a Harrogate working-class population from the census returns
of 1901 and 1911 to form one of the key sources of evidence for this
book. The third is to look at some distinguishing overall features of
working-class life in Harrogate, for example the importance of women's
participation in the workforce or the seasonal nature of much of the work,
be it in hotels or on building sites. The fourth is to look at the extent to
which four key working-class institutions – friendly societies, the Coop,
trades unions and labour politics – were active in this town where the
working-class element was felt by some to be so little in evidence.

Class

At a council meeting in June 1904 there was a lively exchange following
one councillor's objection to the grant of permission to the Harrogate
Temperance Band to play once fortnightly in the Victoria Bandstand on
the grounds that this free music took custom from the Kursaal. Alderman
Fortune, who was in business as builder and plasterer, objected that

they had no right to make the Kursaal the only place of amusement in Harrogate. He pointed out:

'One knew very well that the Kursaal was not a workingman's place – (hear hear) and the workingmen as a body did not go there.'
Councillor Abbott (another builder): 'And they are not wanted to.'
Alderman Fortune: 'Well, I wouldn't put it as strong as that.'
Councillor Abbott: 'But I have heard it stated by Councillors.'
Alderman Fortune: '... working men did not like to mix with those in higher positions of life to themselves, and many kept away because of the class who resorted there. They would not get these two classes to mix together.'[1]

This exchange, which ended with the heavy defeat of the proposal to rescind the permission, prompts two reflections. The first is that these men were acutely conscious of class. The second is that class was real and one's class had a definite impact on one's situation and behaviour. Both those propositions have frequently been asserted by historians. As Jose Harris put it, '... by any standards, late Victorian and Edwardian Britain was a society ridden to its deepest roots by both objective and subjective indices of social class'.[2] Or as David Cannadine argued in a book devoted to the subject of class, society is manifestly unequal and 'the material circumstances of people's existence – physical, financial, environmental – do matter in influencing their life-chances, their sense of identity ...'[3] This study shares those basic propositions.

It is, however, also conscious of the reservations that have been expressed about the concept of class. The idea of any single, homogeneous working class has been questioned, the working class of Eric Hobsbawm, for example, which came of age towards the close of the nineteenth century. In his view, its unity was based on its sheer size in the industrial economy, improving material circumstances and a developing class consciousness. It was a class which possessed a distinctive culture, as he described it, 'of cup-finals, fish-and-chip shops, palais-de-danse and labour with a capital L'.[4] On the contrary, it has been argued, far from being homogeneous, the working class was in fact internally divided in many ways. This was the case at work in the distinction between skilled workmen and labourers. In single industries, like building or railways, there were important gradations based upon levels of skill and manifested in status and wage differentials.[5] The concept of a labour aristocracy, a term actually in use from the mid-nineteenth century, was also developed, particularly by Hobsbawm, to describe the skilled men at the apex of working-class society, with regular, higher earnings and aspirations to social mobility, who felt themselves to be superior to mere labourers. Their separate existence was also questioned from the outset by those, for example Henry Pelling, who simply could not distinguish a labour elite separated from lower strata within the working class.[6]

Differences of status existed too in other ways, it has been argued, by Geoffrey Best for example, between a respectable working class of 'decent' people and a rough one which enjoyed 'rowdyism, beastly drunkenness, dirtiness, cruelty [and] uninhibited vulgarity.'[7] Others, in contrast, have seen this desire for respectability as much more pervasive within the working class. In relation to drink, for example, whilst for some working men of the chapel-going temperance sort abstinence from drink was an essential attribute of respectability, for others, probably most, it was rather expressed in demonstrating the ability to stand one's friends a drink at the pub, thereby showing that you had the small cash surplus which made it possible.[8] Status was also expressed through the goods which people bought, serving as a means of evaluating one's own and other people's position within the working class. This too, as both John Benson and Paul Johnson argued, worked overall to undermine a sense of class identity and to defuse class tension.[9]

This view of the working class as status conscious was presented vividly in Robert Roberts's memoir of his slum neighbourhood in Edwardian Salford. To him, it was 'a stratified form of society' in which individual streets, families and even family members had their own social rating. At its apex was an elite of shopkeepers, publicans and skilled tradesmen, some with aspirations to the lower middle class, then on down through recognized strata to a base of the 'lowest of the low' and those with 'no class'. Richard Hoggart, in his equally well-known evocation of a working-class area of Leeds, similarly urged his readers not to forget 'the great number of differences, the subtle shades, the class distinctions, within the working-classes themselves'. He too perceived distinctions between individual streets and houses within them, between families, one, for example, where the husband was a skilled man with a big order on at his works and with a wife skilled at managing the household and another where she was a 'slattern'.[10] For both writers, however, this did not negate the existence of the working class, rather it stressed its complexity. That view also is shared by this study.

The references here to working-class women alert us to another area which feminist historians have seen as eroding any sense of working-class solidarity, that of relations between the sexes. This has, however, had two differing emphases. In one, as Anna Clark saw them, 'the fatal flaws of misogyny and patriarchy', in which struggles over resources, power and control characterized male and female relations, have been the dominant influence. In contrast, the socialist-feminist perspective of Sheila Rowbotham acknowledged unequal relations between the sexes but stressed the shared aspects of their life experiences. As she expressed it, 'Class exploitation and the cultural indignities which have accompanied it have affected both men and women in the working class. The fate of all women has not been the same.'[11]

In addition to differences based in work, status and gender, there were those based on locality and region. Patrick Joyce has seen these as having 'profound importance', in work, culture and politics and in a 'localism of spirit', so that 'Lancashire towns were just not like Yorkshire towns' be it in their preferred sports, architecture, churches and chapels or ways of speaking.[12] Religion was another identity which divided working people, particularly where migration from Ireland had created large Catholic minorities in cities like Glasgow or Liverpool, but it was also present in those with smaller Irish populations, like Leeds or Bradford. Ethnicity and race could also be divisive. The arrival of thousands of Jews from the 1880s, fleeing persecution in the Russian empire, and on a smaller scale the presence of other European workers, particularly in the hotel trade, provoked hostility.

In addition to highlighting these multiple sources of identity, some historians have also questioned the basic assumptions that class was a social reality in the past or a shared subjective experience. This was based in a belief in the importance of language, the so-called 'linguistic turn'. In this view, taken by for example Joyce or Gareth Stedman Jones, since it is the language that people use that expresses their identity then class is seen as the study of that language. The language of class, further, is just one of many 'discourses', as they are termed, or ways of describing the world. Joyce argued that class 'is seen to be an imagined form, not something given in a "real" world beyond this form'. What is real is not something called class but the discourse of class, one of many competing such discourses. They were therefore the proper subject of study.[13] That the language of class is important is clear, as was seen in the exchange with which I began this chapter. Many historians have accepted the importance of those insights and acknowledge that identities had to be learned from, and expressed through, language. They did not simply appear from their experience. But equally, there had to be that experience in which they were grounded. It did matter what conditions people lived in, what money they had to spend and all the other material facts of life. As Andrew August expressed it in his study of the British working class, 'Class identity thrived among working people because their experiences allowed narratives of class to resonate.'[14]

I return then, after this necessarily brief overview, to my own position. I recognize that class was one of many identities. I recognize too that the working class was divided, along lines of status, gender, locality, religion or ethnicity, but maintain that class was more significant. I believe in the end that class mattered, both as something to be identified with and as a reality. If you were born into the working class then this fact had important implications for the life you would lead. It is one of the central purposes of this book to explore that fact.

The Harrogate working class

For this study I had first to define and then identify working-class people. Of course, one could use all kinds of criteria: source and amount of income or level of education for example, or a combination of criteria. I have followed a definition used by Elizabeth Roberts in her study of working-class women in Preston, Barrow and Lancaster. She found it the most useful because it was the one which was used by those taking part in her oral history:

Men and women believed themselves to be working class because they worked with their hands, were employees not employers, and, in comparison with the latter, were poor and lacked material goods …[15]

Further, if one accepts that occupation is the best guide to social class then systematic analysis is possible using the decennial census which recorded details of occupation for the whole employed population. Accordingly, I used the censuses of 1901 and 1911 for Harrogate.[16] It is necessary to explain first something of how they were taken and second how I created a working-class population from those occupations. In so doing some of the complexities and problems involved will be made clear. It is important to emphasize this. This is in the end a working-class population which I created, using a set of criteria which need to be set out and justified, from a source which in its turn was the creation of other, contemporary, men and women.

The census of 1901 was conducted on lines established in essentials for that of 1841. A schedule, or questionnaire, was distributed to every household prior to census night by enumerators who were recruited each decade for the purpose. He, or she by this time, might offer help where a householder had difficulties. The details on the schedule had to include everyone in the household on census night only. Those away for whatever reason were to be omitted but recorded instead where they were on the night. That night was 31 March in 1901 and 2 April 1911, which was significant for a study of Harrogate as those dates preceded the beginning of the season when much the largest number of visitors were in residence. This was one of the instructions given to householders, which were deliberately kept to a minimum, but clearly some struggled with them. It would take up too much space to detail all such difficulties here but studies make clear that people did not know, for example, their exact age, or falsified it, that they could not remember where they were born or described the place in differing ways in successive censuses, or, pertinent again to this study, they simply did not record occupations, particularly those of women or where it was a part-time job.[17] The schedules were then collected by the enumerators who copied the details into a specially printed enumerator's book. This left open several possibilities of error or misinterpretation. Most simply, they might not be able to read the householder's handwriting, as is evident throughout the books. They might also standardize information, to give the occupation some uniformity, rather than simply copy what they saw.

With the 1911 census, although enumerators were still employed, they no longer had to copy the schedules into books but they did have to check to see that they had been correctly completed. They filled in fields on the schedule omitted by the householder and, as they were instructed, corrected those which 'appear to be erroneous'. We now can view the schedule as it was completed by the householder. In Harrogate this was almost invariably the head of the household himself, or herself in the case of a widow, single woman or married woman where the husband was not present on census night. Only a small number were completed by another member of the household, or by another person because of the illiteracy of the head. This still raises all the problems already noted, of legibility or self-description and straightforward misunderstanding of the instructions but removes to some degree the effects of intervention by the enumerator.

The information requested did differ in minor ways between the two censuses. For occupations that of 1911 sought to identify the type of industry or service in addition to employment status - whether employer, worker or working on one's own account or at home. Increased concern over immigration led to a requirement to state, if not born in England and Wales, whether you were a resident or visitor and a further column on nationality was introduced distinguishing whether you were a British subject by parentage, naturalized or foreign. The disability column was also more detailed, reflecting doubts as to the reliability of the information given. Finally, in response to concerns about declining fertility, details of marriage and the numbers of children were requested.

For all its difficulties it remains a vital source of information. To turn now specifically to occupations, faced with hundreds of different ones, it was necessary to adopt some system of classification. This can be done for economic function, whether for example it be agricultural or transport, or, as here, for social class. For this, like other historians, particularly Alan Armstrong in his study of York, I turned to the one used by the General Register Office (GRO) for the 1951 census, which consisted of five classes allocated 'in relation to the basic criterion of the general standing within the community of the occupation concerned'.[18]

Although a form of social classification had been used since the 1911 census, Armstrong favoured that of 1951 over the one for 1921, which he argued were the two most useful for such analysis, for the practical reason that the former was the most accessible in a single volume. The five classes were, in general terms:

Class I. professional etc., occupations, for example accountant or surgeon
Class II. intermediate occupations, for example, bookkeeper or schoolmaster
Class III. skilled occupations, for example, bricklayer or engine driver
Class IV. partly skilled occupations, for example, gardener or railway ticket collector
Class V. unskilled occupations, for example, charwoman or labourer

In this scheme then, classes III, IV and V make up the working class. Such an enterprise, it must be said, has had its critics. Simon Szreter described the GRO's work as neither theoretically based nor rigorously analytical and necessarily rooted in the concerns of the late 1940s. Nevertheless, as the GRO said itself, it had 'the great merit of simplicity'. Stedman Jones, who used a classification scheme in his work on London, felt it was a 'hazardous project' but 'better than nothing at all'.[19] Although perhaps not a ringing endorsement, it is one with which I concur.

As did both Armstrong and Stedman Jones, I have made some modifications to the 1951 scheme, chiefly to take account of the changed status of some occupations between the Edwardian period and that of the years immediately after the Second World War. For example, clerks in the 1951 scheme were allocated to class III. In my scheme, however, they are placed in class II, as to Edwardians they fell clearly into the lower middle class, differentiated from the manual working class by the nature of their work. Conversely, Edwardian shop assistants, particularly in more high-class establishments, liked to think of themselves as a cut above the working class. H. G. Wells captured this nicely in his autobiography in his mother's view of his own apprenticeship to a draper, 'that to wear a black coat and tie behind a counter was the best of all possible lots attainable by man – at any rate by man at our social level.'[20] Nevertheless, despite the enormous variety of shops, from department stores to street-corner grocers, I have classified all assistants as within my working class, that is class III as they were in the 1951 scheme. As Wells testified, it was after all often hard, physical work, on one's feet for hours on end and, however refined their manners, still service. As to the shopkeeper him-, or herself, Geoffrey Crossick placed them alongside small businessmen as 'the classic petty bourgeoisie'. Others, however, have differentiated between those who catered to a middle-class clientele and small shopkeepers in working-class districts who served its residents and who were therefore more a part of that community. Whilst accepting that point, they were still not entirely of that community and accordingly I have preferred to follow Roberts's view of those in his Salford slum, who had aspirations to lower middle-class status.[21] To them I have also added anyone described as a manager or cashier and the commercial travellers who traded with them.

It would be tedious to detail all such modifications but the following are also worth highlighting. Traders who described themselves as working on their 'own account', such as carters or builders, I have placed in class II, assuming that the former at least owned or rented a horse and cart and the latter hired bricklayers and the rest to fulfil the job. They may in fact have thought of themselves as working class but I have treated them as running a small business. Where it is a skilled workman, such as a joiner, who describes himself as working on his 'own account', I have treated him as class III, a self-employed working man. My exception is where he describes himself as an employer, even though this may have been of only one other man, to whom he may in fact have been related. I have also raised his status to that of small businessman, although once again that may not have reflected how he thought of himself in class terms. Another researcher might have done things differently but I have tried both to have a clear rationale for my decisions and to be consistent.

Finally, I should add that I have always used the social class of the household head as my guide. Other family members may have carried on occupations that placed them in a different social class. In several cases the wife was running a lodging house or letting apartments, an occupation which would place her on her own in the lower middle class. Where that was the case, or where the head had another lower middle-class occupation like small trader or shopkeeper, it was not uncommon for sons and daughters to take class III to V jobs. Equally, one finds the children of working-class household heads becoming clerks or teachers. Clearly, there was blurring at the class edges. Only in a few cases have I not used the head's occupation, when other evidence suggested it was not appropriate. This seemed to me the case with, for example, Theodore Schiendorfer, an Austrian by birth who took British citizenship in 1906. He described himself as the head waiter at a first-class hotel. Their house on Cornwall Road had eleven rooms and other members of his family ran it as a lodging house, which on census night in 1911 took in the type of lodger that included the secretary to the Conservative Party's Primrose League. Whether they thought of themselves as working-class Tories is not known but to me they did not fit into the manual working class as I have defined them.

In total then, my classification scheme produced in 1901 2,669 working-class heads of household, or 45 per cent of all 5,903 household heads in Harrogate and in 1911 3,426 of 7,407, or 46 per cent of all heads. Since the heads of household naturally do not include their children, those who were employed as servants, nor live-in hotel workers, nor workers who were in lodgings, then clearly most of Harrogate's people were working class. This was not a 'bare minimum of "working" inhabitants'.

The Harrogate labour market

There are four features of the town's labour market which are worth highlighting. First was the importance of the work of women. Throughout the Edwardian period, over 40 per cent of the working population were women, compared to a national proportion of some 29 to 30 per cent, and more of the town's women worked than was the case nationally.[22] This was due in large part to the importance of service, the lot of around 3,000 women and girls in any given year. Occupations almost exclusively carried on by women also included laundry work, cleaning and dressmaking or millinery. Women were also well represented among shop workers. Most of this work was also some form of service, or for other women, both long established as areas of women's work. Men's work was dominated by the building trades and transport of all kinds, from the railways to cab drivers. This was a similar employment profile to that of Bath or Oxford and Cambridge.[23] Other areas of importance for men were work in the gas industry, in some form of municipal employment, as gardeners or in hotels. The world of work then was highly gendered. With the minor exceptions of printing and bookbinding and upholstery, which employed a small number of women, only hotel- and shop work and parts of the clothing trade were carried on by both men and women.

It was also often seasonal, although the town naturally hoped for its extension. The *Advertiser* in January 1890, whilst noting that one would not be surprised to find it 'empty' at that time of year, had been pleased to see a 'goodly number of visitors'. And in 1902, welcoming the introduction of weekend tickets by railway companies for the man of business, the professions or commerce unable to take a lengthy summer vacation, expressed the hope that it would also encourage off-season trade.[24] To what extent this hope was realized at this time to any great extent is doubtful, if those lists of visitors printed in the newspapers or the low numbers of guests in the hotels or residents in apartments on census nights are a guide. Other occupations particularly dependent, at least in part, on the season were the cab drivers or bath-chair men, the boys who fetched and carried or took messages, the street hawkers or entertainers and the laundry trade. The weather was a crucial dimension of seasonality, affecting the building trade, the gas industry, gardening and the clothing sector, with the latter also subject to the vagaries of fashion. Intimately connected with seasonality was the casual nature of work, characterized by short periods of employment and others with little or no work. As Stedman Jones noted, writing of the London building trade, 'Very few workers could expect a working life of stable employment in the nineteenth century.'[25]

A third feature of the town's labour market was the opportunities it afforded for what John Benson called 'penny capitalism', where 'a working man or woman went into business on a small scale in the hope of profit (but with the possibility of loss) and made him- (or her) self responsible for every facet of the enterprise'. They included all those who described themselves in the census as working on their 'own account', such as tailors, cobblers, upholsterers, French polishers or watch and clock repairers. In the building trade it consisted of those who found their own work of small jobs and repairs, like building a stretch of garden wall or mending a roof, rather than looking for an employer. The same was true of gardeners, many of whom also described themselves in the census as working on their own account or 'jobbing'. Street entertainers were another group who made the minimal investment necessary to set up as an organ grinder, for example. Similar considerations applied to women in such as laundry work, cleaning, taking in lodgers or basic retailing. For Benson, such activities rarely lifted men and women out of the working class and were essentially defensive against adversity and marked by uncertainty. But for him too it was another layer, along with those of earnings, status or gender, that by fostering individuality was inimical to the growth of a unified, self-conscious working class.[26]

A final observation is of the great heterogeneity of working-class employments. In retailing, for example, there was the high-class James Street store of Marshall and Snelgrove, the little corner shop in Denmark Street or the outdoor flower sellers. The building trade was divided into several trades, each with differing fortunes. The railway industry was characterized by consciousness of status, with an elite of engine drivers at the top. Hotel work too had its hierarchy, clearly differentiating a head waiter like Schiendorfer from those under him and certainly from the kitchen porter and the rest behind the scenes. This too militated against any sense of working-class solidarity.

Working-class institutions

Expressive of solidarity in contrast were four key working-class institutions. The first of these were the friendly societies, to G. R. Searle 'an important source of working-class pride and respectability', in which working men and women sought to secure some protection against the vicissitudes of their lives: unemployment, sickness and the impact of their death. In 1904 they had a membership nationally of some 5,600,000, more than double the figure of 1877, although membership of more than one society makes exactitude impossible.[27] The town shared in this expansion, although it is not possible to give a membership figure. In December 1901 the Harrogate Friendly Societies' Hall was opened in a former chapel under the auspices of the Harrogate Amalgamated Friendly Societies' Association. All but three of the town's societies now met there. In 1906 the *Advertiser* reported the first annual gala promoted by the Harrogate and District Friendly Societies, which attracted a large crowd to Goodrick's fields off Otley Road. In the tradition of friendly societies, a procession made its way there comprising members and their children, the yeomanry and cyclists and the crowd enjoyed a variety of displays and trade exhibits. In addition to big events like this, societies had also long organized excursions. The following year, for example, more than seventy members of the Star of Harrogate Lodge of the Sons of Phoenix Friendly Society enjoyed the nineteenth annual trip to Scarborough.[28]

Membership was boosted by the Liberal Government's insurance scheme to provide protection against sickness and unemployment, which came into operation in January 1913, as it was administered through so-called approved societies, which included the friendly societies, along with trade unions and insurance companies. When the scheme started, the Court Pride of Yorkshire number 7005 of the Ancient Order of Foresters' Friendly Society, Harrogate, which had been founded the previous year, reported a total membership of 532, a gain of 116 for the year. Of these, 368 members were taking the state benefits through the Court, four members had died, seven emigrated and twenty had not kept up payments. There was also a female branch, the Court Mayoress Simpson, with 173 members for voluntary benefits and 330 for state and a juvenile branch of both sexes with 260.[29]

Although there had been earlier attempts at cooperation among workers in socialist communities or in the production and sale of goods, the modern cooperative movement is usually dated to the foundation of the Rochdale Equitable Pioneers Society in 1844. Of its ambitious aims, all designed to make the world a fairer place for working people, the establishment of a shop was the one that was successful. A dividend was paid on purchases and on capital subscribed. Since goods were sold at market price, members in effect got them more cheaply than elsewhere. Customers could also be confident that goods would not be adulterated, as was common by, for example, putting sand into brown sugar or Plaster of Paris into confectionery. In addition, the shops became social centres for meeting people and the exchange of local gossip. By the 1860s the movement was firmly established and in 1863, a buying agency – the Cooperative Wholesale Society – was set up to eliminate the profits of the middleman.[30] In that year an attempt had been made by a group of working men in Harrogate to set up a Cooperative Society in Tower Street but the venture had failed, for reasons not specified in the official history.

The idea was then revived in 1886 when another group of men obtained information from the Cooperative Union. Help was also sought from the town's civic head but, as the official history noted, 'Needless to say the services of the Mayor or any other "prominent townsman" were not available.' In February the following year a public meeting was held at the Saloon in Albert Street, shortly thereafter a provisional committee elected and in March a shop was opened in Beulah Street. The first president was chief clerk at the General Post Office but although the fifty-eight committee members listed in the official history, who served during its first twenty-one years, did include a few men in non-manual occupations, they comprised mostly skilled working men. They included thirteen railwaymen, eight joiners, four postmen, two policemen and two bath-chair men. The 254 members of that first year had passed a thousand by 1895, two thousand by 1900 and by 1913 reached 4,363. In 1908 sixty-two employees staffed the central departments in Albert Street, comprising grocery, outfitting and tailoring, boots and drapery, and the six branches in Regent Parade, Walker Road, Skipton Road at New Park, Gladstone Street at Oatlands, High Street, Starbeck and High Street, Knaresborough. **(19)**

Its activities were not confined to retail. There was an Educational Committee from the outset and from 1897 a Women's Guild, for a time disbanded but revived in 1907 to provide social and 'other interesting gatherings', in the words of the official history. Other events included concerts, lectures, such as one on the 'sweated industries', a choir and for the children lantern slides and a gala. It also ran a library, including works published by the Fabian Society. In the economically difficult year of 1905 a Distress Fund was established to distribute cash and 200 stones of flour to needy members. As the official history concluded, its members belonged mostly to the working class, who had thereby received £60,000 more than they would have if the Society had been a failure.[31] The Society thus offered real material benefits to working-class families but catered also for their social and cultural needs.

19.   The central Cooperative Society departments in Albert
Street, 1908. (Reproduced from Anon, 1887 to 1908: 21 Years
of Progress: the Harrogate & District Co-operative Society.)

A town whose employment was dominated by service of various
kinds and where women made up an above average proportion of the
workforce was unlikely to be heavily unionized. Nonetheless, there was
a significant union presence. In the building trades, although it is not
possible to give details of its extent, workers were certainly organized:
specialist craftsmen, such as carpenters and joiners by the 1880s and the
builder's labourers too had formed a union in 1892.[32] Railwaymen, the
other large group of male workers, were also unionized. An independent
branch of the Amalgamated Society of Railwaymen had been established
at Starbeck in 1890. The North Eastern Railway Company was the
only one of the major rail companies to recognize it and negotiate
with its representatives and, according to its history, its employees 'set
the pace' in the movement at this time. As we shall see, they were
prominent in the national strike of 1911.[33] Other unionized workforces
included the gas workers, the Harrogate and District United Society of

Coachmakers, a branch of the Postman's Federation and a local branch of the Typographical Association. In 1910 the latter claimed that practically 90 per cent of working printers were members.[34] Although shop assistants were difficult to organize, isolated as they were, working long hours, with lots of would-be entrants to the trade, and with a consciousness by some of status, they too had their union. The National Amalgamated Union of Shop Assistants, Warehousemen and Clerks established a branch in the town in 1900 and by the close of 1913 claimed 294 members.[35]

Unions also went beyond the concerns of their trade to a more general pursuit of the interests of labour. In 1901 a meeting was held of those in the building and other interested trades, including a representative from the Typographical Association, with a view to forming a Trades and Labour Council, with the object of putting different workers in touch with each other 'and whose influence could be brought to bear on other public bodies'. The following year a Harrogate and District Trades and Labour Council was duly formed at a meeting in the Clarion Club on Station Parade. Its objects were to secure better organization among established unions, the formation of new ones and the return of labour representatives on all public bodies or of candidates favourable to their programme.[36]

The Council provided support for its constituent unions. In 1905, for example, it agreed a Fair Contracts Clause with the Corporation that its contractors should pay standard rates and observe agreed hours and conditions and in September 1907 organized a mass meeting on the Stray to support the efforts of railwaymen to gain better conditions.[37] The electoral object was pursued but with no immediate success in this period. In 1903 attempts were first made to secure co-opted membership of the Library and Education Committees. Alderman Fortune had proposed the candidature for the former committee on the grounds that 'The Public Library was more for the working population, and it would show they were desirous of being in touch with that body and let them take part in the work.' Neither this candidate, who came bottom of the poll, nor the two for the Education Committee were successful.[38] The following year candidates were put forward for election to the Board of Guardians, the West Riding County Council and Harrogate Borough Council. None again were successful. In the borough election, Henry

Hill, a signalman of Station Parade, came bottom of the poll in the East Ward, which covered Starbeck, but did secure 403 votes.[39] By 1911 Labour candidates were contesting three wards. John Lee, a locomotive firemen, stood in Starbeck, Ernest Broadbank a painter, in East Ward and printer George Flower in Bilton. Although none were elected, Lee ran the Conservative close with 292 votes to 310.[40] This was a creditable result, given that this was not a natural labour town and given also that the electoral system still worked against their potential working-class support. Among those men still without the vote until 1918 were live-in servants, many sons living with parents who could not claim exclusive use of a room and lodgers. In the comparable town of Bath, the level of enfranchisement was less than 70 per cent.[41]

No candidates were put forward in parliamentary elections. The Ripon Division of the West Riding, in which Harrogate was located, returned a Conservative MP at every election save the Liberal landslide of 1906. But working men took an active interest in politics. MP John Lloyd Wharton addressed a 'large attendance' of Trades Council members at their club in Westmoreland Street in January 1905. In a speech covering a range of subjects, he responded to questions on unemployment by expressing support for relief works and for not depriving those who had to apply to the Poor Law Guardians for help of the vote (a further exclusion for working men), which was received with applause.[42] The town also had a branch of the Independent Labour Party, which brought in speakers like Ben Turner, the parliamentary candidate for Dewsbury in 1906, the following year Philip Snowden, the newly elected Labour MP for Blackburn, or at the Kursaal in February 1912, Ramsay MacDonald, the leader of the Labour Party, receiving a 'good attendance' despite the bad weather.[43]

Alongside the politics, the social side was not neglected. There was the socialist Harrogate Clarion Cycling Club, having its annual picnic for about thirty members at Nun Monkton in September 1907. The Trades and Labour Club offered the same pastimes as other working men's clubs: darts, dominoes and billiards. Political difference was no bar to games. In the Harrogate and District Billiard League for 1911, the Trades Club defeated Knaresborough Liberal Club in the final held at the Conservative Club.[44]

Whether it was this social side or the more political which was most important to working men has been debated by historians. Of those who did vote, many cast it for the traditional parties. Socialist ideas made limited progress and their appeal was often rather to the lower middle class. Most working men and women remained unorganized.[45] Nevertheless, the town's working-class institutions were important to the furtherance of their economic and political interests.

Notes to Chapter 2: The Working Class

1   *HH*, 13 June 1904, p. 5.

2   J. Harris, *Private Lives, Public Spirit: Britain, 1870–1914* (1994), p. 7.

3   D. Cannadine, *Class in Britain* (2000), p. 17.

4   E. Hobsbawm, 'The Formation of British Working-Class Culture' and 'The Making of the Working Class, 1870–1914' in his *Worlds of Labour: Further studies in the history of labour* (1984), pp. 184–93 and 194–213.

5   A. J. Reid, *Social Classes and Social Relations in Britain, 1850–1914* (1992).

6   E. Hobsbawm, 'The Labour aristocracy in nineteenth-century Britain', in his *Labouring Men: Studies in the History of Labour* (1964), pp. 272–315; see also his 'Debating the labour aristocracy' and 'The aristocracy of labour reconsidered' in *Worlds Of Labour*, pp. 214–26 and 227–51; H. Pelling, 'The concept of the labour aristocracy', in his *Popular Politics and Society in Late Victorian Britain* (1968), pp. 37–61; and see R. Gray, *The Aristocracy of Labour in Nineteenth-century Britain c. 1850–1914* (1981).

7   G. Best, *Mid-Victorian Britain, 1851–70* (1979), pp. 220–1.

8   E. Ross, '"Not the sort that would sit on the doorstep": Respectability in pre-World War 1 London neighbourhoods', *International Labor and Working-Class History*, 27 (1985), pp. 39–59; P. Jennings, *A History of Drink and the English, 1500–2000* (2016), p. 21.

9   J. Benson, *The Rise of Consumer Society in Britain 1880—1980* (1994), pp. 217–20; P. Johnson, 'Conspicuous consumption and working-class culture in late-Victorian and Edwardian Britain', *Transactions of the Royal Historical Society*, 38 (1988), pp. 27–42.

10 R. Roberts, *The Classic Slum: Salford life in the first quarter of the century* (1973), pp. 13–31; R. Hoggart, *The Uses of Literacy* (1958), pp. 13–26.

11 A. Clark, *The Struggle for the Breeches: Gender and the making of the British working class* (1995), pp. 264–71; S. Rowbotham, 'Search and subject, threading circumstance', in her *Dreams and Dilemmas: Collected writings* (1983), pp. 166–89.

12 P. Joyce, *Visions of the People: Industrial England and the question of class* (1991), p. 219.

13 P. Joyce, *Democratic Subjects: The self and the social in nineteenth century England* (1994), pp. 1–3; G. Stedman Jones, *Languages of Class: Studies in English working-class history, 1832–1984* (1983); and discussed in Cannadine, *Class*, pp. 11–12.

14 A. August, *The British Working Class, 1832–1940* (2007), p. 2.

15 E. Roberts, *A Woman's Place: An oral history of working-class women, 1890–1940* (1984), pp. 3–4.

16 For details of the census returns see the Bibliography.

17 E. Higgs, *Making Sense of the Census Revisited: A handbook for historical*

researchers (2005).

18　W. A. Armstrong, 'The use of information about occupation' in E. A. Wrigley, *Nineteenth-century Society: Essays in the use of quantitative methods for the study of social data* (1972), pp. 191–310; General Register Office, *Census of 1951: Classification of Occupations* (1956).

19　S. R. S. Szreter, 'The genesis of the Registrar-General's social classification of occupations', *British Journal of Sociology*, 35:4 (1984), pp. 522–46; G. Stedman Jones, *Outcast London: A study in the relationship between classes in Victorian society* (1984), pp. 350–7.

20　H. G. Wells, *Experiment in Autobiography: Discoveries and conclusions of a very ordinary brain (since 1866)*, (1934), p. 115.

21　G. Crossick, 'The emergence of the lower middle class in Britain: a discussion', in Crossick (ed.), *The Lower Middle Class in Britain, 1870–1914* (1977), pp. 11–60; C. P. Hosgood, 'The "Pigmies of Commerce" and the working-class community: small shopkeepers in England, 1870–1914', in J. Benson and G. Shaw (eds), *The Retailing Industry, Vol. 2 The Coming of the Mass Market* (1999), pp. 393–413.

22　Census of England and Wales 1901, General Report with Appendices; PP 1904 [Cd. 2174] CVII, p. 76; Census of England and Wales 1901, Area, Houses and Population; PP 1902 [Cd. 1107] CXXI.639, pp. 260–1; Census of England and Wales 1911, General Report with Appendices; PP 1917–18 [Cd. 8491] XXXV.483, p. 151; Census of England and Wales 1911, Vol. X, Occupations and Industries, Part 1; PP 1913 [Cd. 7018] LXXVIII.321, pp. 456–7.

23　G. Davis, *Bath as Spa and Bath as Slum: The social history of a Victorian city* (2009), p. 58; C. V. Butler, *Social Conditions in Oxford* (1912), pp. 46–50; p. 184; Jebb, *Cambridge*, p. 39.

24　*HA*, 4 January 1890, p. 4 and 9 August 1902, p. 2.

25　Jones, *Outcast London*, pp. 52–70.

26　J. Benson, *The Penny Capitalists: A study of nineteenth-century working-class entrepreneurs* (1983).

27　G. R. Searle, *A New England? Peace and War, 1886–1914* (2004), pp. 187–8.

28　*HA*, 7 December 1901, p. 6; 11 August 1906, p. 6; and 20 July 1907, p. 3.

29　*HA*, 25 January 1913, p. 7.

30　E. Hopkins, *A Social History of the English Working Classes, 1815–1945* (1979), pp. 167–9.

31　Anon, *1887–1908 21 Years of Progress. The Harrogate & District Co-operative Society, Ltd* (1908); *HA* 30 January 1909, p.6 and 31 January 1914, p. 5.

32　Jennings, *Harrogate*, p. 425.

33　*HA*, 18 January 1890, p. 7; R. J. Irving, *The North Eastern Railway Company, 1870–1914: An economic history* (1976), p. 53.

34　*HA*, 26 March 1910, p. 6.

35 W. B. Whitaker, *Victorian and Edwardian Shop Workers: The struggle to obtain better conditions and a half-holiday* (1973), pp. 21–4; *HA*, 21 February 1914, p. 4.

36 *HA*, 30 March 1901; p. 5, 29 November 1902, p. 6; and 20 December 1902, p. 2.

37 *HA*, 30 September 1905, p. 6 and 14 September 1907, p. 3.

38 *HA*, 11 November 1903, p. 5.

39 *HA*, 22 October 1904, p. 3 and 5 November 1904, p. 6.

40 *HA*, 4 November 1911, p. 5.

41 R. McKibbin, 'The franchise factor in the rise of the Labour Party', in his *The Ideologies of Class: Social relations in Britain, 1880–1950* (1990), pp. 66–100.

42 *HA*, 14 January 1905, p. 2.

43 *HA*, 7 April 1906, p. 2; 12 January 1907, p. 5; and 10 February 1912, p. 4.

44 *HA*, 6 January 1906, p. 5; 14 September 1907, p. 3; and 11 March 1911, p 5.

45 J. Benson, *The Working Class in Britain, 1850–1939* (2003), pp. 183–201.

CHAPTER THREE

Women at work

THROUGHOUT the Edwardian period women made up 40 per cent of Harrogate's workforce and a little under that percentage of all women worked. This was more than the national figure. Across England and Wales as a whole, fewer than a third of all women worked and they made up less than 30 per cent of the workforce. Those who worked were mostly young and single: over 80 per cent of Harrogate's women workers were unmarried in the two censuses, whilst in 1911, when the status of the remainder is specified, fewer than one in ten were either married or widowed. But whilst only one in ten married women worked, a third of the town's widows did. Although then not a majority of the workforce and comprising a minority, albeit a large one, of the town's women, we begin with their work as service in particular, the occupation of much the greater number of them, was also by far the largest single source of employment in the town.[1]

The broad picture of women's work is set out in the published general reports of the census but they do have several shortcomings. Whilst service itself is relatively clearly demarcated, other sectors, like food, tobacco, drink and lodging, or clothing, include both employers and such as shop keepers, lodging-house proprietors and hotel managers as well as workers like the shop assistants. Further, the employment categories are not wholly comparable across the two censuses. Accordingly, I have based my figures on the individual household returns. The dominance of service is clear, with around three-quarters of all working women in this sector. If we add to them those in laundry work, cleaning (charwomen), shop work and waitressing then clearly most women were performing some sort of personal service. The clothing sector was a far distant second. Over the decade the numbers in all sectors grew, except women taking in washing at home, although this was more than counterbalanced by the growth in the number of women working in commercial laundries. The other main increases were in cleaning and day service, clearly linked, and waitressing but above all in shop work. All those trends will be examined as we look in more detail at women's work.

Service: the private household

Service was by far the most important occupation for women in Edwardian England and this was more markedly the case in a residential and leisure town such as Harrogate. There were over 1.7 million female servants nationally over the period, and around 3,000 in Harrogate. They worked in a range of settings, of which the most important was the private household, where there were over 1.25 million nationally in 1911. But others worked in hotels, pubs, boarding and lodging houses, shops and institutions such as private schools, workhouses, orphanages and hospitals. In total they represented in 1901 41 per cent of working women in England and Wales but 55 per cent of those in Harrogate. Yet in the same period we also see both nationally and locally how service was beginning to lose that dominance, as whilst the total number of servants rose it was by less than the growth of population. By 1911 37 per cent of working women nationally were now servants and in Harrogate 48 per cent. That trend, but also the continuing importance of service within the local economy, was reflected in the proportion of servants per thousand families, which fell nationally over the decade from 189 to 170 and in Harrogate from 401 to 348. With this proportion the town was comparable to other inland and seaside resorts like Buxton, Bath or Bournemouth, or to residential suburbs, notably Hampstead with the highest of all at 737, and far above the much lower figures in industrial towns and cities.[2]

Around seven out of ten of Harrogate's servants worked in private households, well ahead of the fewer than one in five in the accommodation sector. Accordingly, it is with these women that we begin. First, however, which households employed them? The vast majority were middle- or lower middle class. Very few working-class households did so: only seventy-three in 1901, of over 2,600 such households, and even fewer ten years later, and as we will see in several instances the relationship was as likely emotional as one of employment. On the other hand, keeping a live-in servant was not universal among the town's middle class, although of course day servants and cleaners were employed. If it was not therefore essential to middle-class status, as it has often been seen, it was certainly an indicator of it and Edward Higgs's argument that it is unwise to make this link, as lower-class households also kept them, does not apply to the town.[3] To get an idea of the employers we may take a typical residential street of both middle- and lower middle-class households – East Park Road off Victoria Avenue. Employing a single servant were five individuals living 'on their own means', a retired farmer and land agent, an india-rubber dealer, two small employers and the head of a technical school. Employing two servants were a house furnisher, a woollen-cloth manufacturer and a retired lieutenant colonel. If the household head was almost invariably middle class, the family types for which they laboured displayed considerable variety. Looking at over 400 servants in 1901, nearly a third worked for couples with young children but 12 per cent respectively for couples either with no children or whose children were grown up. Some 15 per cent worked for extended or multiple families and, in contrast, one in ten for a widow or single woman living on her own.

The single servant was the most common situation. Throughout the period just under two-thirds of servant-keeping households employed only one, whilst conversely just under 40 per cent of servants worked alone. A further third worked with one other servant. Studies of other towns have shown the solitary servant to be quite typical. One of Lancaster, for example, for 1891, showed that almost three-quarters of households kept just one maid-of-all-work.[4] Households with a large staff of servants were rare in Harrogate. In 1901 just three employed more than six: on Park Road, William Cheetham, a woollen manufacturer, with seven, as had banker Edmund Faber at the Belvedere on Victoria Avenue, whilst Samson Fox, industrialist and three-times mayor of the town, at Grove House on Skipton Road had ten. Both the latter also employed gardeners and coaching staff living in adjoining cottages. Much more typical were, on West End Avenue in 1911, Ann Fairbotham, aged sixteen, working for an accountant, his wife and their three-year-old daughter at number 70, or at number 80, twenty-three-year-old Olive Corner for a single woman of eighty-three years of age with a private income.

Those servants were described in the census returns in a great variety of ways. To analyse them I adapted the functional classification used by Mark Ebery and Brian Preston in their study of domestic service. This in turn had drawn upon Armstrong's detailed work on the systems used by the census authorities and by Charles Booth in his survey of *Life and Labour of the People in London*.[5] My categories comprised: personal attendance; professional service; nursery duties; housekeepers; cooks; and a large group covering the whole range of basic servants' duties, either women specifically described as a kitchen-, house-, or parlour maid, for example, or more commonly simply as a general servant or domestic.

The smallest category was that of professional service. Among them the governess in fact occupied a rather ambiguous social position between that of a 'genteel upper servant' and one who was expected to possess 'the dress and demeanour of a lady'. This 'status incongruence', as it has been characterized, and the other travails which she endured had been debated throughout the nineteenth century, notably in fiction, particularly Anne Brontë's *Agnes Grey* of 1847.[6] But there were few live-in governesses in Edwardian Harrogate, just ten in 1901 and six in 1911. Rather more lived at home and their middle- or lower middle-class backgrounds support the picture of the position's ambiguous status, like the two clergyman's daughters living on West Cliffe Terrace in 1901, respectively a kindergarten teacher and a private governess. Another professional service was that performed by a nurse, variously described in the returns as sick-, monthly-, trained-, hospital- or surgical-, to whom I added those described simply as nurse who were employed in a household with no children aged fourteen or under. From the returns alone it is not generally possible to identify more specific reasons for their presence. Exceptionally, in 1901 a sick nurse was employed where the elderly household head was described, using the contemporary terminology, as feeble minded, or in 1911 similarly to a seventy-year-old invalid. In the latter census there were also four maternity nurses, like fifty-five-year-old

Margaret Cloherty employed by a doctor and his wife living on Norfolk Road, with a twenty-month-old daughter and new-born baby boy. The family also employed a children's maid, cook and housemaid. Such nurses, who were recorded as servants, occupied a similarly ambiguous position to governesses, in that nursing had risen to more professional status by our period, although state registration was not introduced until after the First World War.[7]

The next highest grouping was personal attendance, comprising such as lady's maid and -help or mother's help, but most commonly a companion, of whom there were twenty-four in 1901 and thirty-seven in 1911. The ambiguous social position which they too occupied may be seen in the census returns where the clerks had later amended their relationship to the household head from 'companion' to 'servant' for purposes of classification and enumeration. Almost two-thirds of these women were the companion of a single woman or widow, all but one themselves single, with an average age of thirty-six. The youngest at nineteen was the companion of two elderly sisters, the oldest two, both sixty-two, companions respectively to a lady of sixty and the other, Emma Whitcomb, to a seventy-six-year-old widow suffering from 'softening of the brain' and her fifty-two-year-old son described as of 'weak intellect from birth'. She would therefore have taken charge of the other servants there: the cook, maid attendant and housemaid.

Nursery duties occupied the next highest category, with just over a hundred at each census. They were mostly nurses, with the remainder variously described as under- or upper nurses, nursemaid, children's- or nursery maid and nursery governess. In 1901 there was one kinder maid and in 1911 a school-room maid aged just fourteen, but overall, they were on average in their mid-twenties. Typical then was in 1911 twenty-six-year-old Christina Welsh, nurse to a civil servant, his wife and young children on Walker Road, working alongside a cook and housemaid.

Housekeepers were the next group with around a hundred over the period. These are women recorded as servants but family members like unmarried sisters or nieces also performed this function. In the case of those housekeepers employed by a working-class head, since almost all of them worked for either a single man, a widower or a married man whose spouse was not recorded in the census and many of them were of similar age, it seems likely that some were in fact in a relationship with their 'employer'. In middle-class households some two-thirds were employed by a man similarly placed but were less likely to be the sole servant. The housekeeper as often portrayed, presiding over a large household, was rare. Only four did so in each of the census years: in 1901, for example, a fifty-seven-year-old widow over the nine staff of Samson Fox, or Alice Rainford, forty-one, over Edmund Faber's six servants. As a group housekeepers were mostly single, with a much smaller number of widows and married women and on average aged in their mid-forties.

Ebery and Preston's category of house duties: the kitchen and laundry comprised several specific roles, such as those of kitchen- or scullery maid, but those designations were rare in the Harrogate households. The most common by far was simply cook, with 385 in 1901 and 423 in 1911. Perhaps unsurprisingly very few were employed as the sole servant. More than half in each year worked alongside another woman, typically a housemaid. Their average age of around thirty implies greater experience, although there were some very young cooks, such as seventeen-year-old Kate Long in 1901 working alongside a twenty-nine-year-old housemaid for a bank manager, his wife and their young family in Alderson Road. Like the housekeepers the great majority were single women, also with a much smaller number of widows and still fewer who were married.

The largest category, of over 2,000 girls and women at each census year, worked as maids or general servants. They were predominantly young and single but their overall age and status profiles did change over the period. The number of those under the age of twenty fell but rose among those older, more especially aged twenty-five and over. This was reflected in the increase in the number of those widowed or married. This does suggest that domestic service was becoming less attractive to girls and younger women, although still drawing in many hundreds. (20)

Who were they? The census returns permit analysis of their birthplace, which gives some idea of their backgrounds. The great majority had not in fact come far from their place of birth. In both census years around a quarter had been born in Harrogate itself or, as was more likely, within around ten miles of the town and thus including Knaresborough, Ripon, Pateley Bridge, Otley and Wetherby in addition to numerous villages and smaller settlements. Overall, around two-thirds had been born in

20. Unknown Edwardian Harrogate housemaid. (Courtesy Enid Rispin)

Yorkshire and of those from further afield, about a third of the total, half had originated in the three adjoining counties of Durham, Lancashire and Lincolnshire. Of those having come longer distances, birth in the capital, the county of Norfolk, Scotland and Ireland was most numerous, with a negligible number originating elsewhere. Despite the common assumption that servants were typically country girls, in Harrogate most were not, as in the Lancaster study noted earlier. One in ten were born in cities of over 50,000 inhabitants, particularly Leeds, York and Middlesbrough, and among others born in Yorkshire, half were from towns, although that did include places with only 2,500 people. To add to the confusion, industrial villages, like those in the Durham or south Yorkshire coalfields, were classed as rural. They, like the iron and steel town of Middlesbrough, had limited employment for women compared to textile towns like Bradford, Halifax or Huddersfield from which comparatively few servants came.[8]

To get a more detailed picture of their social backgrounds I traced 276 women employed in service in 1901 back to earlier censuses and marriage registers to find their father's, or where she was the household head the mother's, occupation. As one might expect they came mostly from working-class backgrounds and the wide variety of occupations suggests that going into service was an option for a broad range of families. Fathers included building and railway workers, gardeners, grooms and coachmen, labourers and policemen, and reflected too local employment patterns, as with the miners of south Yorkshire or west Cumberland, the electro plater of Sheffield or the ship's steward of Hull. Of the mothers just under half were employed in some sort of service themselves as charwoman, laundress or cook. Of fathers from a higher social group half were farmers, suggesting again that where opportunities for work were limited, as was increasingly the case in agricultural districts in the latter part of the nineteenth century, service was an option for them too.[9] There were also two daughters of publicans: Rhoda Hardisty, whose father kept the Nelson Inn at Hampsthwaite in 1891 but was also a quarryman and Elizabeth Rayner, whose father had the Green Dragon at Bedale.

Elizabeth was one of eight children and being a girl among many siblings was also important in deciding whether a girl went into service. I looked at the composition of the servant girls' families and, although it may not have been the moment at which she left for service, they were more likely to come from large families of six or more children than were working-class children generally in my case of Harrogate: one third compared to one in ten. Conversely, whereas over a quarter of those working-class children were the only child very few of the servants were.

Whereas most servants came from families, particularly large ones, there were also those raised in institutions: nine in my sample. Two had been in workhouses: Ann Catton, who was in Knaresborough workhouse aged seven with four siblings in 1891, but by 1901 was a general servant to a small employer, his wife and three children in Robert Street; and Dora Johnson, an eight-year-old 'inmate' of Hartlepool workhouse in 1891, who by 1901 was a housemaid with three other servants at Larchfield on Leadhall Lane and ten years later a cook at a Station Parade boarding house. Three had been in orphanages: Julia Kennedy was at St Mary's Convent and Orphanage in Leeds and by 1901 was a general servant in a Valley Drive boarding house. Margaret Tate was at the Port of Hull Society's Sailors' Orphan Home in Hull. Her father, a captain, had drowned in 1866, the year Margaret was born, and she had entered the orphanage in 1873 from the Middlesbrough home of her widowed grandfather. She had left it shortly after the 1881 census was taken, ten years later was in service in Sculcoates, Hull and in 1901 employed as a general servant by a widow on West End Avenue.[10] Henrietta Eden was in 1871 at St Stephen's Orphanage in Newington, south London run by the Anglican order of the Sisters of the Holy Cross, but at the subsequent three censuses was in service in Knaresborough, Pannal Ash and Harrogate.

Four girls had attended what were called Industrial Schools, or Homes, three at one in Ripon and one in Leeds. These institutions dated back to the mid-Victorian period and were aimed, in contrast to reformatories for the criminal young, at what would later be termed vulnerable children. These were, as specified in the Industrial Schools Acts, children found begging, homeless and with no proper guardianship or visible means of subsistence; those destitute, either orphaned or where the parent was in prison; or those who frequented the company of reputed thieves. Children under the age of twelve committing petty crimes, or where the parents represented that they were uncontrollable, might also be admitted. In practice the largest group nationally sent to them were those failing to attend school or 'found wandering'. Nearly a third were orphans.[11] In 1881 Ada Dalby, aged eleven, was one of 105 girls at the Windsor Street Industrial Home for Girls in Leeds but by 1891 was in service in Harrogate. Of the three who had been at the Ripon Industrial Home, two were sisters Annie and Nellie Garner from Pateley Bridge. Their mother had died in 1887, aged just thirty, and their farm labourer father remarried and started a new family with his bride and her own children. Whatever the precise circumstances, and unfortunately there are no admission records for the Home, both girls were there by 1891 whilst their father's new family remained in Pateley Bridge.

We know something of the nature of such institutions and the experience of them from the girls' point of view because one who was at Ripon just a decade later, Alice Collier, has left us a memoir of her time there. Like most such homes this was a charitable, rather than state, institution. It had been founded in 1862 as the Ripon Industrial Home for Girls by the Dean of Ripon in premises in Bondgate formerly a boys' boarding school and was supported by 'a number of benevolent ladies'. Its aim was:

> to befriend poor girls of good character, more especially those that are motherless ... by training then in habits of industry, giving them instruction calculated to fit them for domestic service or as mother of a household of their own, and securing to them religious teaching.

Alice's mother had died in 1909 when she was just four-and-a-half-years-old and the children dispersed from their Scarborough home, as their father was a heavy drinker. Just one week before her fifth birthday she and her older sister Annie were sent to Ripon to join twenty-five to thirty other, mostly local, girls. During her time there she experienced the regimes of three matrons and it seems they very much set the tone for her changing experience. The first had 'lots of kind ways', such as providing hot drinks on cold nights, welcome no doubt as the bedrooms were unheated. She was succeeded by a Miss Orange, 'a regular devil', according to Alice, and four years later by a Miss Hammond, a lot better but still 'quite a tartar at times', including with a stick formed from part of a whip with a steel rod in the middle. The girls' day began at 6.30 with the ringing of a bell and then breakfast of raw oatmeal and warm water. Dinner was a meat dish, with perhaps a milk or suet pudding, and tea a slice of bread and dripping or jam. In their 'awful uniform', of which they were all ashamed, of blue cape, navy blue dress and print pinafore and boater, they attended the nearby Cathedral School. The girls baked their own bread with yeast from a local brewery which imparted to it a beery taste, older girls cooked and they did their own laundry. Bath time was once a week in two tubs, each holding two girls, and in three lots using the same water. For their health there was brimstone and treacle and later Dr Gregory's stomach powder every week. There were prayers three times a day and church on Sunday. Lighter times included the cinema on Saturday afternoons, occasional trips to the seaside or nearby Knaresborough or Brimham Rocks, or to the homes of local 'gentry' families. At Christmas their stockings would receive a few nuts and sweets, an orange and an apple. Prizes of a bible or prayer book or a box of handkerchiefs were given out annually for good conduct, knowledge of scripture, or for skill in such as bread-making or knitting. As Alice commented, 'We were not allowed to lose sight of the gratitude we owed'. As for the whole experience, 'it wasn't too bad', better in fact than that of many girls in their own homes, although there was 'no love'. Finally, at aged fifteen, the girls were 'lent out' for a few weeks as a temporary maid and eventually placed in service to families who paid a subscription to the home of a guinea a year. In their final year they had made up a complete outfit, the cost of which had to be repaid from their wages and provided with a tin trunk for all their worldly possessions.[12]

Service then, perhaps as a life's career, as it was to be for Alice, or more likely before marriage and motherhood, was the aim of all these institutions for its girls. As the much larger Leeds Industrial Home, to which Ada Dalby was sent, put it in its annual report, 'ample accommodation is provided for carrying on industrial work which will fit the girls for domestic service', comprising 'washing, baking, cooking, sewing, knitting and housework in all its branches'.[13] It was the aim also of one further type of institution: the rescue home. The 'rescue' of young women from prostitution or immorality, or the 'prevention' of their falling into it, was a major concern of late Victorian and Edwardian philanthropy. By 1900, according to one estimate, there were nationally 600 charities dealing with girls and young women.[14] A home was set up in Harrogate on West Cliffe Terrace, later moving to nearby Harlow Terrace, by a Prevention and Rescue Association founded in 1905 at the instigation of the Vicar of Christ Church, the Revd Guy, and a number of prominent townswomen and members of the local nobility. Its report for 1911 to 1912 noted thirty-five rescue and twenty-four preventive cases, with a further fourteen maternity and five 'drink'. Twenty-eight girls had been placed in service.[15] 'Placed', as is clear, was usually by prospective employers applying direct to the institution itself, as we saw at Ripon. Similarly, at another home in Leeds helping young women between situations or in poor health, the matron was 'constantly employed in endeavouring to supply ladies who inquire for servants'.[16]

This was but one of several ways in which servants were recruited. There were still in this period, particularly in the north of England, hiring fairs for farm workers. One was held annually at nearby Knaresborough, where in 1905, for example, the 'call for female servants was greatly in excess of supply', but there is no evidence one way or the other as to whether or to what extent it was used by Harrogate households.[17] Advertisements were placed in the local papers by prospective employers or, less frequently, by servants themselves seeking a position. The former might specify age as for example 'a girl about fourteen to assist with the baby', or 'not under twenty'; or allude to a girl's experience, strength or respectability. The latter offered particular qualities, like the nurse 'fond of children ' or, for engagement as a mother's help or lady nurse, a 'good needlewoman' with 'excellent references'.[18] A reference, or character as it was termed, was often specified by both servants and employers and without one it might be difficult or impossible to get a situation. Attesting to its importance, it was a particular grievance of the London and Provincial Domestic Servants' Union, formed in 1890, one of whose objectives was that its provision be made compulsory.[19] One Harrogate servant, cook Alice Doughty, even successfully sued a former employer for libel over a bad character and was awarded £25 damages.[20] Alice had obtained her latest position at a registry office, a further means of recruitment. There were several in Harrogate and they too advertised in the newspapers, as in the following 1900 examples. Willis's Registry in Parliament Street offered 'servants of every description'. Servants registered too and it was an added inducement in some cases, as at a registry run from a house in Valley Mount, that the service was free to them. There was a wider market for servants and this offers some explanation for how girls came to travel to a particular town. Rushforth's Registry in the Market Place, claiming 'servants with good references, suited immediately', was for both Harrogate 'or away'. Conversely, the County Registry, Newcastle was advertising locally in 1911 for servants 'wanting situations'.[21]

It was personal recommendation, however, which was perhaps the most common means of obtaining a position. A contemporary study of domestic service by social researcher and philanthropist Violet Butler cited 'private enquiry' alongside registries and newspaper advertisements, whilst the Lancaster study placed informal recommendation above those two.[22] In Harrogate, family members worked together in the same household, who thus either came to the situation at the same time or one followed the other, like two pairs of Irish sisters in 1901 both serving as cook and housemaid: Molly and Nellie Curran aged twenty-two and seventeen and Kate and Ellen Finnesty from County Sligo, aged twenty-four and nineteen. In many more instances they simply came from the same place, like the thirty-one who were born in Ripon and twenty-seven in Knaresborough in 1901 and it seems likely that informal recommendation secured for many their position. Others came from the same place as their employers and in some cases would have moved with them to Harrogate. All four of the servants of Scottish-born physician Andrew Myrtle and his wife and two Harrogate-born grown-up sons at their Park Parade home were originally from Scotland. Sarah Jane Brackenbury, a fisherman's daughter, travelled with her employer, stock and share broker Reginald Chadwick, his wife and young son to Harrogate from Great Yarmouth and in 1901 was there serving at their West End Avenue home as nurse for this boy and a further young daughter and baby son.[23]

By the later nineteenth century the difficulty of recruiting servants had been elevated to talk nationally of the 'servant shortage' or 'problem'. Certainly, as we saw at the outset, whilst the total number of servants grew there were fewer servants in relation to the number of households. The fall in the proportion of younger servants was only partly attributable to the raising of the school leaving age.[24] Higgs attributed the supply-side crisis from the late nineteenth century partly to a falling rural population reducing the number of available daughters and partly to the fact that urban women were unwilling to enter it, preferring work in cafés, restaurants and shops, although this he felt was a result of the decline of service rather than its cause.[25] The Lancaster study stressed local variation in the timing of changes but found that service remained popular among agricultural workers into the twentieth century.[26] Nor does the Harrogate evidence show any shift away from rural origins over the Edwardian period.

The principal reasons given in the town for the shortage were the attractions of other forms of employment and the lowly status of service. The two were paired by a couple unable to obtain a servant in a letter to the local paper headed 'Pride and Poverty', who declared that if they advertised for a shop girl they would get dozens and dozens of applications 'from respectable young women' who would work long hours for less money 'far sooner than be a domestic servant'.[27] The lack of independence of service, compared to such as shop work, and a 'loss of caste' were both cited by servants themselves in responses to Butler's survey. They talked of the contempt shown to them both by their employers and social equals, the stigma of the uniform, particularly the cap, and the cries of 'skivvy' from passing workmen or errand boys.[28] This low status may have been exacerbated, it has been suggested, by the growth in the number of girls entering service from Poor Law or charitable institutions, particularly of course from rescue homes with their intimations of immorality or worse. It was certainly salient enough for novelist George Moore to use it in a quarrel between his eponymous heroine Esther Waters and another servant who accuses her of being 'no doubt taken out of some 'ouse – Rescue work, I think they call it –'.[29] Finally, the 'servant difficulty' was raised again in 1911 by another Harrogate 'Mistress' with the proposed introduction of health insurance for servants, which also required a contribution from employers. This raised, in addition to hurting thrifty domestics who according to 'Mistress' used the Post Office Savings Bank and the Girls' Friendly Society, the awful prospect of mistresses having to stick stamps on cards, a key part of a vociferous press campaign against the measure, which nevertheless came into force in 1913.[30]

What then was involved in service? Clearly it is difficult to generalize. As we have seen it covered a wide variety both of job titles and of households, upon whose individual size and composition a lot would depend. Since, however, housemaid or general servant was the most common it is to her daily round that we will turn. Mrs Beeton's famous *Book of Household Management* provided details of the duties of the whole range of servants, and whilst these are to some extent ideal types, they do give some indication of the nature and amount of the work involved. The duties of a housemaid are described as 'very numerous', including daily cleaning, dusting and polishing; the clearing, laying and lighting of fires; setting the table for meals, serving and clearing the dishes; bed-making and tidying of bedrooms. Weekly tasks included a thorough clean of all rooms in the house, whilst periodically there were the paintwork, curtains, beating of carpets and spring cleaning. As for the general servant her work in some places, according to Mrs Beeton, was 'never done'. Not only had she the duties of a housemaid but also those of cook and kitchen maid and even tasks performed by a footman or page, taking messages and the like.[31] The hours which all these tasks occupied were long. Butler's survey found that they began at 6.30 and continued to 10 p.m. and even beyond, but that the work was not 'incessant' during those hours.[32]

For this general service the Harrogate couple quoted earlier were offering £22 a year. This was clearly meant to be an attractive wage but the amount is supported by newspaper advertisements. Those from the year 1911 show a range from £18 to £24. For example, an experienced general servant was offered £20 for all duties in a small house, as was a general for another small house and family who could cook but would not be required to do washing. For another general servant 'able to wait' just £18 was on offer, whereas the 8s. 6d. for a strong girl to live-in and assist with spring cleaning was equivalent to £22 a year. At the lower end of the scale, however, there was just 2s. 6d. a week forthcoming to a young girl to be available all day for light housework and to take the baby out.[33] The findings of surveys showed that wages had risen. One prepared for the Labour Department of the Board of Trade in the mid-1890s gave an overall average wage for servants of £15. 10s. There was great differentiation according to age, from just £7 for a young girl under fifteen to over £20 for those aged twenty-five and over, and again according to the nature of the duties performed and the number of servants in the household.[34] A study of London published in 1908 showed that servants' wages there had risen by more than those of other occupations. Similarly, in Oxford domestic service paid better than any other available occupation for young women, at £18–20 a year for a general servant of twenty, which with board and lodging was worth between 10s. and 12s. a week.[35] In addition there were sometimes perks such as cast-off clothing and Christmas gifts. The uniform, however, was rarely provided; indeed, those girls who came from institutions had to cover its cost from their wages.[36]

The accommodation offered had also improved by this time. The Butler survey found that sharing a bed with another servant was 'almost extinct', whilst citing, however, complaints of overcrowding or of sleeping in damp basements. Examples from Harrogate included the cellar, an upstairs room or attic and, in one case at least, the housemaid and cook at Oak Lodge on Cold Bath Road each had their own bedroom with a view. But this contrasted with a Bower Road arrangement where her bed was in a screened-off portion of a landing.[37]

There was then variety in every aspect of service and perhaps no more so than in the relationship with her employing family. Mrs Beeton went out of her way to address this personal dimension, noting that the 'custom of "Society"' was to abuse its servants for not being as good as they used to be and no longer knowing their place, and exhorting employers that 'good masters and mistresses make good servants', who should be treated 'like reasonable beings'; so many mistresses especially 'lacking consideration for their servants.[38] Something of this rarely glimpsed personal dimension, albeit from the employer's and institution's point of view, can also be gleaned, however inadequately, from the records of visits to girls found situations by the Leeds Association for the Care and Protection of Friendless Girls, by which two girls were placed in Harrogate. These range from the 'reliable', 'satisfactory' and 'very satisfactory', 'clean, honest and steady', 'good with children', to 'idle and bad tempered', 'rather sulky', 'can't get on with fellow servants' or that her 'only fault [is] that she is tiresome about getting up in the morning'.[39]

For servants generally the main causes of complaint in Butler's survey were the lack of personal liberty, the feeling of never being off duty and, for girls working alone, the absence of company. Time off was on average one evening a week and half of Sunday, with a fortnight's usually paid annual holiday almost universal and three or four weeks not uncommon.[40] That Harrogate couple were offering three nights a week off in addition to the half-day on Sunday. Although one cannot deny the reality of loneliness for what were often young girls, one must also set alongside this the fact that many lived not so far from home and might well have family in Harrogate or know other girls in service from their home towns and villages. The town of course afforded opportunities with which to spend leisure time, as one journalist noted of their love of dressing up, in a piece typical of the genre on the 'Harrogate Domestic': 'she adorns the Valley Gardens and the Stray Promenade'.[41] The piece also noted how they have 'a young man or two', another cliché of the servant's life. (21, 22) But other evidence does support the view that they

21. Domestic servants were the butt of many attempts at humour; here her pretensions and neglect of duties; another facet of the 'servant problem'. (Contemporary postcard)

22. Here her fondness for 'a young man or two'. (Contemporary postcard)

were able to see relatives and friends and form relationships. Martha Allen, a cook, visited a cousin every year at Ryhill, between Wakefield and Hemsworth, and went home to Middlesbrough to spend Christmas with her family. We know this because she later successfully sued for breach of promise the insurance agent she had met at the former place and taken to meet her father at the latter.[42] Anne Collyer, the housemaid at Oak Lodge on Cold Bath Road, was engaged to a man from her home town of Ilkley whom she had known for some two-and-a-half years. They corresponded and most recently she had spent part of an afternoon and evening with him in Harrogate. Sadly, we know this everyday fact from the inquest into her mysterious death from poisoning with some liniment intended for rheumatism.[43]

Sometimes relationships became sexual. The evidence is the resulting pregnancy. Servants were overrepresented among the mothers of illegitimate children. A survey of 1911 found that almost half of the illegitimate children born in Britain were to women who had been in service, although in relation to the total servant population the numbers were tiny. In Harrogate there were just thirty-five illegitimate births in 1907 and twenty-nine in 1908, compared to the 3,000 servants in the town, low even allowing for the birth having taken place elsewhere and of course an unknown proportion were actually to servants.[44] The Rescue Home, a 'large part' of whose work was with maternity cases, endeavoured to find foster homes for the children and new situations for the girls and to obtain financial support from the father.[45] The babies of some of the girls were baptized at the new church of St Wilfrid on Duchy Road. In each case they were described as a single woman and in none of them was the name of the father given on the birth certificate.[46] I was able to trace further details of just two. In one the daughter of a coal heaver had gone into service in the town, become pregnant and the child been born in 1910. At the census the following year she was back in service but now at Ossett, not far from her hometown of Normanton, where the child was living with her grandfather. In the other the woman was also back in service in 1911, still in Harrogate, whilst the child, aged three months, was a 'boarder' at All Saints Nursery College for the training of nursery nurses at Pannal.[47]

In four cases, documented in the local newspaper, the pregnancy ended in tragedy. In 1902, Beatrice Hill, servant at the Harrogate Hotel at Starbeck, and in fact the half-sister of the landlady, poisoned herself with salts of lemon used for cleaning when her condition became known, as she had earlier said she would. In this case the father was the groom and yard man at the pub who had been dismissed the day before when the relationship was discovered and when Beatrice herself had been prevented from following him. In the second in 1906, Fanny Haggard had given notice to her Beech Grove employers saying she might go to London but had given birth in the lavatory where the baby sustained ultimately fatal injuries striking its head on the stone floor. In two cases she faced trial at Leeds Assizes for the offence of concealment of a birth. In the first the mummified remains of the child had been discovered in a false roof of a house in Ash Grove, Otley Road during maintenance work. The inquest could not determine whether it had been born alive or dead. It had been hidden there by twenty-year-old Elizabeth Walker, who had left her situation some three months after the birth. She was arrested working then as a servant at the Harrogate Swimming Baths, charged with concealment, to which she pleaded guilty, and sentenced to one month in prison. The last girl, Lily Teale, was acquitted when the Grand Jury found no bill, that is no case, to answer. Her baby boy had been born dead in the cellar of her employers' house on Franklin Road. Mrs Thorpe had called the doctor and Mr Thorpe stood surety for her bail and offered to take her back into their service.[48]

The vulnerable young girl subject to the sexual advances of the master or other male members of the household is another popular image of service and is invariably mentioned in its histories, but there is no evidence of its existence or otherwise in Harrogate. A study of service in North Wales asserted that there was 'little doubt' of its prevalence, citing the House of Lords Select Committee Relating to the Protection of Young Girls, which reported in 1881, and local bastardy cases from the mid-Victorian period, although the majority of them actually involved fellow servants or local working men.[49] Certainly in one Harrogate case it was a lodger in the Bower Street household who criminally assaulted the fifteen-year-old general servant who slept on the landing.[50] Memoirs of upper- or middle-class men and the testimonies of servants alike confirm that sexual harassment existed but the history which made this point also asserted that in fact servants were more commonly the vehicle for middle-class vicarious fascination with working-class courtship. The servant as victim coexisted with the 'knowing' servant with active sexual desires.[51]

Petty theft was another source of employer complaint. It is impossible to know to what extent this occurred, except to note that there was some dozen newspaper reports over the period of the appearance of servants for the offence before the borough magistrates. Mrs Tipper of Victoria Avenue testified that she 'had missed so many things by other servants' in giving evidence against her cook who had stolen a pair of candlesticks. She further stated that she had dismissed her as she had been 'very impertinent ... and had not been a sober woman', plus other items had been missed. She was bound over.[52] In contrast, efforts were also made to help the girl, both by the employer and the authorities. In 1902 Lizzie Yeoman, originally from Farnham in Surrey, had a letter both from the vicar of her home parish and her late employer attesting to her good character. The latter also offered to pay her expenses home to her parents. In another case, Minnie Ballard had been born in Ripon workhouse and from the age of twelve been in service in several households prior to appearing in court in June 1905 charged with the theft of a ring, cash and stamps from a fellow servant at their Rutland Road place of employment. She had been arrested at 'a home for fallen girls' in Leeds and the matron came to court, spoke up for her and asked that she might be returned there. In addition, the society which ran it had made some restitution to the other servant for her loss. Minnie agreed to return, promising to behave herself in future, and was also bound over as a first offender.[53] This kind of outcome was the more usual; as perhaps one might expect defiance was rare. When nineteen-year-old Ethel Hodgson from Cockfield, County Durham was arrested for stealing a gold locket from her employer she had gone on hunger strike for three days, stayed in bed and refused either to plead or speak to magistrates and the case remanded due to her 'sulky manner'. The magistrate asserted that in his twenty-seven years on the bench he 'had never seen such stupidity', binding her over for six months in the sum of £5 after she had now pleaded guilty.[54]

Girls who came to grief in such ways were clearly only a small minority of the thousands who went into service in the town over the period of this study. For the majority service was for a relatively short period of time and represented a transitional phase in their lives before marriage. The Board of Trade report found that typically the period of service was short, averaging a little under a year-and-a-half already completed in one situation at the time of the inquiry.[55] I traced 237 servants working in 1901 back- and forwards in time and found that in only just over a fifth of cases was she a servant in two or more censuses and of that fifth the great majority were in only two. It was also very unusual to stay with the same employer, contrary to any idea of the faithful servant. Almost as unusual was the woman for whom service became a career, like Sarah Brackenbury, who later returned to service in her native East Anglia, or Alice Collier, who eventually worked for the Bishop of Blackburn and later for him at the Bishopric of Norwich.

Most servants left for marriage. Indeed, the occupation was held to enhance their eligibility. Helen Bosanquet of the Charity Organisation Society in her 1906 book on *The Family,* asserted that service 'in a well-managed but not wealthy Family' was 'the best possible preparation for married life'.[56] Some historians have echoed the point, seeing that eligibility in personal grooming and the acquisition of skills, savings and middle-class aspirations, which offered in turn the potential for upward mobility.[57] In fact this does not appear to have been generally the case. A study of servants in Cambridge found that significantly more actually married men from a lower social group than their fathers when compared with other working-class women.[58] Using the census and marriage registers I looked at over a hundred servants and found a similar situation in Harrogate.[59] Over a third married husbands of a lower social group than their father's, slightly more married at the same level and just over a quarter married into a higher group within the working class. For other working-class women the position was reversed. Typical then, among marriages for example at Christ Church in 1911, were those of Ada Wood, a general servant, to railway stoker Ernest Fenwick, both their fathers having also been railwaymen, or of Lizzie Anger, another general servant, to labourer Harold Farnell.

Exceptional in rising in the world was a woman such as Ada Dalby, who had formerly been in the Leeds Industrial School. She married in 1902 and by 1911 was with her husband George Almond and their sons at substantial Ringbeck House Farm on the edge of Kirkby Malzeard, north of Ripon. More exceptional still were women who traversed the whole social range and, in the only cases I found, this was through marriage to the son or head of the household. Labourer's daughter Clara Forrest had gone into service in her native Hampsthwaite for the Revd Henry Deck, his wife, their son Henry, a retired solicitor, and daughter. On the vicar's death in 1896 Clara moved with his widow and children to a house in South Drive, Harrogate. After she in turn died Clara then married Henry in 1907, he by then sixty-one and she thirty-three, whom she had therefore known by that time for at least seventeen years. The couple later lived in substantial houses at Dolgellau, west Wales and on the Dunsinore Cliff Estate, Cromer. The other case was that of Annie Baxter, a farmer's daughter of South Stainley, who by 1891 was a housemaid at Grove House, the Harrogate home of Samson Fox, some thirty-two years her senior, whom she married in 1899 after the death of his first wife to return as mistress of her former place of employment.

Domestic service then was a common experience for the daughters of working-class families. Pay and conditions were improving over the period as demand exceeded supply but not sufficiently to offset the pull of other forms of employment. Common to the experience itself was that it was undoubtedly hard work but then this was the lot generally of working-class women. But it was also varied, both due to the size and variety of employing households and, not least, from the unique personalities of those families and servants and the relationships between them. For the majority it was for a more or less short period between home, which for some was an institution, and marriage within the working class.

Service: accommodation, schools and institutions

Service in a wide variety of hotels and other accommodation providers, private schools and institutions was also predominantly female, with the sole exception of hotel work. The proportion of live-in hotel staff who were women fell from just over to just under two thirds over the decade, more than 300 women in each year. Hotel workers who lived out were almost all men. Since the census was taken before the season had begun, this was probably not the full complement of staff. In 1901 seventy servants at the Swan Hydro looked after as many guests, whilst at the Harlow Manor Hydro each guest had two servants and at the Majestic seventeen were looked after by sixty-eight live-in staff. Other types of accommodation similarly had few visitors in residence on census nights. The profiles of staff at the height of the season may therefore have been rather different. In addition, guests brought their own servants: sixty-five at one time at the Majestic, for example, enough to warrant their own special accommodation.[60] Service in pubs, boarding and apartment houses more closely resembled that in private households, as almost all were women. Similarly, most employed a single servant, like eighteen-year-old Kathleen Doyle, originally from West Hartlepool, at the Marlborough Boarding House on Valley Drive in 1911. Only the larger establishments, as one might expect, employed more: the thirteen-roomed Octagon Boarding House, on a distinctive corner site lower down Valley Drive, had a cook, housemaid and housemaid/waitress. **(23)**

Staff at the large hotels naturally had more specialized tasks. Looking at 1911, in addition to the chambermaids, there were hall- and corridor maids, laundry- and staff maids. The Queen Hotel employed lounge- and servants' hall maids. Hotel laundry and linen were also women's work. In kitchens were kitchen maids and still room-, pantry- and vegetable maids. The cooking, in contrast, was done by relatively few women. Also gendered was waiting on tables, also mostly done by men. Exceptionally, the Grand employed a fifteen-year-old bell girl. We know little, however, about the work of all these women beyond what was implied in its description except when tragedy affords us at least a glimpse into their lives. Gertrude Day, aged twenty, had come as a housemaid to the Crown Hotel in April 1911 from Attercliffe, Sheffield and, according to the housekeeper Alice Mortimer, had 'given every satisfaction'. A letter and a postcard home suggested she was happy in her new position and in good health. Just two weeks into her employment she was clearing out a cupboard, when she asked if she could clean the glass in the adjoining domed skylight over the lounge. She got a pail of water and a long brush for the job but must have overstretched and fell through the glass forty feet to her death on the mosaic floor below. At the inquest it was held that no blame attached to anyone, as she had been warned to take care,

Breakfast-time at a Boarding House.

23. More humour in 'Breakfast time at a boarding house' by Herbert Templar (1863-1945), c. 1894. (Courtesy of Harrogate Museums and Arts, Harrogate Borough Council)

but the jury did recommend the provision of some form of protection to prevent future accidents.[61]

Broadly speaking, hotel servants came from the same places as did servants generally, except this was rather less likely to have been Harrogate or within ten miles and somewhat more likely to have been a town or city. No fewer than thirty-five had been born in Middlesbrough, more than twice as many as from nearby Leeds. Four of the twenty staff at the Harlow Manor Hydro came from there and it is tempting to conclude that word-of-mouth recommendation played a part in their recruitment, plus two of them had the same surname. They shared the working-class background of household servants: twenty of twenty-three identified father's occupations, plus two farmers and one publican. They were also more likely to come from large families. Those in more supervisory posts did come from higher status backgrounds. Edith Patchett, the laundry manager at the Grand Hotel, was the daughter of a Bradford Coop clerk and ten years earlier had been a marker and packer in a laundry. Some had previous hotel experience: Sylvia Jarvis at the White Hart in 1911 had ten years earlier been a chambermaid at the Cobden Temperance Hotel in Birmingham; Emma Atherton at the Crown was formerly a still-room maid at the Imperial Hotel, Clifton, Bristol; and Elizabeth Smythe, a chambermaid at the Swan, who came originally from County Meath, had been in 1901 a waitress at the Craiglands Hydro at Ilkley. Hotel work may for some then have been a conscious choice. For most, marriage ended their working life, occasionally from the hotel itself, as Grand Hotel valet Arthur Brown married chambermaid Emma Stretton at nearby St Wilfrid's in November 1911.

Service in private schools was women's work. In 1901, 141 women worked in these schools and in 1911, 153. Their experience naturally would vary with the size of the school. In 1911 at the largest of all – Harrogate Ladies College – in the main 110-room building its staff and 104 boarding girls relied on the services of matron, assistant matron, housekeeper, nine housemaids and two kitchen maids. Unusually, there were also eighteen-year-old page Percy Bentley and fifty-five-year-old porter George Jackson. The seventy-seven boys at Ashville were looked after by two matrons, a cook, two kitchen maids, four housemaids and three laundresses, plus two boots. The exception was Pannal Ash College, whose thirteen servants were all male, except for matron and a single serving maid. At the other end of the scale, Dunmarklyn School on Walker Road, with six girls boarding, was run by two women with the assistance of sixteen-year-old Lily Maynard from Starbeck. A typical life then was that of Elizabeth Robinson, who was the daughter of a Keighley sewing-machine fitter, and in 1891 was a housemaid at a Harrogate boarding house. Ten years later she was a cook at a private school with eight boarding boys, Balliol House in Clarence Drive, working alongside matron, a housemaid and under-housemaid. Six years later she married John Binns, a Harrogate plumber, and the couple spent their married life in Regent Terrace.[62]

Service in an institution was equally, if not more, varied for the thirty-four women in 1901 and the sixty-eight of 1911 so engaged. The Royal Bath Hospital, with eighty-one patients in 1911, employed a cook, two kitchen maids, housemaid, linen maid, two laundresses and four ward maids along with a male porter, supporting two live-in nurses and a married couple who acted as bath attendants. The forty-eight patients at the Yorkshire Home for Incurables were looked after by matron and seven nurses plus the service of a male porter, cook, kitchen maid and three housemaids, two of whom were born in South Bank, Middlesbrough. At the Police Orphanage, the seventy-five boys and girls were looked after by matrons and assistant matrons for each sex, with the help of just a cook and a housemaid and thirty-nine-year-old needlewoman Fanny Abday, who was totally deaf according to the census return. The older girls, however, were 'training in housework'.

Laundry work and cleaning

Whilst some hotels, schools and institutions did their own laundry, there was also a substantial commercial sector, both for them and for private households. It was carried on domestically or, increasingly, by laundry businesses. The number of women described in the census as doing laundry work on their own account at home fell slightly from 85 in 1901 to 78 ten years later but the number of laundry workers almost doubled from 99 to 194. The Oatlands district had a particularly high number of households taking in washing: twenty-four women in 1901 and seventeen in 1911. The women were older, usually widows or single or, if married, there was no husband recorded on census night. Where they were present, the husbands were a retired publican, a house painter and a self-employed out porter at the railway station, the latter two potentially subject to seasonal unemployment. Daughters also often helped but in only one case was it a family enterprise: Samuel and Mary Ascough and their daughter in Devonshire Terrace. For all of them the stages of sorting, washing, rinsing, drying, starching and ironing were therefore carried out in small houses. The attendant smells, of dirty laundry, wet clothes, soap, bleach, bluing and starch, the damp air and heat of the iron would have pervaded the home. But it was a relatively cheap business to get into, with a mangle obtainable for just £1, and clearly attractive to women needing an income.[63]

From the 1890s down to the First World War this hand trade was increasingly superseded by commercial steam laundries. As the Annual Report of the Chief Inspector of Factories and Workshops for 1900 put it, writing of London, the old-fashioned 'washerwoman' was being replaced by a 'laundry proprietor' with a factory and sub-division of labour.[64] This change also took place in Harrogate. At Starbeck, for example, were located both Provincial Laundries and the Harrogate Corporation Steam Laundry; near Oatlands on Leadhall Lane was the Pannal Laundry Company, 'under royal patronage' as it proclaimed; and at New Park a laundry was built on Euclid Avenue. In 1907 the latter employed between fifty and sixty people and with the laundries at Starbeck accounted for 40 per cent of all laundry workers in 1911.[65] (24, 25, 26, 27, 28)

24. New Park Laundry, Euclid Avenue, 1911.
(This and other laundry photographs courtesy Terry Williams, the New Park Heritage Centre.)

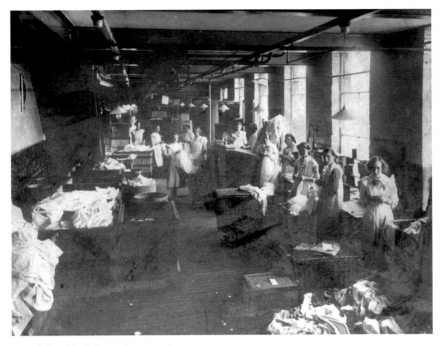

25. New Park Laundry: sorting.

26. New Park Laundry: washing.

27. New Park Laundry: pressing and ironing.

28. New Park Laundry: folding and packing.

Except for the van men who picked up the dirty laundry and delivered the clean and those who worked the boilers the work was done mostly by young women. The median age of fifteen living in New Park, for example, was twenty-three. Of the now subdivided stages, washing, drying and ironing for all but the most difficult items had been mechanized but the work for the women tending the machines was still hard. The Chief Inspector's Report had noted the lack of guards on machinery at some premises, the working conditions of steam and heat and the physical consequences of constant standing: varicose veins, leg ulcers, rheumatism, bronchitis and pthisis (tuberculosis) and inflammation of the hands and arms caused by the soap, soda and other chemicals used.

All this was made worse by the long hours, especially at peak times. During this period in Harrogate there were several prosecutions for permitting women to work for more than the lawful hours, which had been extended to laundries by legislation in 1907. The Provincial Laundry Company was fined several times. In August 1909, for example, for allowing two women and three girls to work beyond the lawful Saturday hours of 7 a.m. to 3 p.m. The assistant manager explained that as this was a Bank Holiday week there was a rush of work and all 'hands' were finished by 4 p.m. In 1913 the Jubilee Steam Laundry on Roseville Road was also fined for working three girls till 4.40 p.m. on a Saturday. The Factory Inspector had heard them running upstairs to a private room when she turned up. The defence was that a big order had suddenly come in and that in any case the girls had volunteered. An earlier case gives us further details of laundry work. Two calendar hands, girls who worked a machine which pressed cloth under rollers, had been taken to court by the Provincial Laundry Company for money in lieu of a week's notice and damages. The pair, Lily Cant and Lizzie Beech, had left work, it was claimed, to go to Scarborough for the day. As this was the height of the season two replacements had had to be brought down from the main laundry at Newcastle and washing also sent to the Leeds branch. The company was claiming damages including the girls' train fares from Newcastle and the cost of providing lodgings for them. The court, however, only awarded their wages of 10s. and 11s. a week. For their part, they complained of long hours and being forced to fold having already completed their calendar work.[66] Those wages would seem to have been typical of much of the work; only the most skilled, like some ironers, could earn more, up to 16s. a week as was reported in a study of women's work in Birmingham.[67]

Women who went out to clean were similarly placed to those who took in washing. In 1911, of the seventy-five women described as cleaner or charwoman, fifty-five were either single, widowed or with no husband present, a larger proportion than ten years earlier when more were other family members or lodgers. Their average age was forty-five. Union Street, in the town centre, was home to some of them. Ellen Ormsby's husband was not there on census night. She was a forty-two-year-old charwoman, whilst three of her five children were day servants, as was another girl who boarded with them. Similarly placed was thirty-four-year-old Ellen Dent, who lived with her mother and sister, who must have looked after her two young children. Emma Thirkell, a forty-five-year-old widow also had two boarders. A husband out of work or in irregular employment, or in a low-paid job like labouring or carting or, as with most of the women, the basic need to make a living on their own sent them out to clean. This was confirmed in a study of charwomen undertaken by the Women's Industrial Council, which in 1898 had founded the Association of Trained Charwomen and Domestic Workers to secure better conditions and higher wages. Nationally in 1911, 70 per cent of cleaners or day servants were unmarried or widows. Married women only did it out of necessity. Such was the varied nature of the work that it was difficult to generalize about earnings but the study cited a cleaner at a boarding house who was paid 2s. for a nine-hour day, whilst another at an 'institution' received 13s. a week for daily work from 6 a.m. to 12.30. The Birmingham study quoted earlier gave average earnings for charwomen of around 4s. 2d. a week and slightly better for those cleaning council offices, for example.[68]

Shop work and the clothing trades

The diversity of the retail sector in Edwardian Harrogate meant that the term shop assistant covered a variety of roles, from the saleswoman at Marshall and Snelgrove's prestigious store to the grocer's assistant in a small shop in a working-class district. Shops were typically family businesses, with or without other paid staff. As it did nationally, the number of shop assistants in Harrogate expanded, from just over 400 in 1901 to just over 700 ten years later. There were always more male assistants than women but growth was greatest among women, whose ranks more than doubled, from 153 to 315. These figures are sound estimates but it should be borne in mind that in the census returns it is not always clear, particularly in such as confectionery or millinery, whether an individual worked behind the counter or in manufacture. Most of them lived away from the premises. The live-in assistant, who featured so prominently in the literature of the period, was only a small fraction of those totals, fifty-two in 1901 and thirty-nine in 1911, of whom twenty-three and twenty-four were women.

Shop work was largely gendered, with women in 1911, when the type of shop was specified in the census, concentrated in dress and drapery, boots and shoes, confectionery, stationers, newsagents and book stalls and as photographers' assistants. Also increasing in number were women who worked as waitresses in cafés and restaurants, doubling from twenty-four to forty-eight over the decade. In contrast, grocers, greengrocers and fishmongers almost invariably employed male assistants. The women were young, those living out in their 'teens or early twenties for the most part and the few living-in slightly older on average, and almost invariably single. A sample of fathers' occupations showed them to be almost all from working-class backgrounds, but with only one from class V, the eighteen-year-old daughter of a general labourer working for a fancy-goods dealer.

The hours of both male and female assistants were long. In Harrogate they could be as much as seventy-five a week. A letter from some assistants to the *Advertiser* in September 1905 cited hours of 8 a.m. to 8 p.m. on weekdays, and longer on Saturday when a 10 p.m. or even 11 p.m. finish was the norm. This represented only the most marginal improvement on the situation twenty years earlier when 9 o'clock closing on weekdays was usual during the season. Already the 'Over-Taxed Shop Assistants' who cited those hours were calling for the establishment in the town of an Early Closing Association.[69] This problem of long hours, focusing on the provision of half-day closing, persisted throughout the period. A committee to further this object was in fact set up at the beginning of

1900 but progress over the succeeding years was tortuous, hindered by the difficulty of getting agreement among the town's traders. That such agreement was necessary was voiced by the members of the Harrogate Traders' Association, representing 140 of the principal shop keepers, at which it was resolved by a large majority to close on Wednesday or Saturday afternoon, but only outside the season from November to April. But within a month, those same traders were hearing at their annual general meeting that the confectioners were still open.[70]

Shop workers were difficult to organize, partly because their hours were long but also because they did not stay in one post for any length of time, many women wanted to do it and an element of status consciousness inhibited such action. Nevertheless, a union had been set up in London in 1889 and in 1891 a National Union of Shop Assistants was formed at a conference in Birmingham with the twin aims of reducing hours and securing adequate wages. Margaret Bondfield, who had herself been a shop assistant and was in 1929 to be the first woman in a cabinet as Minister of Labour, became its assistant secretary in 1898. In that year the union claimed nationally over 3,000 members in 86 branches.[71] One was formed in Harrogate in 1900 and by 1905 had between sixty and seventy members.[72] By this time the Shop Hours Act of 1904 had made some move towards half-day closing on one day a week but this was dependent upon an order from the local authority, which had also to be approved by at least two-thirds of the affected shops. The union canvassed a wide range of the town's tradesmen and found that of 398, only 79 were against the change but the Corporation refused to take any action on the grounds that there was no clear majority for any of the specific options for closure put to traders in its own canvass. In fact, this was usual; the Act 'achieved little', according to its historian, and few orders were made under its provisions.[73]

One modest improvement, however, had been to close on the Monday and Tuesday following Christmas Day in 1904. But the movement for regular half-day closing continued and now succeeded, following the example of places like Leeds and Bradford. By the end of 1909 almost all shops were following the lead earlier taken by the Harrogate and District Grocers' and Provision Dealers' Association by closing on Wednesday afternoons out of the season.[74] Then in 1911 a further Shops Act made half-day closing compulsory but offered exemptions (as had the earlier legislation), including of four months a year for resorts and for a number of trades including those in perishable goods, newspapers and tobacco. These provisions 'were to cause a lot of uncertainty and many possibilities of evasion', as was to be the case in Harrogate, which availed itself of those exemptions following yet another ballot of traders, and the town's shops remained open during the season.[75]

The pay for those long hours differed widely between the lowest and highest rates, according to a 1909 report of the Minimum Wage Committee of the shop assistants' union, which was based on replies from 10 per cent of members. Women in drapery, for example, were paid from 1*d*. to 7¼*d*. an hour, less than the rates for men of between 2*d*. and 1*s*. 0¼*d*. an hour. In confectionery they were paid between 2*d*. and 4½*d*. an hour. The report also described conditions: the poor ventilation of many shops; the confined spaces in which staff worked; the strain of standing up all day; and the 'nervous irritation' produced by the need to pander to customers. Another study found that meals were rushed and staff were subject to irksome rules and fines for such as gossiping, losses and breakages. The Birmingham study, in contrast, found that there were very few rules or fines and the pay for assistants in medium and small shops averaged 10*s*. 6*d*. a week, whilst in Oxford it was typically 12. to 15*s*. a week. It could also be an uncertain trade. Reduction of staffing levels out of season, the bankruptcy of businesses, the competition to enter and the threat of redundancy for those too weak or too old all contributed to this. The number of union members, of both sexes, receiving unemployment benefit in the Edwardian period was high: over 9 per cent of members in six of the ten years from 1906, reaching a high in 1908 of almost 16 per cent, when an estimated 150,000 shop workers in total were unemployed.[76]

Despite advances, however, they remained largely unorganized. Over 21,000 members nationally in the National Amalgamated Union of Shop Assistants, Warehousemen and Clerks in 1910 represented just 2 per cent of the workforce.[77] The Harrogate branch at the close of 1913 had 294 members of both sexes, but these were of course not solely shop workers. During the year forty-two members had received state sickness benefit, twenty-four trade union sickness benefit and fifteen unemployment benefit. Its women officials included Miss Jessopp on the Finance Committee, Miss North, one of two sick visitors, and Miss Applegarth, the delegate to the Yorkshire Women's Council.[78]

Women also worked at making the goods for sale in shops. J. Farrah, grocer and confectioner, manufactured at its Crescent Road premises. Hours here could also be long. The firm was fined in August 1911 for illegally employing three girls to pack toffee for more than the permitted hours on Saturday of 6 a.m. to 2 p.m. In fact, two had begun work at 4.30 and another at 4.45. This was due to high demand at that time of the season, the need for the toffee to be fresh and, according to the firm in further extenuation, the girls did so voluntarily to avoid the heat of the day. The penalty was a fine of 10s. and costs for each case.[79] But most of the women on the manufacturing side were in dressmaking or millinery. The number of women who described themselves as workers in dressmaking, rather than working on their own account, rose from 146 in 1901 to 237 in 1911 and of milliners from 42 to 83. Here too the hours were long and there were also prosecutions for exceeding those permitted. E. J. Clarke, a James Street milliner, was fined in May 1905 for having women still in the work room after 5 p.m. on a Saturday. In November 1911 a costumier in King's Arcade was prosecuted for allowing women to begin work at 6.15, nearly two hours before the permitted start time. The importance of the time of year to the availability of work, compounded by the dictates of custom or fashion, was highlighted in such cases: May was one of the busiest times and costumier Nelson of the King's Arcade shop had explained in mitigation how they had been 'exceptionally busy'.[80] These effects might be worsened by the unexpected, as with the collapse of the summer 'boom' on the death of Edward VII in May 1910.[81]

To obtain more detail on the women, I looked at those who worked for Emmatt's mantle makers and costumiers on Westmoreland Street, where twenty-eight live-in dressmaker's assistants were employed. Their average age was just twenty-one. None had been born in Harrogate, within ten miles or in rural Yorkshire and over two-thirds of them had origins some distance away. Where the father's, or in one case the mother's, occupation was traced, half were in class II, four were skilled workmen but another four were semi- or unskilled. Three of the women had ten years earlier also worked in the clothing trades. Ellen Phillips, aged twenty-seven in 1911, was a dressmaker in her native Birmingham where her father had a hosiery business. Rosey Metcalfe had also been a dressmaker back in 1901, whilst still at home in Sunderland with her father, a pawnbroker, and two of her sisters who were also dressmakers. Elsie Corby, fourteen in 1901, was an apprentice mantle maker in her native Northampton, where her father was a manager in the boot and shoe trade. This does lend support to the findings from Birmingham, which described them as '"high-class" working girls', who were skilled and required to dress well. But the rewards were not necessarily commensurate: they still had to work for three years before earning 5s. a week.[82] **(29)**

29. Showroom of Emmatt & Son, Mantle Makers and Costumiers, Westmoreland Street. (Reproduced from Robinson's *Harrogate, Knaresborough, Ripon, Pateley Bridge and District Directory* 1902, p. 70.)

Prostitution

Prostitution, or sex work as it is now sometimes described, was another source of income for women. A resort town like Harrogate, however genteel it felt itself to be, must have generated a demand for commercial sex. The Revd Ogle, formerly the vicar at Starbeck, said as much in a speech praising the work of the Prevention and Rescue Home: 'Many who came to Harrogate, alas! did not enjoy themselves in an innocent way.'[83] But to what extent the Home was working with women who had resorted to prostitution is not clear; many seem to have been unmarried mothers or who were leading what were seen as immoral lives, which might be somewhat broadly defined. The 1912 meeting certainly heard details of the number of rescue cases and made reference to 'fallen women' but the London vicar who addressed it also noted how young girls hearing a street piano might 'give vent to their natural feelings by waltzing ... or acting in a somewhat frivolous manner'.[84]

What is clearer evidence is when a woman was taken to court for soliciting. In 1891 it was stated in the *Advertiser* that members 'of the unfortunate class' visited Harrogate every night of the week. This was in the case of Annie Wright of Knaresborough, going on twenty years old, alias 'The Riverside Beauty', who was given fourteen days for being drunk and disorderly whilst soliciting on Station Parade, after several previous cautions.[85] Over the Edwardian period there were some twenty-five cases reported, chiefly of soliciting but also of disorderly conduct. The women were taken up at a variety of locations, usually in the town centre, with West Park the most often mentioned. It looks to have been a part-time occupation. Three were described as charwomen, and one each as laundress, cook and housemaid. Where their address was given four were from Harrogate, including two from Oatlands and one from New Park but five were recorded as of no fixed abode. Where status was given, seven were married, three single and one widowed. It was also possible to trace a small number of them in the census. For example, Rose Mary Gibson, given one month for soliciting in July 1911, was a twenty-nine-year-old charwoman, married but with no husband present on census night at their Christina Street, New Park home.[86]

This, admittedly limited, evidence does confirm some of the findings of a detailed contemporary investigation of prostitution in London and the provinces, which collected over 1,200 case histories, of which however some 400 had been rejected as merely promiscuous or kept women. By far the greatest number had formerly been domestic servants, including many who had for whatever reason been unable to get a reference, or had become pregnant, with such as laundry workers, shop assistants or dressmakers a long way behind. Unemployment or seasonal underemployment, low wages and poor working conditions were also cited. But their domestic situation was also important: whilst nearly a quarter had come from 'good' homes, twice as many were from those 'definitely bad'. One in ten had been brought up in an institution and one in five had been homeless at some point in their lives. Bad and overcrowded housing, premature acquaintance with sexuality and abuse were also partly responsible.[87]

How many brothels the town supported is unclear but they certainly existed, as evidenced in two prosecutions. In 1910 Margaret Chapman, aged sixty-seven, was gaoled for keeping a disorderly house in Chapel Court, along with two other women for assisting her, one of whom had been previously convicted of soliciting. In 1912 Nellie Day, a married women separated from her husband, was fined for keeping a disorderly house in Ash Grove. The court heard evidence, to some amusement among the spectators, of known 'street-walkers' taking men to the house, of a 'jolly party, singing, drinking and dancing' and of men arriving at and leaving the house almost nightly, including one who 'fell into the bushes'. Day admitted 'noisy concerts' but no 'immorality'.[88]

Prostitution was a feature of life in the town at odds with its reputation for gentility and the self-perception of its residents. Similarly, most well-to-do residents and visitors alike seemed to be unaware of, preferred to ignore, or simply accepted the long hours, drudgery and unpleasant working conditions of the women who made possible their comfortable and leisured lives. Most of those women worked because they had to, whether sent into service as young girls or, as widows or women alone, compelled to go out and clean. On marriage most gave up work unless necessity forced them. This is not to say that work offered no satisfactions, of companionship for example, or that women were without choice, as their preference for shop work or waitressing over service shows. Nor were they necessarily passive accepters of their fate, as the mobility of servants suggests, providing they had that all-important reference. In the end, however, they were in predominantly low status jobs, working long hours for small reward.

Notes to Chapter 3: Women at Work

1   As Chapter 2, note 22.

2   PP 1917–18 [Cd. 8491], pp. 106–8; PP 1902 [Cd. 1107], pp. 260–1; PP 1913 [Cd. 7018], pp. 456–7; the figures for servants in Harrogate are derived from the census returns rather than the reports; M. G. Ebery and B. T. Preston, *Domestic Service in Late Victorian and Edwardian England, 1871–1914* (1976), pp. 35–7.

3   E. Higgs, 'Domestic servants and households in Victorian England', *Social History*, 8:2 (1983), pp. 201–10.

4   S. Pooley, 'Domestic servants and their urban employers: a case study of Lancaster, 1880–1914', *Economic History Review*, 62:2 (2009), pp. 405–29.

5   Ebery and Preston, *Domestic Service*, pp. 114–15; Armstrong, 'The use of information about occupation'; C. Booth, *Life and Labour of the People in London* (1902).

6   L. James, *The Middle Class: A History* (2008), p. 219; A. Goreau 'Introduction' to A. Brontë, *Agnes Grey* (1988), pp. 40–5; M. J. Peterson, 'The Victorian Governess: Status incongruence in family and society', *Victorian Studies*, 14:1 (1970), pp. 7–26.

7   L. Holcombe, *Victorian Ladies at Work: Middle-class working women in England and Wales, 1850–1914* (1973), pp. 68–102.

8   Pooley, 'Domestic servants'; PP 1904 [Cd. 2174], p. 80.

9   P. Horn, *Labouring Life in the Victorian Countryside* (1987) pp. 69 and 88–9.

10 Port of Hull Society's Sailors' Orphan Homes, Girls Admission Register, 1863–1916 and Mixed Leaving Register, 1874–1900, Hull History Centre.

11 M. G. Barnett, *Young Delinquents: A study of reformatory and industrial schools* (1913), pp. 49–50 and Appendix B, p. 205.

12 M. Younge (ed), *Echoes from Ripon's Past* (2004), pp. 107–9; M. H. Taylor (ed.), *Alice's Story: This was my childhood* (1991).

13 Leeds Industrial School for Girls, Reports, 1860–1886, 11th Annual Report (1871), p. 9.

14 F. Prochaska, 'Female philanthropy and domestic service in Victorian England', *Bulletin of the Institute of Historical Research*, 54:129 (1981), pp. 79–85.

15 *HA*, 25 November 1905, p. 2 and 27 April 1912, p. 3.

16 Female Servants' Home Society, Leeds, Annual Reports, 1890–1901, 26th Report 1890 (1901), p. 3.

17 *HA*, 25 November 1905, p. 5.

18 See for example *HA*, 24 February 1900, p. 8 but I looked at such advertisements throughout the period.

19 A Servant, *How to Improve the Conditions of Domestic Service By a Servant. A Book for Masters, Mistresses and Servants* (1894), pp. 2 and 17.

20 *HA*, 25 July 1908, p. 7 and 1 August 1908, p. 3.

21 *HA*, 24 February 1900, p. 8 and 18 March 1911, p. 7.

22 C. V. Butler, *Domestic Service: An enquiry by the Women's Industrial Council* (1916), p. 72; Pooley, 'Domestic servants'.

23 I thank Enid Rispin for the Brackenbury details.

24 Butler, *Domestic Service*, p. 130.

25 E. Higgs, 'Domestic service and household production', in A. V. John (ed.), *Unequal Opportunities: Women's employment in England, 1800–1918* (1986), pp. 125–50.

26 Pooley, 'Domestic servants'.

27 *HA*, 27 October 1906, p. 6 and 21 January 1905, p. 5.

28 Butler, *Domestic Service*, pp. 13–17.

29 Prochaska, 'Female philanthropy'; G. Moore, *Esther Waters* (2012), p. 52.

30 *HA*, 4 November 1911, p. 6; D. Read, *England, 1868–1914* (1979), p. 471.

31 I. Beeton, *The Book of Household Management* (1891), pp. 1471–98.

32 Butler, *Domestic Service*, pp. 48–9

33 *HA*, 1911 *passim*.

34 Wages of Domestic Servants, Board of Trade (Labour Department), Report by Miss Collet on the Money Wages of Indoor Domestic Servants; PP 1899 [C. 9346] XCII.1.

35 W. T. Layton, 'Changes in the wages of domestic servants during fifty years', *Journal of the Royal Statistical Society*, 71 (1908), pp. 515–24; Butler, *Social Conditions*, p. 63.

36 Pooley, 'Domestic servants'; see for example the Leeds Ladies' Association for the Care and Protection of Friendless Girls Annual Reports, 1884–1914 (1914).

37 Butler, *Domestic Service*, pp. 44–5; examples in *HA*, 26 April 1902, p. 5; 30 March 1901, p. 5; 28 November 1908, p. 7; 17 June 1911, p. 5; and 14 June 1913, p. 3.

38 Beeton, *Household Management*, pp. 1453–4.

39 Leeds Ladies' Association for the Care and Protection of Friendless Girls, Records of Girls in Service, 1889–1940, West Yorkshire Archive Service, Leeds.

40 Butler, *Domestic Service*, pp. 49–50.

41 *HA*, 21 January 1905, p. 5.

42 *HA*, 18 March 1905, p. 5.

43 *HA*, 17 June 1911, p. 5.

44 J. R. Gillis, 'Sexual relations and the risk of illegitimacy in London, 1801–1900', *Feminist Studies*, 5:1 (1979), pp. 142–73; Borough of Harrogate, Reports of Medical Officer of Health for 1907 and Medical Officer of Health and Sanitary Inspector for 1908, NYCCRO.

45 *HA*, 16 May 1914, p. 6.

46 I thank the Registrar at Harrogate for confirming this fact.

47 St Wilfrid, Register of Baptisms, 1902–1967.

48 *HA*, 20 September 1902, p. 6 (Hill); 15 December 1906, p. 3 (Haggard); 30 March 1901, p. 5 and *Yorkshire Evening Post*, 8 May 1901, p. 3 (Walker); *HA*, 26 April 1902, p. 5 and *Leeds and Yorkshire Mercury*, 28 July 1902, p. 5 (Teale, also given as Teal).

49 A. Williams, *A Detested Occupation? A history of domestic servants in North Wales, 1800–1930* (2016), pp. 104–9.

50 *HA*, 14 June 1913, p. 3.

51 L. Delap, *Knowing Their Place: Domestic service in twentieth-century Britain* (2011), pp. 174–205.

52 *HA*, 7 July 1906, p. 5.

53 *HA*, 20 December 1902, p. 6, where Farnham is given as in Hampshire, and 17 June 1905, p. 5.

54 *HA*, 14 March 1914, p. 4.

55 PP 1899 [C.- 9346], p. 25.

56 H. Bosanquet, *The Family* (1906), pp. 292–3.

57 T. M. McBride, *The Domestic Revolution: The modernisation of household service in England and France, 1820–1920* (1976), pp. 83 and 98.

58 P. Wilcox, 'Marriage, mobility and domestic service in Victorian Cambridge', *Local Population Studies*, 29 (1982), pp. 19–34.

59 For details of the registers see the Bibliography.

60 *HA*, 11 January 1902, p. 2.

61 *HA*, 29 April 1911, p. 2.

62 I thank Valerie Chadwick for the Robinson details.

63 For these and other details see P. E. Malcolmson, *English Laundresses: A social history, 1850–1930* (1986).

64 Annual Report of the Chief Inspector of Factories and Workshops for the year 1900, PP 1901 [Cd. 668] X.1, pp. 381–2.

65 Robinson's Directory 1912; *HA*, 5 January 1907, p. 3.

66 *HA*, 4 September 1909, p. 6; 4 October 1913, p. 6; and 3 September 1904, p. 3.

67 E. Cadbury *et al.*, *Women's Work and Wages: A Phase of life in an industrial city* (1906), pp. 106–7.

68 L. Wyatt Papworth, 'Charwomen', in C. Black (ed.), *Married Women's Work* (1915), pp. 105–13; Cadbury, *Women's work*, pp. 112 and 173.

69 *HA*, 16 September 1905, p. 3 and 16 June 1883, p. 6.

70 *HA*, 6 January 1900, p. 5; 26 January 1901, p. 5; and 23 February 1901, p. 2.

71 Whitaker, *Shop Workers*, pp. 21–4.

72 *HA*, 18 February 1903, p. 4 and 4 February 1905, p. 5.

73 *HA*, 10 December 1904, p. 3 and 16 September 1905, p. 3; Borough of Harrogate, Shop Hours Act 1904, NYCCRO; Whitaker, *Shop Workers*,

p. 143.

74   *HA*, 10 November 1906, p. 2; 23 January 1909, p. 3; 30 October 1909, p. 7; and 6 November 1909, p. 5.

75   Whitaker, *Shop Workers*, pp. 163–4; *HA*, 16 March 1912, p. 2 and 25 May 1912, p. 2.

76   J. Hallsworth and R. J. Davies, *The Working Life of Shop Assistants: A study of conditions of labour in the distributive trades* (1910), pp. 24–57 and 103–7; Butler, *Social Conditions*, p. 64; Cadbury, *Women's Work*, pp. 107–10; Whitaker, *Shop Workers*, pp. 18–20.

77   C. P. Hosgood, '"Mercantile monasteries": shops, shop assistants and shop life in late Victorian and Edwardian Britain', *Journal of British Studies*, 38:3 (1999), pp. 322–52.

78   *HA*, 21 February 1914, p. 4.

79   *HA*, 26 August 1911, p. 6.

80   *HA*, 18 November 1905, p. 5 and 27 May 1911, p. 6.

81   B. Drake, 'The West End tailoring trade' in S. Webb and A. Freeman (eds), *Seasonal Trades* (1912), pp. 70–91.

82   Cadbury, *Women's Work*, pp. 102–4.

83   *HA*, 16 May 1914, p. 6.

84   *HA*, 27 April 1912, p. 3.

85   *HA*, 7 March 1891, p. 6.

86   *HA*, 8 July 1911, p. 6.

87   Anon, *Downward paths: An inquiry into the causes which contribute to the making of a prostitute* (1916).

88   *HA*, 27 August 1910, p. 7 and 23 November 1912, p. 6.

CHAPTER FOUR

Men at Work

THE MOST IMPORTANT areas of work for men in Harrogate were the building trades and the transport sector. Much of this chapter will necessarily be concerned with the workers in those key industries but it makes sense to begin with those few areas where both men and women were employed in the otherwise highly gendered world of work: the hotel trade, retail and clothing. Following building and transport, I then examine the gas industry and the vital services provided by municipal and postal workers and the police. The chapter concludes with a look at some of those who in their way were also an essential part of the leisured life of the spa and, not least, the amusements of its workers: street musicians.

Service, shops and tailoring

The number of men employed in household service was negligible. In 1901 there were just six butlers, the largest group of male indoor servants, and seven in 1911. Only three in each year were described as footman. The butlers were a varied lot. Five of the seven were married, ranging in age from twenty-nine to sixty-three and the two single men were seventeen and forty. There were also three butlers living in their own homes, all married men. Of those living-in, Arthur Bannister, originally from Chertsey in Surrey, presided over a cook, kitchen maid, housemaid and parlour maid at Willaston, the home of William Benn.

Bannister's wife was not with him on census night, unlike the wife of William Cranston who worked alongside him, together with a housemaid, at Wellfield on Pannal Ash Road, the home of professional violinist Montagu Montagu-Nathan and his wife. More numerous were the gardeners, coachmen and grooms, some of whom, as we saw at Grove House for example, lived in cottages in the grounds of the main house. Over the decade the chauffeur largely replaced the coachman and groom, although at both censuses few lived at their employer's residence.

Much more important for men was hotel work. In 1901 the 159 men working at hotels represented nearly a third of the live -in staff, which in 1911 had risen to 189 men or nearly 40 per cent. There was also a substantial rise in the number of hotel workers living out, from 44 men in 1901 to 156 ten years later. They were employed as bar staff and waiters, hall- and night porters and in the kitchen as chefs, kitchen porters, knife- or plate men and plate washers. At the Crown in 1911, for example, the male staff comprised the hotel clerk, night porter, four cooks, two kitchen porters, plate man, two cellar men, a page boy, three waiters and a billiard marker, plus the boiler- and engine men. I traced a small sample of hotel workers to an earlier census and found that most came from a working-class background. Alfred Marshall, a twenty-five-year-old porter at the Swan Hydro was the son of an agricultural labourer and had been an errand boy in his native Lincolnshire at the 1901 census. The chef at the Harlow Manor Hydro, Walter Eyles, was the son of an Oxford billiard-table keeper who had been a cook in his hometown. His assistant, Richard Gelder, also from Oxford, was the son of a compositor. (30)

The most striking thing about the hotel staff was the number from Europe, thirty-five men in 1901 and fifty-seven in 1911, over a third of the total male hotel workforce, of whom in turn two-thirds were of German or Austrian descent. At the Crown, the four cooks were respectively two Germans, an Austrian and an Italian; one kitchen porter was Italian; the luggage porter Swiss; and the waiters German, Austrian and Italian. There were also a further thirty European workers living around the town, like head waiter Hermann Valentine from Hamburg, on Stonefall Avenue, Starbeck with his English wife and three children, the youngest of whom had been born there. Although working in a range of hotel jobs,

30. Commercial Hotel, West Park, *c*.1900, showing the recently added iron canopy. Its male staff in 1901 comprised a waiter, boots and page boy. The sign indicates it was the headquarters of the Bicycle Touring Club. Its name was shortly after changed to the West Park Hotel. (Courtesy the Walker-Neesam Archive)

waiting on tables was most common, especially for Germans. As waiters they had the advantages of formal training, including some who were sent to England by the owners of hotels in Germany and Switzerland as a form of apprenticeship, and the ability to speak a foreign language. They no doubt also added a certain continental flair to an establishment and were widely employed in major hotels in London and in cities and resorts around the country. Their presence, however, generated hostility. A music-hall song about the Royal Naval Exhibition of 1891 attacked foreigners in general but singled Germans out:

> The work they didn't attempt to halve,
> They hired German waiters to wait and carve,

While English waiters are left to starve,
Through German competition.

In 1910 a Loyal British Waiters' Society was set up, with its own newspaper *The Restaurateur*, which aimed to provide 'employment for British waiters who are reliable and loyal'. Harrogate was not immune to this resentment. In that year John Crest, a waiter of no fixed abode, pleaded guilty to begging at houses on West Park but complained that 'he could not get employment because the Germans were cutting them out'.[1]

Waiters particularly, but hotel staff generally, were said to earn good money, especially at those larger hotels which attracted richer clients, but in return for long hours during the season.[2] But it was not all work. They socialized in the town's streets, as the *Advertiser* noted in September 1906 of those in great numbers in Walker Road creating a disturbance. More formally, there was an annual ball of the Harrogate Hotels and Hydros Employees and by 1913 it had become 'quite a feature of the Harrogate Winter season'. That year the fancy-dress ball was held at the Kursaal, with around 450 dancers and 370 spectators in the gallery and dancing till 3 a.m., whilst the following year some 500 took to the floor.[3]

Shop work employed more men than women and they worked especially in grocers and greengrocers, butchers, fishmongers, ironmongers and chemists. (31) A small number lived on the premises, like the three men employed at Handford and Dawson's chemist on Station Bridge, but most came daily into work. Of a sample of ninety of these men, twenty-nine were married, two were widowers and fifty-nine single, of whom thirteen were boarders. Of twenty-eight whose father's occupation was identified, all but two were from working-class backgrounds. As we saw, the men were better paid than their female counterparts and for some at least shop work might provide a comfortable life. Living on West End Avenue, a street with many middle- and lower middle-class households, were in 1911 William Robinson, a fifty-nine-year-old assistant at a jeweller's and his wife and William Bell, a forty-year-old draper's assistant with his wife and mother-in-law and a general servant.

In the clothing trades tailoring was largely the preserve of men. In the census returns they are described either as working at home on their own account or as workers. Some of those workers were in turn

31. Preston family butcher, Chapel Street, 1898. (Used with permission from Harrogate Library, North Yorkshire County Council.)

specified as cutter or cutter's assistant. The number in the first group rose from just 11 in 1901 to 23 ten years later and in the second from 76 to 112. Work for an employer could also be done at home or in a small workshop. They were either paid a wage or by the piece. One high-class ladies' tailor, Sim Hart of Chapel Street, gave his workers the choice of either method. We know this from claims which were made against him in 1906 for non-payment of a weekly wage of £2 2s., or a daily rate of 7s. 6d. The following year, in a similar case, Charles Ballman was awarded £1 5s. 6d. from Stokes and Peel for two coats which had taken eight days to make. Ballman had had his rail fare from London paid and an earlier case against Hart also suggests that employers actively sought men. Harold Silverberg had been sent for, and given up his employment in Bradford, for a year-round wage of £2 a week. He was, however, sacked after just three weeks for alleged incompetence and now claimed the week's notice that had been denied him. Despite evidence from Hart's foreman that Silverberg had refused to do work and spoilt a coat collar, the court awarded him the money.[4]

Silverberg's surname indicates an important development of these years, the entry of Europeans into the trade, particularly Jews, who left the Russian Empire in huge numbers in the years of persecution following the assassination of Tsar Alexander II in 1881. From that year until 1914 some two million Jews left Russia, which then included Poland. By 1911 the more than 95,000 Russians represented the largest foreign-born group in the country, well ahead of the more than 53,000 Germans. Key areas of settlement were London, Manchester and Leeds. In the latter city, 12,000 were there by 1901–2 and 25,000 by 1914. Tailoring was much the largest occupation among them.[5]

In 1901 there were just three tailors of European birth in Harrogate: an Austrian and a Frenchman, both single men boarding, and David Brightstone, aged thirty-six, who was born in Poland. The fact that his wife Ann was born in London suggests something of his journey to Harrogate, where he was then living on Grange Avenue with her and their three young children, all born in the town. By 1911 just under one in five of those employed in tailoring in the town were of European birth. Of those twenty-six men, twelve were born in the Austrian or German Empires and eleven in the Russian. Of the former group, on

Chatsworth Avenue lived Adolf Langer and his wife Bertha, both born in Germany, their daughter Wilhemina, born in London and baby Adolf born in Harrogate itself. Of the latter, three families of Russian Jews lived in Valley Mount. The census again suggests their passage to the town. Hyman Andorski and his wife were both Russian-born Jews but the two children were born in Stepney, east London, the heart of Jewish settlement in that city. The two young children of Sam and Minnie Dofsky had been born in Leeds. Similarly, living on Strawberry Dale Avenue, Harris Rozenblaum had been born in Minsk but his wife and children also in Leeds.

The building trades

The late-nineteenth-century building boom in Harrogate provided work for hundreds of men, making it their largest source of employment in the town. But in the Edwardian period they experienced the country-wide vicissitudes of the trade. Nationally, numbers peaked in 1901 at 1.3 million, or nearly 8 per cent of the total workforce but thereafter the trade contracted sharply and did not recover, and then only in part, for another ten years.[6] This trend was mirrored in Harrogate as the census reports show. In 1901 22 per cent of employed men were in building and 15 per cent in transport. Ten years later those positions had been reversed: transport now occupied 18 per cent, whilst building had fallen to 14 per cent, although exact comparison is not possible due to a shift in the location of the category of work on roads and those figures also include employers and men in managerial positions.[7] Although residential building continued in the Edwardian period, it was not on the former scale, and large-scale projects effectively ended with the construction of the Grand Hotel.

The contraction of building is clear also from the census returns. Overall numbers of workers fell from 1,343 to 1,044 over the decade. The number of those described as mason, stonemason, stone dresser or stone waller, for example, fell from 234 in 1901 to just 93 ten years later. Paralleling this fall was that of quarry and brick workers, from 88 to 55. Only the numbers of plumbers and glaziers and of painters, decorators and paper hangers showed an increase, which is probably explained by the continuation of improvements to existing property. Upgrades of furnishings would similarly explain the rises in the number of upholsterers from 29 to 42 (of whom three and five were women, their sole presence in all these trades) and French polishers and the relatively slight fall in that of cabinet makers. Less easily explicable is the rise in the number of those describing themselves simply as building worker from 49 to 89, although it may reflect men looking to pick up any kind of building work.

The industry consisted mostly of small employers of fewer than ten men, who might also hire for specific contracts. A directory listed fifty-six builders and contractors in the town at the beginning of the decade but work was also given to firms from further afield. The major work on the Crown Hotel in 1900, for example, was completed by six general contractors from Harrogate, Bradford, Leeds and Shipley employing respectively masons, slaters, joiners, plumbers, plasterers and painters.[8] There were some larger local firms like that of David Simpson, whose work included Valley Drive and the Duchy estate. In the summer of 1900, before the boom ended, he took around seventy employees on their annual excursion to Scarborough where they had lunch at the Grand Restaurant, at which foreman Clark proposed the toast to Simpson, 'who always did what was right to his employees'. (32, 33) Two years later builder and contractor H. A. Holmes also took more than thirty of his workmen there for dinner at the Salisbury Hotel and then to enjoy the sea bathing or scenic drives.[9] On the furnishing side, some men were employed in workshops, like that of cabinet maker W. H. Slater on West Park, 'the oldest furnishing house in the town' as it styled itself, whilst others tried to make a living on their own from small individual jobs.[10] (34)

A report published in 1900 indicates wages in the relatively good times. In Harrogate they ranged from those of bricklayers, masons and plasterers of 9½d. an hour; carpenters and joiners 8½d.; slaters and plumbers 8d.; painters 7½d; to labourers on just 6d. Those rates were above the lowest level on offer in Yorkshire and the top rate was at the highest. They were for summer hours of 49½ to 50 a week and, if all those hours were worked, ranged from 15s. to around £2. The report noted that these were standard rates but some with greater levels of

32. Workers for Charles Dawson, builders, at the Royal
Baths, 1897. (Courtesy the Walker-Neesam Archive)

skill, or engaged in more difficult or dangerous work, might earn more.
Conversely, those who had not yet mastered their craft, or who were too
old, might get less.[11] They were also summer rates and the trade was
one subject to seasonal variation. Brief winter daylight, heavy rain and
fog hindered all work. Frost and damp particularly affected bricklayers,
plasterers, painters, masons and other labourers. The winter months also
saw reduced demand for repairs.[12]

In good times rates of pay could go higher. Such was the demand
for labour on the Majestic Hotel project that the rates for all men were
raised, the highest, for plasterers, to 10½d. an hour. Men accordingly were
attracted to Harrogate for work from places like Leeds, Bradford and
Middlesbrough. Conversely, in the more difficult times of 1901 employers

33. Building workers at St Luke's Church, Walker Road,
1897. (Courtesy the Walker-Neesam Archive)

34. Cabinet shop of W. H. Slater, upholsterer, house furnisher and
undertaker, West Park, 1904. (Reproduced from the Gentleman's
Journal and Gentlewoman's Court Review, 28:192, 1904.)

now pressed for both a reduction in rates and a relaxation of working rules to bring them into line with those of other towns, for example that they should work shorter hours in winter like masons, joiners, painters and plumbers, instead of trying to work by candle- or lamp-light. The dispute seems to have been one of some bitterness, with claims that it was a lock-out not a strike and the law brought into play. George Crossley was fined £2. and 18s. costs for the unlawful intimidation of a fellow plasterer, who was in the union but had continued to work. He had gone into the Golden Lion Hotel on West Park asking if there were any 'scabs' or 'blacklegs' and whether the landlord encouraged 'lepers' to drink there.[13] In the end, however, they returned to work at the old rate. The painters in 1902 were similarly met with the threat of a reduction in the rate of ½d. an hour. Although this also was not implemented, neither was a sought-for increase forthcoming.[14]

In general, rates of pay seem to have remained broadly stable. Although I found no further figures specific to Harrogate, this is confirmed by a 1908 report giving weekly pay for England and Wales for places said to have been selected for their typicality.[15] It needs to be stressed once again, however, that the availability of work had become increasingly uncertain, with reports in October 1904, for example, of its limited availability since the completion of work on the Prospect Hotel, and always seasonal, all of which reduced actual hours worked.[16] Furthermore, these were also years of rising prices, after a long period in the late nineteenth century when the cost of basic foodstuffs and many other goods had been falling, so that the real incomes of workers were now in decline.

Although the painters had averted an actual reduction in their rate of pay, they had had to accept a new code of rules which 'met with the strong disapproval of all the men'. One specific objection was the question of labourers doing the work of competent men. This deterioration in the conditions of work was experienced across the building trades. Their worsened situation was reflected in declining union membership, which further weakened their bargaining position. As the trades' historian Raymond Postgate concluded, 'the burden of the bad trade was almost entirely shifted on to the operatives'. Furthermore, individual trades were affected by the introduction of new techniques, products and processes. Concrete and steel were increasingly used in building. The introduction of prefabricated woodwork similarly reduced the amount of carpentry work. In plumbing lead was being replaced by iron piping and there was a big rise in the use of manufactured earthenware for sanitary purposes.[17]

One constant was that the work was hard. Robert Tressel's account, based on his own experience, merits consideration. It begins with work on 'a large old-fashioned three-storied building standing in about an acre of ground', wherein we find about twenty-five carpenters, plumbers, plasterers, bricklayers and painters, besides several unskilled labourers, engaged on their various tasks. As he tells us, 'The air was full of the sounds of hammering and sawing, the ringing of trowels, the rattle of pails, the splashing of water brushes, and the scraping of stripping knives used by those who were removing the old wallpaper.' But as he continues, 'besides being full of these sounds the air was heavily laden with dust and disease germs, powdered mortar, lime, plaster, and the dirt that had been accumulating within the old house for years.'[18] Set this alongside the following report from Harrogate in December 1896. It is of an inquest into the death of George Griffith, aged thirty-six. He was from Bradford and had come to the town seeking work, leaving his wife of fourteen years at home, and taken lodgings in Belmont Avenue, off Cold Bath Road, where he shared a bed with another stonemason. They both obtained employment on the new baths. The work was described to the jury as 'heavy', and they heard also how Griffith coughed all day and was not really fit but could not afford to rest. He later had his supper of a little bacon, bread and cheese and two cups of cocoa. Next morning, he woke up coughing blood and died within a quarter of an hour. It was stated that he was 'wasting away' with what was termed 'mason's consumption' and a verdict of sudden death from natural causes was returned. The jurymen donated some of their fees to his widow.[19] The jury were similarly generous to the mother of Alfred Mills, aged twenty-three, killed in an accident at the Majestic Hotel site. He worked nights from 6 p.m. to 6 a.m. as a general labourer looking after the fires, as this was January, but had fallen down the well-hole of a staircase and fractured his skull.[20]

The potential dangers, and in some cases unsafe working practices, are further illustrated in two more inquests from one week in 1904. The first was into a death at the Diamond Brick Company's works at

Starbeck. Bricklayer William Appleton, aged forty and from Starbeck itself, had worked there just five or six weeks and was at the top of a new brick kiln when it collapsed. Although a verdict of accidental death was returned, the jury added a rider that it was unfortunate that the work had not been inspected by a fully qualified architect in addition to the Corporation's inspectors. The other was into the death of Wilfrid Scaife, aged twenty-nine, a quarryman at the Sandy Bank Quarry at Pannal, where he was killed in a fall. Once again an accident verdict was returned but it was also recommended that a code of rules be adopted and displayed at all quarries after the coroner had observed how with quarrymen 'familiarity breeds contempt' of danger and that Scaife had put himself in a dangerous position in his haste 'to get the face down'.[21]

Transport

The transport sector was also vital to the life of the town, for bringing in visitors, facilitating commuting and the import of goods and for meeting the daily needs of visitors and residents alike. Railway workers were the largest group. The total number of men employed rose by over a third from 338 in 1901 to 465 in 1911, although the 1911 figure is inflated by the fact that in that year more bricklayers and joiners were specifically identified as working on the railway. Of that total around 70 per cent lived in Starbeck: 235 men in the former year and 336 in the latter. Like building it was a male trade; the only women in the sector were two lavatory attendants. It encompassed a range of different occupations. Most numerous were the porters who did the fetching and carrying and the platelayers and renewal men who laid and maintained the track. Then came the engine drivers and firemen, who almost all lived in Starbeck, close to the engine sheds. Also mostly living close to their work there were the ancillary staff, including engine fitters and engine- and carriage cleaners. Essential to the safe running of the trains were the signalmen and associated workers like signal fitters. Guards manned both passenger and goods trains, whilst shunters carried out the work of moving passenger carriages and goods waggons. Also involved with goods were the various railway carters and van men. At stations porters were joined by such as ticket collectors and the booking clerks and managerial staff, although these last two are not included in my figures, which are of manual workers on the railways.

These varied employments had differing status levels, which was reflected in the rates of pay. Those of the North Eastern Railway Company, which enjoyed a near monopoly of rail services in the region, had been set by a general settlement agreed between the company and its men at the beginning of 1900. This had secured increases to all jobs and grades of the around 25,000 staff which it employed. At the top of the scale were the engine drivers, with average weekly earnings in 1907 of over 49s., and the firemen who worked alongside them on 31s. 4½d. At the bottom, the men who cleaned the engines earned just 16s. 2d. In between was a complex array of rates depending on the role and its specific tasks. Plate-laying, for example, comprised three grades rising from over 22s. to over 25s. and porters, similarly, earned 20s. 4d. on the platform but over 24s. if dealing with goods. Whilst average earnings for most grades did rise over the years 1907 to 1911, those of drivers, firemen, cleaners and goods porters fell and those of all were eroded by inflation. (35)

The 1900 settlement had also brought a reduction in hours. The case of the signalmen illustrates this and something further of the complexity of the wage structure. At 127 signal boxes the shifts were reduced from twelve to ten hours and at a further twenty-one from ten to eight. The rate of pay was also linked to the number of train movements which they oversaw and overtime was paid at the rate plus a quarter. Similarly complex changes were made for passenger guards, shunters and platform porters, the latter seeing a reduction in their hours at some stations from sixty-six a week to shifts of ten-and-a-half hours, excluding meals, whilst at others, including Harrogate, the change was from sixty-three hours to ten-hour shifts.[22]

Nevertheless, these remained long hours. In addition, in a uniformed service the men were subject to military-style discipline, partly justified by the companies for safety reasons. But the fatigue produced by such long hours was itself a cause of accidents. For the railways were a dangerous place to work. In 1906, for every 10,000 men employed eight lost their lives in the course of their work. The highest number of casualties was among shunters, the most dangerous grade of all, goods

117

35. Staff at Harrogate station, 1900. (Used with permission from Harrogate Library, North Yorkshire County Council.)

guards and brakemen, men working on the track and then drivers and firemen. This was the experience of Harrogate's railwaymen. In March 1900 William Hattersley, a shunter who lived on Mount Street, Oatlands died after being hit by a train. The census the following year shows his widow Mary, then thirty-nine, taking in washing to provide for daughter Ethel, aged eight and son George, just five. Also sharing the home were her widowed sister, aged twenty-five, and her two-year-old daughter. In April 1911, goods guard James Sharp, with twenty years' service, was hit by a passenger train at Stonefall siding, although there was no evidence given of anything to prevent him getting out of the way. And in a third example, of many reported in the local paper, two platelayers, William Whincup and Frederick Hood with over sixty-years' service for the NER between them, were killed near Dragon Junction, hit by a train whilst trimming ballast. The train's driver, William Steele of Regent Place, Starbeck, was unaware of the accident until he reached Leeds, having not seen them due to a sharp bend and a passing goods train, which the two men had gotten out of the way of only to be hit by his train. The coroner in this instance raised the desirability of a look-out man in future.[23]

There had in fact been an improvement by this time in the number of accidents. In 1875, nationally 767 men had been killed and getting on for three thousand injured. At the close of the century, fatalities were now 532 but 4,633 were injured. In the succeeding two decades greater improvement was achieved by pressure from the railway unions and legislation in 1900 which gave the Board of Trade greater powers over the companies. By 1920 the total number of men killed was less than half and the number injured less than one third of the figure for 1899.[24]

The NER was the only major railway company which recognized a trades union and allowed its permanent officials to negotiate on behalf of the men. This was the Amalgamated Society of Railway Servants, which was the oldest and the largest of the railway unions, formed in 1871 to improve the conditions of all classes of railwaymen, with over 62,000 members by 1900.[25] A local branch covering Harrogate, Starbeck and district was set up after a meeting at the Harrogate Hotel, Starbeck in January 1890, employees up until then being associated with the Leeds branch.[26] In addition to negotiating pay and hours the union also provided assistance from a Benevolent Fund at times of accident, sickness or distress, to raise money for which an annual concert was held at the Winter Gardens.[27] The branch also supported with an annual service and procession the union's Orphan Fund, which had been set up in 1880 to support widows and their children after it had lost control of the management committee of an orphanage at Derby to prominent citizens of that town, some of whom were connected with the Midland Railway Company. In 1902, for example, the service was held on a September Sunday at Christ Church, followed by a procession from Starbeck to Harrogate centre behind the association's banner, supported by the Harrogate Borough and Volunteer Bands.[28]

Nonetheless, pay and conditions remained central to the men's grievances, exacerbated by the rising cost of living, which fuelled widespread union militancy in these years. This had been encouraged by the restoration in 1906 by the new Liberal Government of the legal immunity of trade unions and their freedom to engage in peaceful picketing, which had been challenged by the House of Lords' decision in the Taff Vale Railway case. This had arisen in 1900 from a strike in South Wales over the alleged victimization of a signalman who had led a movement for a pay rise. The decision held that the funds of a trades union were liable for damages inflicted by its officials, in this case those of the Amalgamated Society of Railway Servants which had organized pickets to prevent the use of blackleg labour.[29] Now in 1907 a national 'all grades' movement was initiated and the companies approached to discuss a general rise in wages. In support of this, demonstrations were held at all the large railway centres in the country, including Starbeck. In the event, only the NER accepted this proposal and the union members then voted for a strike, which was averted following the intervention of Lloyd George who persuaded the companies to accept Boards of Conciliation for each railway and each grade, on which both company and employees would be represented. Recognition of the unions, however, was not conceded and it was lack of progress by the Boards and growing rank-and-file discontent which led to the first national rail strike in August 1911.[30]

Although the NER was not directly involved in the events leading up to the strike, the strength of feeling ensured that the company's men participated fully. The region, according to the historian of the NER, was 'paralysed'. From Harrogate there were just one or two trains going north and traffic from the south was 'practically at a standstill'. The *Advertiser* regretted intensely the 'jeopardising of the season', claimed the men had been led into the dispute against their better judgement and lamented that the lack of early trains from Knaresborough meant that those who lived there but worked in Harrogate had had to walk. After just two days, and with a further intervention from Lloyd George, a compromise was reached and the companies now conceded union recognition. The NER men, however, had already achieved this and stoppages continued in the region for some time for redress of their own special grievances, although not all the men took part. The *Advertiser* noted the 'Loyal Knaresborough Railwaymen', who to a man stayed at their posts at the town's station, and that a Loyal Servants' Fund had been set up to support them, which included Harrogate's mayor among its subscribers, to whom donations might be made.[31]

The strike was followed by a surge in union membership: that of the Amalgamated Society of Railway men, the largest rail union, quadrupled from 1900 to reach over 270,000 by 1914. As to wages, the year following the strike an NER survey acknowledged the effect of inflation and increased the rates of all men on grades earning less than 24s. a week by up to 2s., covering about half its employees. Despite this, railwaymen remained comparatively poorly paid and still worked long hours, in a normal week exceeding the already long standard amounts. It was also dangerous, as we saw. All of this, however, was offset by some benefits. It was steady and regular work, unlike that in the building trades, and it offered the prospect of long service. It was not unusually a family trade. The father of brothers Robert and Edward Lancaster, both living in Victoria Terrace, Starbeck in 1911, had been a fireman. Robert was a signalman and Edward had progressed from engine cleaner to driver. Most grades received up to six third-class travel passes a year and some got paid annual holiday, although six days was offered to only 6 per cent of men and three or four days to 45 per cent, with the rest getting nothing. There was sick pay and an old age pension, although the last was very patchy in its coverage and modest. A modest pension was the reward of George Croft, whose photograph was featured in the *Advertiser* in December 1911. He was retiring after forty-eight years working for the NER, forty of them at Harrogate station. He had been appointed foreman porter there in 1871. Just six years before his retirement he had had his left leg amputated after an accident at work but had continued as a lavatory attendant until he retired on reaching the age limit for employees. The paper praised his 'genial and obliging disposition'.[32] **(36)**

Transport within the town changed significantly over the period with the development of motor vehicles alongside the existing horse-drawn provision. The motor car's arrival had been highlighted by an early accident in October 1899. Ambrose Valentine of the Bradford Automobile Club was fined for driving 'furiously' (the legal term) down Parliament Street and hitting a little boy, one of a number who had been running alongside, suggesting the then novelty of the event.[33] Its impact on employment was also evident over the decade. The number of men

36.   Railway workers' housing built for the North Eastern Railway
Company in Station Parade in the mid-1880s, photographed shortly
before demolition in 1937. A bus station was built on the site. (Used with
permission from Harrogate Library, North Yorkshire County Council.)

employed as coachmen, or in support roles, declined, the former from
139 to 106 and those described as groom, ostler or stableman from 92
to 69. In contrast, there were seventy-two chauffeurs or drivers by 1911.
Supporting the motor car there were by then nine garages listed in
a directory and the census returns recorded over fifty garage men or
mechanics. In addition to private coaches and now cars, the hansom cab
continued to ply for hire alongside the new taxis. The number of men
described in the census returns as cab driver rose from sixty-seven in
1901 to eighty-one in 1911, but there were by then fourteen motor- or
taxi-cab drivers and some of the former group were probably in fact
driving taxis. The Corporation had included taxi cabs within its licensing
powers from 1908, when it also provided sixteen stands for twenty taxis.[34]

There was also a fall in the number of bath- or cycle chairs for the elderly and invalid, the number operating them almost halving over the decade from sixty-seven to thirty-four.

Hackney carriages and taxis were either operated independently or the driver worked for someone else. Regarding the former, the census returns distinguished between cabman, cab driver working on his own account and cab proprietor. They might then rent or own outright their own cab or work for someone else who might own and manage several cabs, although the returns may well have blurred those distinctions. In 1901, for example, at 13 Valley Mount the head of the household was a cab proprietor and lodging-house keeper. One of his four lodgers, Harry Moxon aged twenty-five, was a hansom-cab driver, although it is not clear whether he drove his landlord's cab or worked for someone else. Mindful of this difficulty, I excluded the proprietors from my figures. With taxis the picture is also unclear but there was a branch of the Provincial Motor Cab Company based in the town and several drivers gave it as their employer.

Hackney cabs, bath chairs and taxis were regulated by the Corporation and subject to the oversight of an Inspector of Hackney Carriages. The rates and fares of cabs were fixed according to distance, time, whether drawn by one or two horses or by a pony and the number of passengers. For example, the fare for a hackney coach or carriage drawn by one horse, conveying not more than two persons and not exceeding a mile in distance was 1s., with 6d. for every additional half-mile or portion thereof. The hirer could opt to pay for time or distance. Similarly, to hire a bath chair cost 1s. 3d. for the first hour or portion of an hour, whilst a cycle chair cost 2s. Taxi cabs could charge 1s. per mile and 3d. per quarter mile thereafter with a 4s. an hour waiting charge.[35] The Inspector also dealt with complaints, which were heard before the Stray, Pleasure Gardens, Entertainments and Hackney Carriage Committee. Such was the volume of these that, following several of disorderly conduct and using abusive language it was resolved in July 1900 to recommend the establishment of a special Hackney Carriage Complaint Sub-Committee.[36] They continued to be made against cab- and bath-chair men throughout the period. Most seriously, in May 1902 three cabmen were convicted at Leeds Assizes of unlawful wounding, inflicting grievous bodily harm and common assault on a police constable who had remonstrated with them for making insulting remarks to passing women and again later for using disgusting and bad language in the middle of the road. For this assault, which involved a heavy stick and kicking the constable until he lost consciousness, the men were given penal servitude for three years, later reduced to fifteen months with hard labour as it was not a premeditated attack.[37] Bad language, this time by bath-chair men in their shelter, resulted in the Committee's chairman being despatched to Prospect Hill to 'warn them against a repetition of the offence'.[38] Offenders could have their licence suspended or revoked. That the cab drivers and bath-chair men were, however, on the whole a respectable body is suggested by their annual dinner, as in 1900 for example, when the men of the Harrogate Cabmen's Association were joined by the mayor and other aldermen and councillors at the White Hart Hotel.[39]

Larger coaches to take residents and visitors further afield were similarly joined by motor buses. Of the former, Frederick Harrison, for example, had several coaches based at the Little Wonder Inn stables at New Park, like the one for thirteen passengers which plied for hire from Low Harrogate to Ribston Hall. He employed a guard whose job it also was to collect the fares, a workaday fact we know as in July 1904 Thomas Dugmore received a month in prison for embezzling them.[40] But by 1907, the NER, among other operators, was running charabanc tours around the district. They could also be hired by private parties. Timetabled motor-bus routes were also now licensed by the Corporation to run from Station Square to half-a-dozen destinations around the town.[41]

The movement of goods also began to be switched to motor vehicles, although once again the extent of this over the period is not clear: the term van, for example, was used for both a horse-drawn and motor vehicle. The total number of all types of goods driver rose from 181 to 225. Some of the latter were certainly driving motorized vans, as this is specified, but this probably underestimates the actual number. In addition, much day-to-day movement of goods and information within the town was done on bicycles or on foot by boys. The number of errand-, shop-, delivery- and newsboys, and a tiny number of girls, nearly doubled from 100 in 1901 to 184 ten years later. In addition to such as delivering for shops to customers, boys would wait at the station to carry visitors' luggage, a service not in fact welcomed by the NER, which was willing to take them to court. In March 1906, for example, it prosecuted five boys for trespassing at the station, who were described in court as the 'leaders' of up to forty who surrounded passengers and became abusive if their services were refused. And in September the following year, in a similar case, police were said to drive boys away from the station ten to twelve times a day.[42] Taking and delivering messages was another important service, among whom those working for the Post Office were said to be 'the aristocracy of the messenger world', with minimum educational and health standards specified for the job.[43]

Gas and municipal workers

The provision of the essential services of gas, electricity, water and sewerage employed significant numbers in the town. Whilst gas remained the responsibility of private enterprise, the others came to be provided, as was more generally the case, by the local authority. The Improvement Commission had from its creation power to provide gas lighting. The local paper thought that its provision would 'be a great inducement to Visitors to prolong their stay, and thus extend the Season very considerably'. Rather than provide it, however, the Commissioners agreed not to oppose the legislation of a private company, set up in 1845, to obtain the necessary powers, on condition they retain an option to purchase the undertaking in the future. The company built its gas works at New Park and provided lighting for the town under contract to the Commissioners. Although the service was the subject of repeated dispute between the company, local authority and residents over price, quality and damage to the town's streets by its traction engines bringing coal and although at one point the Commissioners did announce their intention to exercise their power to take the company over, nothing came of it and it remained privately run.[44]

The provision of water, similarly, was first undertaken from the mid-1840s by a private company, which constructed reservoirs, beginning with one on Harlow Hill. In this case the company was bought out by the Corporation in 1898 for £205,000, which went on to build the Roundhill reservoir on a tributary of the River Burn, near Masham, providing on its completion in 1912 capacity well above the town's current needs.[45] Adequate sewerage came rather later. Into the 1860s, for a growing town of over 5,000 inhabitants and thousands of visitors a system was 'virtually non-existent' and raw sewage instead went into the various watercourses and ultimately into the River Nidd. Finally, however, by the close of the 1860s the town's sewers were linked to an irrigation treatment works on a 300-acre farm in lower Oakdale.[46] The provision of electricity was from the first a Corporation venture. Works were also built on the Oak Beck site and became operational from 1897.[47]

Of the utilities, the gas industry was the largest employer. Increasing demand for gas as the town grew and its use was extended to heating and cooking led to the considerable enlargement of the New Park works in 1894–95 and again in 1914.[48] There were in 1901 98 gas workers of all types, including 19 labourers, rising to 116 in 1911, including 21 labourers, although employment was subject to seasonal variation. There were twice as many retort-house men in December as in June, when the days were longer. Conversely, the yard men were busiest in summer with maintenance and repairs, although the overall impact was by this time being reduced by those newer uses of gas.[49] Not surprisingly, a majority lived in New Park, sixty-three men at the latter census. On Electric Avenue, for example, one of the new streets built just outside the borough boundary after 1901, at numbers 14 and 38 lived John Hardcastle, aged 32 and John Towser, 34, both labourers at the gas works. At numbers 49 and 53 were John Day, 40, a gas stoker and George Lancaster, 31, foreman stoker. At number 54 was Charles Barker, a stationary engine man at the works and at 35, Frank Hayes, a light-railway engine cleaner. One of the engine drivers, George Potter, lived further out of town on Ripon Road towards Killinghall. The latter pair worked on the narrow-gauge railway which had been opened in 1908 to provide a link to the works from the coal depot on the main line at Bilton Junction. Elsewhere in New Park lived a platelayer for this line, blacksmith, firemen, fitters, carters and meter inspectors. One of the carters was Henry Daniel, whose wife Nora ran a fried fish shop close to the works at the corner of Leedhams Terrace and Ripon Road.

The men who lit the gas lamps were employed by the Corporation: thirteen were described as lamplighters in the census in 1911. They performed just one of the great variety of jobs being undertaken by the municipality by the Edwardian period, which it is impossible to detail here. The electricity industry employed over sixty men in 1911, although not all would be council employees. One who was so employed was Luke Pearson, aged in his mid-thirties, who lived in lodgings in Nydd Vale Terrace. A native of Castleford, he had been a miner before coming to Harrogate seeking work. By day he was a bath-chair man and at night a switchman. One late November night in 1902 he was electrocuted when switching off the arc lights which illumined West Park and adjoining streets.[50]

For the men in the Highways Department a committee report of wage increases in 1910 provides an insight into one area of the Corporation's work. For example, thirty-eight 'ordinary sweepers' were given a rise from 22s. to 22s. 6d. a week. At the same time, an age limit of fifty regulating the weekly wages of sweepers was abolished and the special cases of those too old or infirm were to be instead considered separately and dealt with on merit. The wages of six men were then set at 21s. a week, whilst another was granted a weekly pension of 5s. There were also rises for, among others, mason's labourers, road makers and repairers, stone breakers, tar macadam mixers and spreaders and roller attendants.[51] In addition to general road maintenance and sweeping, the department was responsible for snow clearance, which could be quite a task. In January 1913, in what was said to be the worse snow since March 1909, it reached a depth of fourteen-and-a-half inches. On the Sunday, 147 Corporation- and 34 extra men worked to clear it and on Monday over 100 extra men were employed, with half as many again on subsequent days.[52]

Other work carried out by the Corporation included emptying and cleansing ashpits and dustbins and the maintenance of drains, sewers and water works. Keeping up the public gardens was another important job. Indeed gardening, for public and private gardens, was a major employer in the town. In the 1901 census returns, thirty-six men described themselves as jobbing gardener or working on their own account and in 1911 no fewer than 121 did so, indicative of demand for their services and perhaps too the difficulties of finding employment at that date. Over the decade, the number of those describing themselves as gardeners working for an employer, including for the municipality, rose from 188 to 208. This was over and above those designated as servants or who lived in houses adjoining that of their employer.

The Corporation's spa facilities also employed men and, in another unusual exception to the generally gendered nature of employment, women, including as pump room or bath attendants, even one shampooer, and ticket collectors. In 1901 there were forty-three such workers, of whom twenty-one were women and in 1911 thirty-nine, including seventeen women. No detail was to be overlooked in securing the comfort of visitors, as when it was resolved in March 1913 that a 'youth' be engaged from Whitsuntide at 12s. a week to wash and dust seats.[53]

Finally, two other important groups of workers need to be mentioned: postal staff and the police. In 1907 the Harrogate General Post Office had a total staff of 180. This included indoor staff of twenty-three sorting clerks, five telephone operators and seventeen season assistants. The outdoor staff included forty-seven town and four rural postmen, nineteen assistant and auxiliary postmen and porters, fifteen boy cycle messengers and twenty-four additional boy messengers plus six additional postmen during the season. The men were represented by the Postman's Federation and that same year, at a 'smoker' for the uniformed staff, a toast was proposed to the Postmaster General Sydney Buxton for the 'good feeling' existing between him and the staff. They were now recognized as trade unionists and 'treated like reasonable human beings, instead of being looked upon as mere machines', in Buxton's 'generous and liberal treatment' in granting them concessions that for years they had been fighting for. The Federation had inaugurated an annual supper back in February 1897 and the social side seems to have been important to them as for other workers. They supported a brass band and an annual whist drive and dance was also introduced.[54]

Edwardian Harrogate was policed by the West Riding of Yorkshire force. It was part of the Claro Division which also covered Ripon and Pateley Bridge, described in 1901 as the largest police division save one in England.[55] Following the incorporation of the town in 1884 a new police station and court house was built in Raglan Street. Around a third of the Division's officers lived in Harrogate: twenty-one men, including three sergeants, in 1901 and twenty-nine, including four sergeants, in 1911.

Street musicians and entertainers

As we saw earlier, the town afforded opportunities for street sellers but
another group who made their living in the streets were also a feature
of life in the town: street musicians and entertainers. Like street sellers
they were not welcomed by all. In the eyes of the town's authorities and
respectable citizens there was a definite hierarchy from the acceptable
to those considered a nuisance. At the apex were musicians like Otto
Schwarz and his German band. They came from Rhineland Palatinate,
a German state known as the 'land of musicians' from its tradition
of sending men throughout Europe to perform. They were trained,
professional musicians with a repertoire which included classical and folk
music, as well as marches, waltzes and contemporary music-hall tunes.
Their first Harrogate season was in 1898, after which they were regular
annual performers in the town's hotels, at the Kursaal and at various
outdoor locations, including the Valley Gardens and the Pier Head at
the top of Montpellier Hill. They also performed for charity and in 1912
gave an open-air concert in the Crescent Gardens for the victims of the
Titanic disaster. Otto's friend, violinist Wallace Hartley, a member of the
Kursaal Orchestra, had led the ship's band and Otto attended his funeral.
At this time they were renting a house in Valley Road and in 1911 we find
Otto, then aged thirty-four, the band master, his wife Amalie 'assisting
in the business' and their little boy Berthold plus his brother Gustav and
four nephews who together made up the band.[56] (37)

The permissions granted to performers on the Stray also indicate
what was deemed acceptable entertainment. In 1908, for example, it was
granted to Messrs Brown and Walker's Scotch Concert Company and to
Tom Carrick's Original Scarborough and London Pierrots. According to
their historians, these pierrots of the Yorkshire coast 'possessed a certain
refinement', in contrast to the more 'brash' minstrel shows. Carrick's
troupe had been formed in the early 1890s. Carrick himself 'had a quirky,
clown like, smiling face, and always spoke in a broad northern accent'
as he delivered his comic songs at breakneck speed, as in this example:

He knew all about etymology,
Hebrew, Shebrew and phrenology,

37. Otto Schwarz and his German band performing on the Stray below the Prospect Hotel. They were among the elite of entertainers from 1898 to the First World War. (Courtesy the Walker-Neesam Archive)

> Syntax, tin tax, hobnailed boot jacks
> etc. etc.

The audience was invited to join in. Starting at normal speed, this was increased until they were left laughing and gasping for breath.[57] Pierrots, however, also indicate the mixed feelings in the town towards some forms of entertainment. In July 1905 those using the bandstand in the Valley Gardens were the subject of countervailing petitions. One councillor cited the objections of local lodging-house keepers to the noise, their lowering of the tone and collecting boxes 'stuck in one's face'. Another mounted a 'spirited defence', arguing that anyone might take their wives and children to see them 'and hear nothing but a most refined entertainment'. Again, in July 1908 councillors received a letter complaining about pierrots and their attendant crowds causing annoyance to visitors in Harlow Moor Drive. In March 1912 councillors voted to continue a ban on pierrots performing on the Stray, which had been introduced two years previously. Alderman Shepherd thought they should be allowed for the amusement of the poorer classes and those visitors who could not afford the Kursaal whilst a fellow alderman claimed they were a nuisance to residents and a threat to its profits. Councillor Mallinson weighed in with 'disgraceful sights', 'not fit for children and nurses and other young people' before expostulating: 'It might do for a continental town but would not do here.' Despite such condemnation, they remained popular. One of the best-known troupes was Tom Coleman's Pierrots, formed in 1902, and regular performers thereafter. For a record attendance at the Pierrot's Annual Benefit Concert in August 1913 at the Harlow Moor bandstand, they were 'seen at their best' with baritone, elocutionist, dancer and treble.[58] **(38)**

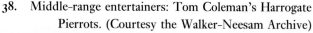

38.   Middle-range entertainers: Tom Coleman's Harrogate
Pierrots. (Courtesy the Walker-Neesam Archive)

Some forms of entertainment, however, were unequivocally unacceptable. These were itinerant musicians. Their presence on the Stray had been one of the reasons the Corporation had taken it over, although they did not immediately disappear. Nor were they without supporters. One letter to the *Advertiser* in July of 1894 defended 'nigger' performances and found such 'street minstrels' 'highly amusing' and 'perfectly respectable'. And in June the following year another correspondent had professed to be no foe of them so long as they kept clear of 'nastiness'. This appeared to cover songs such as one heard recently which told a veiled story of the seduction of a 'simple country maiden' by a 'young philanthropist', the 'friend' of a lady who had been prominent in a crusade against certain prurient entertainments in London, which had caused 'quite young women' to exchange 'meaning looks at the most indecently suggestive parts'.[59]

The 1893 legislation which gave control of the Stray to the Corporation and with that powers to regulate entertainment there also introduced them over street performers. Under Section 85 any householder or his servant, either directly or through a constable, might require them to depart from the neighbourhood. Failure to comply would render them liable to a penalty not exceeding 40s. The first case came the following year. Angello Fasicone (*sic*), a street organ grinder, had been asked by the residents of Oak Lea to move on. When he failed to do so they went to the police station and brought two constables to remove him. Since he was the first to be convicted, he was fined in mitigation just 1s., as the *Advertiser* put it 'A Warning to Street Organ Grinders'.[60] They faced something of the hostility experienced by German waiters, one correspondent to the *Herald* in 1906, for example, complaining about foreigners being treated more leniently over noise than English pierrots.[61] (39)

Although not the only street musicians, Italians were prominent among them in the many cases brought either under the act or highways legislation. In 1901 there were several living in Knaresborough and working in Harrogate. These were two branches of the Crolla family and the Fassionis (*sic*). In May 1902 Mary Fassioni was fined for allowing a donkey attached to a barrel organ to stray eighty yards in front of her. Her brother Michael escaped punishment in November 1910 when the new mayor exercised his prerogative and dismissed a case of assault on

39. Unknown street organ grinder on the Dragon
estate, *c*.1900. (Courtesy the Walker-Neesam Archive)

an inspector of the Valley Gardens.[62] Members of the Crolla family were
often in trouble it would appear. Mary and Rose, for example, in August
1901 were fined for not moving on when requested from Prospect Place.
In 1902, and again in 1903, Anthony was fined for using obscene language
when similarly requested.[63] There is a suggestion of some rivalry between
the two families. In 1907 Michael Fassioni and Angela Crolla were fined
for not moving on from in front of the Crown Hotel. According to
Superintendent Keel there was 'some friction' between them and they
followed one another about playing opposing tunes.[64] By 1911 Antonio, as
he was in the census, was in business as a confectioner in Gateshead, later
returning to Harrogate in the ice-cream trade. That census indicates he
was born in Picinisco, south-east of Rome. In that year, another Crolla,
Alfonso, was living in Harrogate in Grove Place, making and selling ice
cream but providing lodgings for four organ grinders, only one of whom
was Italian. In that same small street were also an elderly Italian couple
called Montano, Joseph being listed also as the head of an adjoining

133

lodging house. Their other neighbour was Michael Fassioni, still an organ grinder, with his wife of three years Lilian from Belfast.

Although not welcome by some in the town, street entertainers like these were a colourful feature of the resort, with an appeal to its working-class residents as much as visitors. The participation of some women made it, with hotel work, retailing and, to a small extent, printing and upholstery, one of the few areas of employment that was shared by both sexes. Overall, the world of work was highly gendered and no more so than in those key sectors of building and transport. What the sexes shared as workers, however, was the key contribution they made to Harrogate's success both as an international spa and a desirable place to live.

Notes to Chapter 4: Men at Work

1   D. Russell, *Popular Music in England, 1840–1914: A social history* (1987), pp. 119–20; P. Panayi, 'Sausages, waiters and bakers: German migrants and cultural transfer to Britain, c. 1850–1914', in S. Manz *et al* (eds), *Migration and Transfer from Germany to Britain, 1660–1914* (2007), pp. 147–59; B. Drake, 'The waiter', in Webb and Freeman, *Seasonal Trades*; *HA*, 19 November 1910, p. 6.

2   Jennings, *Harrogate*, p. 425.

3   *HA*, 8 and 22 September 1906, p. 6; 11 January 1913, p. 5; and 17 January 1914, p. 5.

4   *HA*, 23 and 30 June 1906, pp. 6 and 5; 18 May 1907, p. 6; and 8 December 1900, p. 5.

5   Census of 1911, vol. IX Birthplaces of Persons Enumerated in administrative counties, county boroughs etc and ages and occupations of foreigners; PP 1913 [Cd. 7017] LXXVIII.1, pp. xviii and xxi; N. Grizzard, 'Demographic: the Jewish population of Leeds – how many Jews?', in D. Fraser (ed.), *Leeds and Its Jewish Community: A history* (2019), pp. 35–46.

6   Benson, *Working Class*, p. 20; R. W. Postgate, *The Builders' History* (1923), p. 369; R. Price, *Masters, Unions and Men: Work control in building and the rise of labour, 1830–1914* (1980), p. 187.

7   Census reports as Chapter 2 note 22.

8   Benson, *Working Class*, p. 20; Robinson's Directory, 1902; *HA*, 7 July 1900, supp.

9   *HA*, 28 July 1900, p. 2 and 19 July 1902, p. 3.

10   *The Gentleman's Journal and Gentlewoman's Court Review*, 28:192 (1904), p. 9276.

11   Report on the Standard Time Rate of Wages in the United Kingdom in 1900; PP 1900 [Cd. 317] LXXXII.335, pp. ix and x and 4–6.

12   A. D. Webb, 'The building trade', in Webb and Freeman, *Seasonal Trades*, pp. 312–93; N. B. Dearle, *Problems of Unemployment in the London Building Trades* (1908), pp. 67–81.

13   *HA*, 6, 13, 20 and 27 April 1901, pp. 2, 5, 2 and 6.

14   *HA*, 18 January 1890, p. 7 and 22 March 1902, p. 3.

15   Report of an Enquiry by the Board of Trade into Working Class Rents, Housing and Retail Prices, together with the Standard Rates of Wages Prevailing in Certain Occupations in the Principal Industrial Towns of the United Kingdom; PP 1908 [Cd. 3864] CVII, p. xxxiii.

16   *HA*, 29 October 1904, p. 4.

17   Postgate, *Builders' History*, pp. 369–73.

18   Tressell, *Philanthropists*, pp. 3–4.

19   *HA*, 5 December 1896, p. 5.

20 *HA*, 20 January 1900, p. 6.

21 *HA*, 6 February 1904, p. 5.

22 *HA*, 27 January 1900, p. 2; Irving, *North Eastern Railway*, p. 72 and Appendix XIV, pp. 304–5.

23 *HA*, 31 March 1900, p. 3; 15 April 1911, p. 6; and 9 May 1914, p. 4.

24 P. S. Bagwell, *The Railwaymen: The History of the National Union of Railwaymen* (1963), pp. 94–125.

25 Bagwell, *Railwaymen*, pp. 52–3 and 309–10.

26 *HA*, 18 January 1890, p. 7.

27 *HA*, 30 November 1901, p. 5.

28 Bagwell, *Railwaymen*, p. 122; *HA*, 13 September 1902, p. 3.

29 H. Pelling, *A History of British Trade Unionism* (1971), pp. 123–4.

30 Pelling, *Trade Unionism*, pp. 133–4 and 136–7; *HA*, 18 May 1907, p. 3.

31 Bagwell, *Railwaymen*, pp. 289–308; Irving, *North Eastern Railway*, pp. 69–71; *HA*, 19 August 1911, pp. 2 and 5; 26 August 1911, p. 2; and 2 and 23 September 1911, pp. 3 and 2.

32 Irving, *North Eastern Railway*, pp. 72–4; *HA*, 9 December 1911, p. 5.

33 *HA*, 21 October 1899, p. 3.

34 Borough of Harrogate, Stray etc. Committee, 6 May 1908.

35 Robinson's Directory, 1902 and 1912.

36 *HA*, 14 July 1900, p. 6.

37 *HA*, 10 May 1902, p. 9.

38 Stray etc. Committee, 9 December 1907.

39 *HA*, 6 January 1900, p. 5.

40 *HH*, 6 July 1904, p. 6.

41 T. M. Leach, *'Twopenny Single to Starbeck': Early public transportation in the Harrogate area* (2000); Stray etc. Committee, 9 December 1907.

42 *HA*, 24 March 1906, p. 5 and 7 September 1907, p. 6.

43 J. G. Cloete, 'The boy and his work', in E. J. Urwick (ed.), *Studies of Boy Life in Our Cities* (1904), pp. 121–2.

44 Jennings, *Harrogate*, pp. 345–6, 408 and 411–12; and Walker, *Improvement Commissioners*, pp. 90–122, 166–8 and 393–5.

45 Jennings, *Harrogate*, pp. 346 and 422.

46 Walker, *Improvement Commissioners*, pp. 259–75; Jennings, *Harrogate*, pp. 351 and 408.

47 Jennings, *Harrogate*, p. 422.

48 M. P. F. Hallows and D. H. Smith, *Harrogate Gas Works: Its railways and other transport systems* (1995), pp. 6 and 10.

49 F. Popplewell, 'The gas industry', in Webb and Freeman, *Seasonal Trades*, pp. 148–209.

50 *HA*, 29 November 1902, p. 2 and 6 December 1902, p. 6.

51 Highways Committee, 28 February 1910.

52   *HA*, 18 January 1913, p. 2.

53   Stray etc. Committee, 31 March 1913.

54   *HA*, 9 and 16 March 1907, pp. 5 and 3; 6 February 1897, p. 7; and 14 February 1914, p. 3.

55   *HA*, 4 May 1901, p. 5; G. C. East, *The Constables of Claro: A History of policing in Harrogate and district* (1996).

56   D. K. Schwarz, *The Waves Roar: A kapelmeister's journey, the biography of musician Otto Schwarz of Hinzweiler, Rhineland Palatinate* (2011); The late Mike Hine was kind enough to loan me his copy of this book and discuss it.

57   Stray etc. Committee, 27 January 1908; M. and B. Chapman, *The Pierrots of the Yorkshire Coast* (1988), pp. 10–11 and 39–41.

58   *HA*, 15 July 1905, supp.; Stray etc. Committee, 27 July 1908; *HA*, 16 March 1912, p. 7 and 30 August 1913, p. 7; M. Neesam, *Music Over the Waters* (2017), p. 60.

59   *HA*, 7 July 1894, p. 5 and 29 June 1895, p. 2.

60   *HA*, 7 July 1894, p. 3.

61   Neesam, *Music*, p. 76.

62   *HA*, 24 May 1902, p. 6 and 19 November 1910, p. 6; the spelling of their surname varies.

63   *HA*, 31 August 1901, p. 2; 26 July 1902, p.6; and 1 July 1903, p. 4.

64   *HA*, 21 September 1907, p. 7.

CHAPTER FIVE

Neighbourhood, Community, Housing and Health

THIS CHAPTER brings together several important aspects of working-class life. It begins with those working-class neighbourhoods which I identified in Chapter 1 and asks to what extent they might be characterized as communities. How do we define that elusive term community and how might we seek to measure it? It then focuses on the houses in those districts. In Thomson's fictionalized account of Edwardian Harrogate, just as his Nidvale had only a bare minimum of 'working' inhabitants so also had it 'no slums and only two poor streets'. This was echoed by Neesam, who whilst noting the existence of sub-standard housing similarly observed that in the real Harrogate 'slums have never existed'.[1] To what extent was this the case? The chapter then goes on to explore a question directly linked to housing conditions, that of the health of Harrogate's working people, with a focus on their children.

Neighbourhood and community

By the Edwardian period there were several working-class districts in the town. The earliest had been developed in the centre along Tower Street and in courts off Chapel Street. To these had been added much larger ones a little further to the north of the centre between Walker Road and Smithy Hill west of Skipton Road, and, to its east, the Regents, plus some smaller developments such as that at Harlow Hill. There were also large districts at New Park, Oatlands and Starbeck. In the Edwardian period, streets were added to several existing districts but the only major new development was the Bilton Grange estate.

These were working-class districts in that they consisted wholly or largely of housing built for working people but to what extent might they be characterized as working-class communities? Community has proved to be a singularly elusive concept. As cultural historian Raymond Williams put it, it is a 'warmly persuasive word' that 'seems never to have been used unfavourably'.[2] One thinks, for example, of its use with religions, ethnic groups, localities, hobbies and lifestyles. It has been used widely in this nostalgic way to characterize an important phase in the history of working people but it has also been detected by historians, as did Mike Savage and Andrew Miles, for example, seeing 'the rise of the working-class neighbourhood' in the period 1880 to 1920.[3] It does therefore merit attention. Although I accept that 'defining "community" has been a long-standing challenge', I have turned to a pioneering text of the mid-1960s for guidance. For Ronald Frankenberg:

> Community implies having something in common ... Those who live in a community have overriding economic interests which are the same or complementary. They work together and also play and pray together. Their common interest in things gives them a common interest in each other.[4]

That interest may not have been positive. Neighbours and groups can equally display hostility towards, and come into conflict with, each other. This was certainly evident in working-class districts, as in banal incidents like that of the Denmark Street neighbours fighting over the taking down of a clothesline in the yard.[5] There is also something of a fine line between neighbourliness and intrusion, or between closeness to each other and lack of privacy. A sense of community may also produce hostility to excluded groups, be they those of other religions and ethnic groups, for example, or with marginal lifestyles like rough sleepers or beggars.[6]

Other indicators of community have been sought in the extent to which individuals were born in a particular city or town; whether they lived over time in the same street or district; their choice of marriage partner; the extent to which they were near to other relatives; and whether they lived close to their place of work. All have presented problems to the researcher, as two social geographers expressed them, 'Taken in isolation every statistical index of community structure is ambiguous and taken together different indices may be contradictory.'[7]

Mindful of the difficulties, I looked at some of those indicators in relation to Harrogate's working class. But first, areas like Smithy Hill, New Park or Oatlands were working-class neighbourhoods in the simple sense that almost all their residents were working-class people. The only exceptions were shopkeepers, small employers, lodging-house keepers and, exceptionally, clerks, like those on Mount Street at Oatlands for example in 1911. Shopkeepers, although they might perceive themselves as of a higher status than their neighbours, like those of Roberts's Salford, were also very much a part of the neighbourhood.[8] Joseph Lilley was a greengrocer, trading on Denmark Street at the 1911 census. His was a house with just four rooms which, although he himself was single, he shared with a married woman who gave her occupation as charwoman and her two children. We do not know how he viewed his status but both in the small scale of the business and its reliance on local working-class custom, plus her occupation as a cleaner, they were not greatly distinguishable from their working-class neighbours. This was likely also the case with Ann Fitzpatrick, who kept a lodging house there. Her boarders, three of whom were from Ireland, comprised a cook, labourer and three old-age pensioners. More conscious of status perhaps was John Littlewood of the Denmark Tavern, the district's pub, whose son Joe had left Grove Road Council School in 1907 aged twelve for a private school. (40)

Nevertheless, this was a beerhouse, rather than a fully licensed public house, in a district which, like Tower Street, had something of a reputation in the town for drunken and disorderly conduct. This is evidenced in characteristic newspaper headlines such as 'Another Tower Street Incident' or 'Brawling in Denmark Street – Another Drunken Episode'.[9] This was so much the case that eventually, at the time of the George V's Silver Jubilee in 1935, its residents petitioned the council for its name to be changed. The vicar of St Luke's, who chaired their

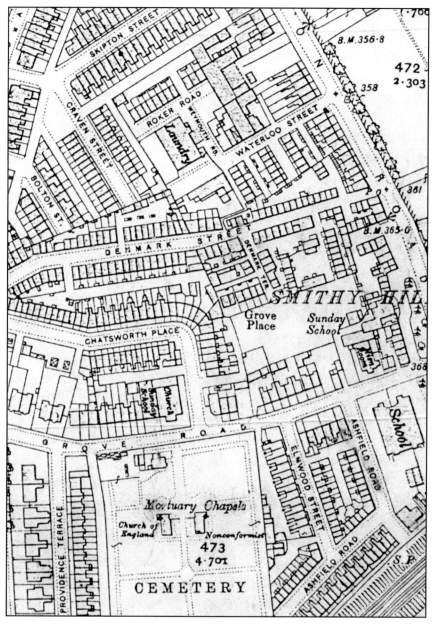

40. Smithy Hill with the 'low down quarter' of Denmark Street at centre. Skipton Road is to the right and Walker (from 1910 King's) Road at top left. Grove Road School is to the right. Note the Sunday schools. (Ordnance Survey, 25″ to the mile, revised edition 1907, reproduced with permission of Ordnance survey.)

meeting, observed that 'in years gone by this street had a very bad reputation as a "tough spot" and a "low down quarter"', which slur still gave tradesmen difficulty in obtaining contracts and others in obtaining work of any kind. The request was granted but the change was to Chatsworth Road and Terrace rather than the suggested Windsor Road and Terrace.[10]

Status differences within the working-class are rather difficult to detect from the census alone. Looking at Denmark Street again, of the sixty-nine working-class heads of household whose occupation was recorded in 1901, 42 per cent were in the skilled class III, including several building workers, 44 per cent in semi-skilled class IV of such as carters and gardeners and just 15 per cent in the lowest, unskilled, class V of labourers. In Union Street, however, another of those regarded as the poorest in the town, there was more of a presence of the semi- or unskilled, with nearly three-quarters of residents in classes IV and V. Conversely, in Archie Street at New Park, one of four terraces which were named in alphabetical order from family members of the gas company, just under three-quarters of household heads in 1901 had class III occupations and rather more in Duncan Street. In Christina Street, however, located between those two streets, over half had class IV or V occupations. This could well have translated into perceptions of status difference between streets. Yet ten years later, by which time Baldwin Street had been completed, only Duncan Street now had mostly class III household heads and the other three all had around three-quarters of heads in classes IV and V. And if there were perceived status differences between streets, they were all clearly still working class. (41)

In other areas of the town we find more of a mix of working- and lower middle-class families. This was the case, for example, in those streets between Grove Road cemetery and the town centre: Mayfield Grove and Terrace and Nydd Vale Terrace, although the latter's view over the railway line cannot have helped its desirability to some. It was the case also in the streets built on the west side of Walker Road, such as De Ferrieres- and Grange Avenues or Dawson Terrace, whose residents in 1911 included the manageress of a shop, a clerk, and a licensed lay reader for the Church of England. Similarly, on the Bilton Grange estate, King Edward's Drive had only a minority of working-class families;

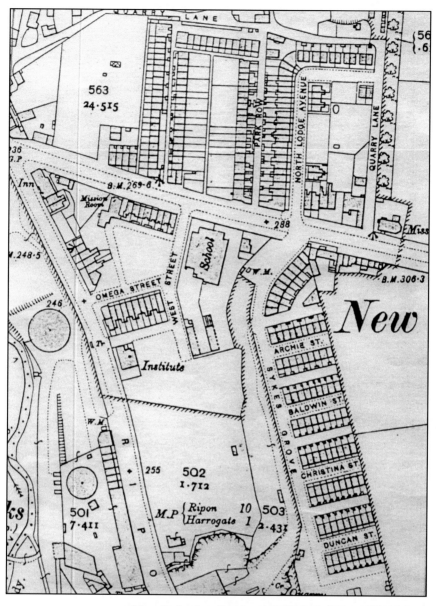

41. New Park, showing the alphabetical streets. Skipton and
Ripon Roads meet at the Little Wonder Inn. Part of the gas
works is to the left and at top, Quarry Lane leads to Knox
Quarries. Note the Institute, school and two mission rooms.
(Ordnance Survey, 25″ to the mile, revised edition 1907,
reproduced with the permission of Ordnance Survey.)

143

Albert Road was more mixed; and Birch-, Chestnut-, Poplar- and Willow Groves almost wholly working-class streets. In those districts the occupational evidence, and the size and quality of the houses, does perhaps suggest that status differences between individual streets may indeed have been perceived by their residents.

Linked to status are the related questions of movement into and out of the working class and the permeability or otherwise of the boundary between it and the lower middle class. I sought to measure this social mobility using the evidence of marriage registers and the census returns.[11] With the first, one can compare the groom's occupation with that of his father and for brides her father's occupation with that of her new husband. Similarly, with the census returns one can look at the occupations pursued by children compared to those of their father or mother. The evidence of both sources shows that in Harrogate most working-class men and women remained in that class but that there was some limited movement into the lower middle class. Among working-class grooms, just twenty out of 278, or 7 per cent, had lower middle-class employment on marriage. Among working-class brides, however, 14 per cent married into the lower middle class, although slightly more common was movement in the other direction, as the daughter of a Princes Square dentist, for example, married the son of a bricklayer of Northumberland Court. The census returns of fathers' and children's occupations show the same picture. Some 7 per cent of sons had a lower-middle class occupation but 9 per cent of daughters did. For the sons, to be a clerk was the most likely move and among daughters nearly half went into teaching and getting on for a third became a cashier or bookkeeper. Most girls nevertheless went into the jobs I described in Chapter 3: in shops, dressmaking, laundries or service. Both sources show more movement within the working class. For example, over a quarter of Class IV grooms and a third of those in Class V had moved into Class III by their marriage, although in both cases more had stayed where they were or moved down. The census returns show the same pattern.

The 'frontier' between the lower middle class and the working class was not therefore impenetrable, although as F. M. L. Thompson pointed out, it could scarcely be otherwise since the working class were so numerous.[12] But the Harrogate evidence confirms the conclusion of a much larger study of social mobility using marriage registers that the barrier between the classes was high, with only limited working-class interaction with the non-manual world. Movement was rather within the working-class, with those from unskilled manual backgrounds moving up into higher status, better-paid work. This represented greater mobility than that experienced by the working class of seventy-five years earlier, which had been based in the subsequent growth of white-collar employment, but still 'both the stability and coherence of the Victorian and Edwardian working class remained virtually undisturbed'.[13] Further, as Frankenberg suggested, it may be that such social mobility as took place served not to weaken but to strengthen the class system as a whole, as the mobility of individuals 'emphasizes the rigidity of the class system through which they move', as the revolt against the bad king strengthens the kingship.[14]

Turning now to the origins of Harrogate's workers, they were very much incomers. At both censuses, only around 15 per cent of male household heads had been born in the town. This was a low proportion compared with the much higher ones in industrial cities like Leeds or Bradford, but at a similar level to that of other resorts like Blackpool, Bournemouth or Eastbourne and growing suburbs like Acton in west London.[15] Those high levels of the locally born in industrial cities have been taken to be an indicator of community. Does this therefore mean that it would be absent in Harrogate? First, it surely does not follow that newcomers cannot form communities or become part of an existing one. Second, most of those incomers had not in fact travelled far from their place of birth. One in five had been born within ten miles of Harrogate and getting on for two-thirds elsewhere in Yorkshire. Third, whilst they might have moved, most of their children were born in the town. It may be inferred therefore that they had quickly settled into family life in their new place of residence. Moreover, many of them had connections in Harrogate, either relatives or people from their hometown or -village, as we saw with servants. To take two examples: in 1911, sisters Maria and Lois Briggs, originally from Fishlake near Doncaster, by then both widows, lived next door to each other in Beech Street, Starbeck and brothers George and Robert Allinson, originally from Masham, also next door to each other in Elmwood Street, off Grove Road.

Length of residence in one street, or 'residential persistence' as social geographers have described this measurement, has been used as another indicator of community. George Allinson had been in Elmwood Street in 1901, with his wife Julia and their young son William. As both Julia and William were born in Cuckney, near Mansfield, they were at that point new arrivals in the town, where their three other children were then born. A cousin of George's from Masham was living with them. This residential persistence was, however, varied in the town. Looking, for example, at those alphabetical streets at New Park, very few of the residents lived there across the decade: of the three, there was just one household in each of Archie and Duncan Streets which did so. This represented quite a contrast with Union and Denmark Streets. In the former, 41 per cent of household heads living there in 1901 were still there in 1911 and in the latter 38 per cent. Those rates are quite high in comparison with those calculated for other cities and towns.[16] Its usefulness as a way of measuring whether there was a sense of community is based on the assumption that living in the same street for a decade at least may have contributed to its development. But of course, the residents may have had no choice but to stay, trapped by their low incomes. It is perhaps significant that of fourteen householders who stayed in Union Street, half that number were women: one was a widow at both censuses, four had been married in 1901 but were widowed ten years later and two others had also been married, and were still married in 1911, but had no husband present on census night. (42)

In addition to living in the same street, people moved to another street within the same district or to another part of Harrogate. Frequent but short distance movement was common among working-class people, facilitated by the fact that most rented their home.[17] Of those two Fishlake sisters, Maria had been living in Pannal village with her husband, a signal fitter, in 1881. Ten years later they were in one of the railway houses in Station Parade in Harrogate itself, before moving at some point to Beech Street by 1901, where they remained ten years later. I traced several individuals living at Oatlands in 1901 and found similar movements. William Ellis, a house painter, came from Leeds with his wife at some point in the 1890s. In 1901 they were in Gladstone Street and ten years later had moved the short distance to Mount Street. Samuel Pickersgill

42.   Surviving cottages at the bottom of Union Street, behind
Parliament Street; in the Edwardian years it was characterized as one of
the town's poorest streets. Photographed in 2018. (Author's photograph)

had been a railway porter in Leeds before moving to Harrogate, also
at some point in the 1890s. By 1901 he was a ticket collector living on
Hookstone Road and ten years later had moved to Station Parade. Also
on Hookstone Road in 1901 was Robert Deighton, a gardener originally
from Moor Monkton, where ten years earlier he had been a postman. In
this instance, movement was away from the town and in 1911 we find him
and his family running the Post Office at South Otterington, just south
of Northallerton. Finally, local all his life was Frederick Yates, born in
Pannal, the son of a quarryman. He eventually became a self-employed

147

tailor and by 1891 was living in Gladstone Terrace and at the same address ten years later, just moving to Gladstone Street by 1911. One son worked with him as a tailor, but another, Francis, went to work at the Kursaal, first as a programme boy, then as a stage electrician and latterly as an assistant stage manager.[18]

Finally, in addition to residence shared local employment might be taken to indicate the presence of community and this was certainly the case in Harrogate's working-class districts. At Oatlands, men worked in the brickworks or women in laundry work, either at home or at the industrial laundry. In New Park many families had members who worked in its principal industries of gas, quarrying and laundry work. At Starbeck, similarly, there was employment in the two laundries but especially on the railways, although we should be mindful of status differences between the various grades. But surely overriding them to some extent were the struggles and sometimes griefs which families faced in common.

In the succeeding chapters I will pursue this theme of common experience when I look at working-class family life and living standards, their experience of school, leisure time pursuits and religious observance. But here I turn to the houses they lived in.

Housing

A useful way to approach discussion of working-class housing is by looking at a report to the Local Government Board, published in early 1909, into the sanitary condition of Harrogate and of the Knaresborough urban and rural districts.[19] The prospect of such an inquiry had in fact caused some alarm in Harrogate. In April 1907 the Town Clerk wrote confidentially to the Local Government Board asking for it to be postponed, arguing that the season had just begun in what he termed 'the principal Inland Health Resort in the UK' and that the inspector's visit would become known 'and cause unjustifiable alarm, preventing a large number of visitors to the Town, causing great financial loss to the Corporation, Hotel Proprietors, Boarding House Owners and Occupiers, and the Owners and Occupiers of property generally'.[20] This plea was accepted and the inspection deferred until February of the following year. The report affords us a detailed picture of the town's housing and sanitary provision, which I have supplemented with evidence from a range of other sources.

Its key conclusion was that, 'Compared with many other places, the working classes are comfortably, if somewhat expensively, housed in Harrogate.' Unlike in most industrial, or indeed market towns like Knaresborough, very little of its workers' housing was built either back-to-back or in courts. There were some of the former in Tower Street, a pair for example comprising kitchen and pantry, two bedrooms and an attic, with a yard to the rear in which were a washhouse, shed and two WCs. There were some also at Smithy Hill, in Beresford Place, similarly with living room, scullery and two bedrooms above and outside toilets.[21] There was also some courtyard housing in the centre in Chapel-, Northumberland- and School Courts. Some was also constructed in 'squares', as they were named, as at Kensington Square off Cold Bath Road (43) or Mowbray- and Myrtle Squares off Westmoreland Street. At New Park, off the junction of the Skipton- and Ripon Roads, some houses were constructed in the shape of a horseshoe. (44) But most workers' housing was built in terraces of 'through' houses, either with the front

43. Early nineteenth-century workers' housing in Kensington Square off Cold Bath Road, drawing by George Walker. They were demolished in the 1970s. (Courtesy Harrogate Museums and Arts, Harrogate Borough Council)

44.   Early workers' cottages at New Park in Skipton Road,
drawn by George Walker. They were demolished in clearances
in the 1960s and 1970s. (Courtesy Harrogate Museums and
Arts, Harrogate Borough Council)

door opening directly on to the street or into a small yard or garden. In
the alphabetical terraces at New Park, those in Baldwin Street opened
directly on to the pavement, whilst those of Christina Street had a small
yard to the front. (45, 46) At Smithy Hill, houses in Denmark Street and
Roker Road, built in red brick, opened on to the street, whilst stone-built
houses in Bilton- or Skipton Streets had small gardens. (47, 48, 49) This
mix, of materials and styles, was replicated throughout the town. On the
cemetery side of Grove Road, houses in stone-built Ashfield Road opened
to the street, whilst those of Providence Terrace had a small garden. (50,
51) Red-brick houses at Starbeck, like those in Beech Street, opened to
the street. (52) Finally, to return to Tower Street, there were those also
with a small garden and others in Oxford Terrace of red brick with their
front door opening directly to the street. (53)

The internal arrangements of all those houses afforded space for only
limited variation on a basic theme. In Omega Terrace in New Park, for
example, a typical house had sitting- and living rooms, scullery and three

45. Workers' housing: Baldwin Street, New Park, the last of the alphabetical streets to be completed. Photographed in 2018. (Author's photograph)

46. Workers' housing with small yard, Christina Street, New Park. Photographed in 2018. (Author's photograph)

bedrooms. At a house in Coronation Avenue, one of the newer streets built after 1900 at Oatlands, there was also a bathroom.[22] Model cottages built by Samson Fox at Stonefall had either four or five rooms, the latter having a parlour as well as a kitchen, scullery and two bedrooms.[23] The Omega Terrace house was rented at 6s. 3d., but that in Coronation Avenue at 7s. 9d. The Stonefall model dwellings, however, were let for 4s. 10d. a week for five rooms and just 2s. 5d. for four, although the latter rent seems to have been exceptional. Those housing types and their rents are comparable with those of York, for example, cited in Rowntree's well-known study of poverty in that city. The rent for the best working-class housing, usually with sitting room and kitchen/living room and three bedrooms above, plus scullery and yard with a WC, was typically 6s. a week. Most households paid between around 4s. and 6s. a week. Unfortunately, I was unable to

47. Red-brick workers' housing in Denmark Street built in the 1870s. Photographed here as Chatsworth Road in 2018. (Author's photograph)

48. Red-brick workers' housing in Roker Road. Photographed in 2018. (Author's photograph)

49. Workers' housing with small garden, Bolton Street. Photographed in 2018. (Author's photograph)

50. Workers' housing: Ashfield Road off Grove Road by the school. Photographed in 2018. (Author's photograph)

51. Providence Terrace, off Grove Road. Superior workers' housing with small garden, adjoining the middle-class Franklin Road area. Photographed in 2018. (Author's photograph)

find rents for the very poorest housing in Harrogate. In York, 2*s.* to 2*s.* 6*d.* was charged for a two-roomed house in one of the city's narrow alleys or courts but there was very little indeed of such housing in Harrogate.[24] A Board of Trade survey published in 1908 found that in provincial towns weekly rents ranged from 3*s.* to 3*s.* 6*d.* for a two-roomed house, up to 5*s.* 6*d.* to 6*s.* 6*d.* for one with five bedrooms.[25] That there was considerable variation was confirmed by the rents revealed in a survey done a little later in the period of four medium-sized towns around the country: in Northampton and Reading they were typically 6*s.* to 7*s.* a week, in Stanley from 5*s.* to 6*s.* and Warrington 4*s.* to 5*s.*[26] Allowing for that variation, rents in Harrogate were then broadly comparable with those in other towns outside London, where they were indeed much higher.

53. Oxford Terrace off Tower Street. Later nineteenth-century workers' housing in this district which had been developed from the 1830s. Photographed in 2018. (Author's photograph)

52. Workers' housing at Starbeck: Beech Street. Photographed in 2018. (Author's photograph)

There was little overcrowding in Harrogate, as defined in the Registrar General's standard of more than two persons per room. In 1901 just over a fifth of houses had fewer than five rooms, which compared with a county average of just over half and well below the proportion in industrial cities and towns like Bradford or Huddersfield at over two-thirds. Of the 1,253 Harrogate dwellings in 1901 with fewer than five rooms, only 70 were overcrowded by that two-room standard. It is, however, a generous standard when one looks at the reality behind the statistic. Six persons shared a three-roomed house in Union Street, for example, but they comprised a young couple, William and Sarah Cundall and their one-year-old son, plus William's brother Robert and sister Ann and her husband George Bentley. Similarly, at another three-roomed house Joseph Bowes, a fifty-six-year-old widower, lived with his three daughters aged twenty-five, twenty-four and seventeen and sons aged twenty-two and thirteen. In 1911 there were 120 overcrowded dwellings, but home to over a thousand people.[27]

The sanitation of those homes was now provided almost exclusively by water closets, although in the poorer districts two houses might share one WC, and the town possessed comprehensive sewerage totalling over sixty-four miles, of which just a few short lengths were not deemed efficient. This was certainly a big improvement. At Smithy Hill, sewage had formerly run under Skipton Road into a ditch before discharging into Bilton Beck and flowing ultimately into the River Nidd and on downstream to the Ouse and York. Similarly, the effluent of the Oatlands district had originally drained into an open water course which passed under the railway before flowing into Hookstone Beck, thence into Crimple Beck and the Nidd.[28]. Although the enlargement of the borough boundary of 1900 had led to the conversion of many privies in those districts to WCs, their sanitary condition still did 'not yet reach a very high standard', according to the report. 'Tippler' conveniences still in use at some properties at New Park, for example, were 'out of order, inaccessible, or in an extremely filthy state'. Overall, 'defective sanitary arrangements' remained one of the principal shortcomings of the town's workers' housing and was a constant concern of the Corporation, detailed in the minutes of its Sanitary Committee. For example, the owners of five cottages in Chapel Court and ten in Northumberland Court were required in April 1908 to provide additional WCs for the occupiers. The following year sanitary works were ordered to be carried out at various properties in Denmark Street but in 1913 it was again reported that at many houses they were still defective and not intercepted from the sewer. At Oatlands, the Inspector of Nuisances was ordered in 1910 to look at the sanitary arrangements and open out drains at houses in four streets. In some instances, properties had to be put into such a state as to be 'reasonably fit for human habitation', as for example at Tower- and Union Streets or Primrose Hill off Skipton Road. Nor were problems confined to the poorer streets. Defects at houses in Valley Road, many of which were let in apartments, were also ordered to be remedied in 1911.[29]

Defective drains, along with unpaved backyards, were the principal shortcomings of workers' housing. The report highlighted what it clearly perceived, if it did not unequivocally state, was a root cause of the problem. This was the overrepresentation of builders and those in related trades on the two relevant council committees: Sanitary and General Purposes and Plans. Noting that as many as ten of the eighteen members of the former and six of twelve of the latter were so employed, it observed that this 'must at times render the task of the officials of the Corporation needlessly delicate or difficult'. The occupations of committee members were 'liable to hamper their judgements when questions of strict application or interpretation of the building bye-laws or of nuisances are at issue'. Over the previous ten years, it reported, 552 building plans for houses submitted by members of the council had duly been approved, as had 108 plans prepared by a member who was an architect but submitted by non-members of the council. Presumably those comments were noted but there is no record of any action taken in response.

As most of Harrogate's workers' housing was built from the 1880s, by which time minimum standards were now enforced and expectations had risen, the town did not have slums comparable to those of industrial cities, or even of small towns like neighbouring Knaresborough. There was nonetheless substandard housing. Eventually, after a delay due to the Second World War, many properties at Tower Street and Smithy Hill were demolished in slum clearance schemes, along with older housing at New Park and Starbeck. (54) But it is something of a testament to the overall standard of workers' housing in the town that so much of it remained in habitation into the twenty-first century.

Health

The report was also critical of the town's Medical Officer of Health, Dr Ward, for deficiencies in his record-keeping, the procedure which he had followed regarding smallpox and for the lack of detail provided in his annual report. That those reports were not printed for public consultation and his was only a part-time appointment were also deemed unsatisfactory. The contrast between the generally positive tone of Ward's reports with some of the findings of the inquiry is also noteworthy. Whereas, for example, he could find the town's dairies 'quite satisfactory', the inquiry observed that 'No doubt if consumers of milk in Harrogate

54. Housing in the Skipton Road Clearance Area, 1938; not demolished until after the Second World War. (Used with permission from Harrogate Library, North Yorkshire County Council.)

were to pay a visit to some cowsheds they would hastily change their milkman.' Overall, it concluded that although there had been a large expenditure on water and sewerage, 'In several respects ... public health administration has failed to reach that standard of efficiency which may reasonably be expected.'

Part of that reasonable expectation was of course the fact that Harrogate was a health resort and the same criterion was applied to the health of its inhabitants. Looking at infant mortality first, although the rate was lower than that of the country as a whole and lower also than that prevailing in smaller towns generally of between 20- and 50,000 inhabitants, it had been 'somewhat high in recent years' and was 'not as low as it should be in a health resort'. It highlighted particularly 'an excessive amount of diphtheria'. In 1900, 153 cases had resulted in eighteen deaths and over the eight years from then to 1907, 576 children had been affected, leading to a total of 59 deaths. The majority were children at the town's public elementary schools: the children of the working class.

It is on the health of children that I will focus here, for two reasons. First, whilst adults are not separated by class in local statistics, children in public elementary schools were almost all from working-class backgrounds. Second, the logbooks which heads of schools were by law required to keep provide ample documentation on the children's health.[30] Although rates of infant and child mortality were improving generally over these years, and those of Harrogate compared favourably with other places, there was still everywhere much sickness and general ill health among children.[31] The diphtheria outbreak of 1900 led to the closure of schools for up to five weeks at the beginning of the year. The head of Western, James Hammond, was himself off with diphtheria, although on his return he was happily able to write in the logbook that 'By God's mercy I have returned to my well-loved life's work, very little the worse for my illness.' Five of his staff were also absent suffering from influenza. Towards the end of the period in 1913 Starbeck school was again closed due to diphtheria from the 25 November until Christmas. At various times schools were also closed due to outbreaks of measles, mumps and chicken pox. Bilton, for example, was closed for three days in October 1907 after an outbreak of chicken pox which led to the isolation of sixty children, plus a further twenty suffering from fever. It was again closed in 1910 for three weeks from September to October due to an outbreak of measles.

Apart from diphtheria, however, there were fewer actual deaths in these years from disease, reflecting national trends. Those from smallpox had been virtually eliminated, with just one in Harrogate, although precautions were still necessary: in 1904, following two cases at Starbeck, all the classrooms at the school were disinfected in addition to the 'Tablets' which always hung there. There were twenty-four deaths from measles over the period 1901 to 1907, including a spike of fourteen in 1906. Scarlet fever, which formerly had been a real killer, claimed thirteen lives, in line with the fall nationally in the death rate from the disease.[32] In 1898 a girl at Bilton had died from croup and in 1904 another girl at St Robert's Infants from whooping cough and bronchitis. Whooping cough, however, did claim the lives of twenty-six infants under one-year-old over those years. Other diseases and illnesses noted in the logbooks were a case of nettle rash at St. Peter's, but more commonly swollen glands, eczema, scabies, ringworm and diarrhoea. The latter could still be fatal to babies, accounting for seventy-nine deaths between 1900 and 1907.

Most common were colds, coughs and sore throats, complaints to which, along with diarrhoea, the schools' environment, over and above the proximity to each other of large numbers of children, contributed. In early December 1907 the drains of all the council schools were inspected. This resulted in the closure of Oatlands until the end of the first week of the new year so that the sewers could be taken up and re-laid. The following month the Medical Officer of Health closed Grove Road for ten days to inspect and put the drains there in order. The cold was also a problem. In February 1906 it was reported that Bilton school had been very cold for the past fortnight, with temperatures as low as 42 degrees (5.55 Celsius) at the start of the day. In 1908 new radiators were installed at Grove Road due to inadequate 'warming' in cold weather, although the Infants was still reported to be 'cold and draughty' later that year. The same measure was necessary at Western in 1913, where in December it was reported that the temperature in the classrooms had also fallen to as low as 48 degrees (8.88° Celsius) but was now much warmer with the installation there too of new radiators. Bad weather also resulted in children arriving at school cold and wet. In February 1912, for example, due to the 'severest snowstorm for some years', just fifty-three children made it into Western, 'the majority of them soaked to the skin', only to be sent home when the school was closed. Many children simply did not have adequate clothing, as was recorded for example in the Bilton Infants School logbook in November 1904, 'Many children are away today because their boots are so worn they cannot come.'

Western was one of several schools which did make efforts to deal with the root causes of ill health. In so doing they were reliant on voluntary effort. In December 1904, during a period of some distress in the town as a result of an economic downturn, Hammond wrote to the

Advertiser describing how the richer parents provided warm clothing for the children of the poorer and that children in actual want of food were fed 'as quietly and privately as possible'. Twenty-five had also been provided with new boots and others with second-hand. He noted that the greatest distress in the district was at Harlow Hill, where 'A relief kitchen seems badly needed ...' Several other schools provided free breakfasts and some also dinners. St Peter's began giving breakfasts in December 1904 to children whose parents were out of work with donations of food and money from parents who could afford it, 'so that the scheme so far has been worked without any appeal to the outside public'. At Starbeck soup was given out at the head's expense, at others at that of private benefactors, which at Grove Road was the Chairman of the Education Committee, Amos Chippindale, to whom his committee loaned the use of the school's cookery room.[33]

The committee itself was slower to take action to improve the health of the children for whom it was responsible and when it came this was usually as a result of legislation. In December 1904 it issued a circular giving advice on eyesight, hearing, breathing and general health and in January 1906 it was agreed to propose teachers for attendance at courses of lectures offered by the West Riding Education Committee to enable them to detect early indications of epidemic diseases and afflictions such as defective eyesight.[34] Medical inspection came with legislation of 1907 which made it compulsory for local education authorities to carry it out, although other authorities, notably Bradford, had already introduced it some years before. In March of that year the committee resolved to appoint a medical officer at a salary of £100 to carry out inspections four times a year. A school nurse was also appointed in July 1909 to assist him and to treat minor ailments and advise parents. Three years later she was provided with a bicycle, providing it did not cost more than eight guineas. Negotiations were also begun in that year with the town's Infirmary over their terms for treating children with defective teeth, eyes, ears, tonsils and the like.[35]

From this time the logbooks regularly record the visits of those officials to inspect, weigh and measure children. These naturally uncovered problems. In September 1909, for example, the school nurse visited Bilton Infants regarding cases of ringworm, which led to the exclusion of several children from school, and examined those with dirty heads, whose parents she then went to see. The following year four children were sent home on the nurse's advice, 'until such times as their respective mothers found time to wash their bodies and clothing'. Similarly, in February 1914 two girls were excluded from St Peter's school owing to 'the verminous condition of their heads' and the parents threatened with proceedings if they did not clean them up.[36]

Legislation in 1906 had also given local authorities the power to provide free school meals to poor children. In December 1908 the Education Committee sent a report on the number of underfed children to the Medical Officer for his consideration. Again, in February of the following year a deputation from the Citizens Guild of Help, a locally-based organization which sought to coordinate charitable provision as part of a more scientific approach to the problem of poverty, gave evidence that from their enquiries 198 children were unable to take advantage of the education they were offered due to lack of food and urged the committee to make use of its new powers. No action was immediately forthcoming, however, and the committee preferred to continue to rely on voluntary effort. Whilst acknowledging that there was distress amongst some of the children, its chairman, Councillor Raworth, hoped it could be met through 'private agency' and offered to write to the local press asking townspeople for subscriptions. By the end of that year, however, in the absence of sufficient voluntary funding, a Canteen Committee was now established and applied to the Board of Education for sanction to use the power to provide meals out of the rates 'for so long as distress exists'. Meals were now provided for 260 children.[37]

By the close of the period, improvement had taken place. The Education Committee had acted to institute medical inspection and treatment of children and to provide meals to those in need. Problems at the schools with sanitation and heating had been addressed. When the plans were unveiled for a new council school at the junction of Skipton Road and Bilton Lane, the future Bilton Grange, it was stressed that the buildings would get the benefit of sun and good ventilation and incorporate the most modern systems of drainage and heating.[38] Although children remained vulnerable to sickness and disease, things were improving. There were still ill-clad, dirty and verminous children but they were a relatively small number among the total school population and steps were taken to help them. Statistically, Harrogate had always been a healthier place and that position was maintained as the health of the whole country improved. This was particularly significant in the most vulnerable group – the very young. In 1900 the infant mortality rate was 144 per thousand in Harrogate and 154 for the whole of England and Wales. By 1907 it was 70 per thousand in Harrogate, albeit after having risen in 1905 and 1906, compared with a national figure of 118, the then lowest figure ever recorded. By 1913 it was down to 64 per thousand in Harrogate and 95 nationally. At that date the overall death rate was 9.3 per thousand in Harrogate, again lower than the figure for England and Wales as a whole, enabling the characteristic comment that Harrogate was 'one of the most, if not the most, favoured health resort in the country'.[39]

Some of that improvement had been brought about by medical intervention, as with inoculation against smallpox and the inspection and treatment of children. Some was down to better sanitation and improved housing. Some also was brought about by the general rise in working-class living standards, including the consumption of more and better food. But there were also, as Harris maintained, less quantifiable influences on health such as conditions of work, length and flexibility of working hours, high or low alcohol consumption, cigarette smoking, local access to institutional care and the strength or weakness of family and community support.[40] Some of these influences have been commented upon in earlier chapters, others will receive attention below.

Improvement should also be kept in perspective. This was a society with great inequalities in health as in other aspects of life. Although with school children we were able to make some comment on Harrogate's working class, in the statistics generally, as was noted, it is not possible to separate them within the town's total population, which had a high proportion of the well-to-do and an above average number of the elderly. There is no reason to suppose, however, that they did not share the inequalities of health and well-being present in the population at large. Height was one indicator of this. Boys at public, or rather private, schools, for example, were taller on average than their state-school counterparts. They were already as tall in fact as they were to be in modern times.

The height of the average Englishman was around five feet seven inches and it was exceptional to reach six foot.

Nor should we forget some further salient points about our Edwardians. Those death rates, although improving, were still much higher than in modern Britain. Up to the age of forty-five, the death rate for men was six times higher than by 1980, and for women ten times higher, not because women had been more vulnerable but because their pre-existing advantage over men was to open out over the century. For Edwardians old age came some ten to twenty years sooner than for modern Britons. And although from about 1870 each cohort of children grew taller and more quickly, the rate of change only became striking from around 1930. Edwardian young people aged five to thirty-five faced a chance of death which later in the century was only approached well into middle age. Finally, although the life expectancy of infants improved considerably over the Edwardian years, it changed most dramatically thereafter, falling to just 12 per thousand by 1980.[41]

Notes to Chapter 5: Neighbourhood,
Community, Housing and Health

1   Thomson. *Exquisite Burden*, p. 24; Neesam, *Chronicle*, p. 377.

2   R. Williams, *Keywords: A vocabulary of culture and society* (1983), pp. 75–6.

3   M. Savage, and A. Miles, *The Remaking of the British Working Class, 1840–1940* (1994), pp. 62–8.

4   G. Crow, *What Are Community Studies?* (2018), p.1; R. Frankenberg, *Communities in Britain: Social life in town and country* (1965), p. 238.

5   *HA*, 13 October 1900, p. 5.

6   J. Bourke, *Working-class Cultures in Britain, 1890–1960: Gender, class and ethnicity* (1994), pp. 142–3 and 150–1.

7   R. Dennis and S. Daniels, '"Community" and the social geography of Victorian cities' in M. Drake (ed.), *Time, Family and Community: Perspectives on family and community history* (1994), pp. 201–24.

8   Roberts, *Classic Slum*, pp. 17–18.

9   *HA*, 4 February 1893, p. 5 and 30 May 1891, p. 6.

10   Denmark Street, Change of Name to Chatsworth Road 1935, NYCCRO.

11   For the registers see the Bibliography.

12   F. M. L. Thompson, *The Rise of Respectable Society: A social history of Victorian Britain, 1830–1900* (1988), pp. 94–5.

13   A. Miles, *Social Mobility in Nineteenth- and Early Twentieth-Century England* (1999), pp. 28–34.

14   Frankenberg, *Communities*, p. 264.

15   PP 1913 [Cd. 7017], pp. 248-0, Table 11; this was concerned with the relationship between birthplace and residence in counties and urban areas with a population of over 50,000. Since it would include children, it is not strictly comparable with Harrogate but the pattern is clear enough.

16   R. Dennis, *English Industrial Cities of the Nineteenth Century: A social geography* (1984), pp. 250–69.

17   Dennis, *Industrial Cities*, p. 262.

18   Neesam, *Music*, p. 135.

19   Report of Dr J. Spencer Lowe to the Local Government Board on the Sanitary Circumstances and Administration of the Three Sanitary Districts within the Knaresborough Registration District (1908); also detailed in *HA*, 13 February 1909, p. 5.

20   Letter from J. Turner Taylor, Town Clerk, to the Local Government Board, 10 April 1907, NYCCRO.

21   Tower Street and Belford Square Clearance Area and Skipton Road Individual Property Reports 1949, NYCCRO.

22   *HA*, 25 March 1905, p. 7.

23   Jennings, *Harrogate*, p. 426.

24 B. S. Rowntree, *Poverty: A study of town life* (2000), pp. 147–58.

25 PP 1908 [Cd. 3864], p. xiv.

26 A. L. Bowley and A. R. Burnett-Hurst, *Livelihood and Poverty: a study of the economic conditions of working-class households in Northampton, Warrington, Stanley and Reading* (1915), p. 18.

27 Census of England and Wales 1901, County of York, Area, houses and population etc.; PP 1902 [Cd. 1107] CXXI.639, pp. viii and 164; Census of England and Wales 1911, Vol. VIII, Tenements in administrative counties and urban and rural districts; PP 1913 [Cd. 6910] LXXVII.1, p. 408.

28 P. Barnes ed., *Bilton with Harrogate – Forest, Farms and Families: Report of a community archaeological project* (2008), pp. 38–9; *HA*, 8 August 1891, p. 2.

29 Borough of Harrogate, Sanitary Committee, 27 April 1908, 22 February 1909, 30 June 1913, 28 November 1910, 31 March 1913, 29 May and 25 September 1911 and 31 July 1911.

30 For the logbooks see the Bibliography.

31 D. Dwork, *War is Good for Babies and Other Young Children: A history of the infant and child welfare movement in England, 1898–1918* (1987), p. 167.

32 Harris, *Private Lives,* p. 52.

33 Harrogate Education Committee Minute Book, 1904–1921, 29 November 1904, NYCCRO.

34 Minute Book, 20 December 1904 and 30 January 1906.

35 Minute Book, 22 March 1907, 1 March and July 1909 and 1 May 1912.

36 Minute Book, 25 February 1914.

37 Minute Book, 31 December 1908, 24 February 1909 and 22 December 1909; *HA*, 3 April 1909, p. 6 and 25 December 1909, p. 5; K. Laybourn, 'The New Philanthropy of the Edwardian Age: The Guild of Help and the Halifax Citizen's Guild, 195–1918', *Transactions of the Halifax Antiquarian Society*, 23 (2015), pp. 73–94.

38 *HA*, 17 May 1913, p. 7.

39 Lowe Report and Medical Officer of Health Report in *HA*, 19 July 1913, p.2.

40 Harris, *Private Lives*, pp. 52–3.

41 P. Clarke, *Hope and Glory: Britain, 1900–2000* (1997), pp. 40–1.

CHAPTER SIX

Family, Household and Making a Living

T HE FOCUS of this chapter is the working-class household. Most families consisted of husband, wife and children so we begin with marriage and go on to look at the numbers of children couples had and how this was changing. Some marriages failed and there were children who were alone or vulnerable, to use the modern term, for a variety of reasons. What was the response of the state and voluntary bodies to their situations? There were also many households which did not fit the familiar picture. Widowed parents brought up children alone. Some contained other relatives and many also provided accommodation for lodgers. Lodgers contributed to the household income and the chapter goes on to look at how working-class families made a living. For some this might be a precarious one. There was certainly poverty in this genteel resort but what was its extent and how did the town and society seek to alleviate it?

Family and household

To begin with I analysed the composition of working-class households at each of the censuses of 1901 and 1911, using the following suggested guidelines. These classed them as: households consisting of a single individual, either unmarried or widowed; households with co-resident siblings or other relatives; conjugal family units, that is married couples with and without children and the widowed with children; extended families with other kin living with them; and multiple family households, those with two or more kin-linked conjugal family units.[1] There were a total of 2,669 households in 1901 and 3,426 ten years later.

In both years around 80 per cent of all households were conjugal family units. Around 90 per cent of them in turn were married couples with and without children. The next highest group were extended families, around 13 per cent of the total. They were extended in a variety of ways: upwards to include mothers, fathers, aunts and uncles; downwards with grandchildren or nieces and nephews; sideways with brothers, sisters or cousins; or a combination of these. Downwards extension was the most common in each year but by 1911 the presence of older kin like parents was more common than that of siblings. Finally, there were multiple family households, sixty-seven in 1911, 2 per cent of the total, and a smaller number of households where siblings or other relatives lived together.

Although there were at this time more men and women who never married than was later the case, most did, so it is with marriage that we begin.[2] To determine their choice of partner, I looked at the details of some 300 marriages.[3] Most chose from within the working class, as we saw in the previous chapter. The entries give the address of the parties, which may not of course be where the couple met, but which show, perhaps unsurprisingly, that partners were mostly found locally.[4] Nearly three-quarters were from Harrogate itself, with over a third from the same neighbourhood. A typical couple then were Albert Scott and Rose Wheatley, married at Christ Church on New Year's Day 1900, of neighbouring Avenue Place and Grove Street, Starbeck. The groom was a fireman and both their fathers also worked on the railway. As we saw, some brides had originally travelled to Harrogate for places in service. One such was Mary Scrivener from Essex, a cook in an Otley Road household, who in April 1902 married plumber Frank Chipchase, who lived in nearby West End Avenue, at St Mark's on Leeds Road. Fewer than one in five married a partner whose address on marriage was further than ten miles away.

Grooms were aged on average twenty-seven years and their brides twenty-five. There were just nine teenage brides, either eighteen or nineteen, but no grooms. Those ages are in line with national figures, as is the fact that in Harrogate working-class men married at a younger age than did middle-class professionals. Grooms who were architects, school masters or solicitors for example married on average at thirty, an age when their incomes would support a family in the required comfort. Their brides were also slightly older at twenty-six on average than working-class young women. Those ages at first marriage were higher than they had been earlier in the nineteenth century but they were to fall again to historic lows in the 1950s and 1960s.[5]

The families which these couples went on to have were large by modern standards. To measure fertility, the 1911 census asked how many children had been born to the present marriage, how many had died and how many therefore survived. This shows first that the death of a child before its parents was a common experience. Over half of the those who married in the 1870s and 1880s and just under half of those marrying in the 1890s had experienced the loss of at least one child. In some cases the losses were severe: James and Martha Richardson of Cecil Street had lost nine of their fourteen children in the twenty-four years of their marriage. Such very large families, however, were not the norm. In the decade 1880 to 1889, when they were married, only two other couples had had fourteen children. It was most common to have four or five, with just under a quarter of all couples having this many. This represented a decline in the number of children born to a marriage: average numbers fell from seven to those marrying in the 1860s (although this is based upon the relatively small number who had survived until 1911) to six in the 1870s and five in the 1880s. This was in line with the national trend, which then continued downwards into the inter-war years.[6]

Edwardian marriages were now for longer as mortality rates fell: 91 per cent lasted at least ten years, with three quarters for twenty-five years and 44 per cent for forty or more.[7] It was still death which parted couples at this time and the widowed spouse was common. In 1911 twenty-three widowers lived alone and thirty-six widows, whilst a further seventy-six and 178 respectively were living with their children. Together they accounted for 9 per cent of working-class households.

Divorce was almost unknown. There were on average nationally fewer than 600 annually at the beginning of the period, although this did represent a rising trend. The process was difficult and expensive and eligibility was hedged around with limitations. Not until 1923 could wives divorce on the grounds of adultery alone and not until 1937 were the insanity of the spouse, cruelty, or desertion for three years allowed as causes.[8] Adultery by the wife was another matter. This was the cause in the only Harrogate case involving a working-class couple I came across. This was of a joiner of Oatlands who had married in June of 1899. By the following year he was complaining to his wife about her and another young woman going about with soldiers, after which she had promised not to do so again but failed to keep it. Prompted by an anonymous letter he kept a watch and confronted her with another man, for whom she then left him the following day. Their divorce was granted in 1902.[9] Both partners remarried, she to her new lover, and were still in the area in 1911, the former husband living with his second wife and their twins at his father-in-law's in Knaresborough and the former wife now keeping house for her uncle in Station Parade, although her husband is not recorded there in the census and their two children had both died.

Although divorce was rare, separation was becoming more common. Earlier reforms had been consolidated in legislation of 1895, which provided for separation in cases of aggravated assault, desertion, persistent cruelty or neglecting to maintain her and her children so as to cause her to leave. Adultery by the wife was not a valid reason, unless the husband had condoned it or connived at it by his wilful neglect or misconduct. The act also provided for the wife's legal custody of the children and financial maintenance.[10] Around ten thousand orders for maintenance were granted annually by the Edwardian period, chiefly to working-class women.[11] Cases were reported with some regularity in the local newspapers and convey not only the difficulties which some women faced in their marriages but also those involved in seeking redress. In January 1900 Walter Edmondson, a mason, was charged by his wife Eleanor with neglecting to maintain her and a separation order requested. The couple had married in 1895 and had lived apart on three occasions since. He claimed that there was no cause of difference between them, except her mother, that he gave her nearly all his earnings, but that in bad weather these might be only half of the usual 25s., that he was sober and had never struck her. In addition, 'He had his own socks to mend, ties to wash, and had to make his own bed.' For her part she denied that regular payments were made and had been forced to apply for poor relief and go live with her mother. The bench made an order of 18s. a week and gave her custody of the children. Three months later he had paid nothing and was now bound over to give a reasonable instalment or go to prison. The next month he paid £2, which was all he could get, and arrears at £1 a week, or again face prison.[12]

Other cases documented adultery, drinking and violence. John Birkinshaw had ill-treated his wife of twenty-four years, Elizabeth, introduced into their home 'a lady who should have been foreign to the house' and kept her without money, forcing her and their five children to go to the workhouse at Knaresborough. She did go back to him but his 'intemperate habits and conduct' persisted: he had threatened to push her down the steps having again taken home another woman. He admitted taking beer and that he 'was not one of the best' but denied anything beyond threats. A separation order was granted with custody of the children and 10s. a week maintenance.[13] There were some men who evidently preferred prison to maintaining their families. Fish hawker John Acomb was charged by the Poor Law authorities with deserting his wife and four children, leaving them to their support when they had no money and nothing to eat. Rather than pay the fine he told the bench he would 'do the month' instead.[14]

The children of course suffered in these situations and their general welfare was increasingly becoming the concern of the state and charitable bodies. The Poor Law authorities were the support of last resort for families in difficulty and they were now given the power to assume all the rights and responsibilities of a parent over a child in their care till the age of eighteen.[15] The laws protecting children were tightened up in a series of measures, which were consolidated and extended in the important Children Act of 1908. But the key body involved in child protection was the National Society for the Prevention of Cruelty to Children, established in 1889, following local initiatives. Through local committees it investigated cases of suspected cruelty and by the late nineteenth century its inspectors 'had become neighbourhood institutions in many English towns', the 'cruelty man' as he was known.[16]. From about 1904, it shifted its strategy from punishment of the parents to the reformation of parent-child relations in their own homes, with permanent removal of children very much a last resort.[17]

There was an inspector covering Harrogate and district, whose work illustrates the society's approach and the sad lives some families led. In June of 1905 Eliza Bailey of Tower Street pleaded guilty to neglecting her three children causing them unnecessary suffering. The family had been under observation for more than a year, warned and then cautioned. Her husband had been written to, which led to some improvement, but then 'things got worse than ever' and on the last inspector's visit Eliza was drunk and the almost naked children running about 'in a miserable condition'. She was fined on promising to do her 'duty' to the children.[18] This was the pattern in other cases reported in the local paper: families under observation, with prosecution as a final step leading usually to a fine and a promise to do better by the children. Only aggravated cases led to more severe punishment. In March 1912 coal porter Herbert Smith was charged with the neglect of his two children, spending his wages on drink and 'in other ways'. His wife had done her best but on one occasion when Inspector Offord visited there was only a crust of bread and some margarine in the house. With seventeen previous court appearances, Smith was now given three months in prison.[19]

These were extreme cases, but as we saw in the previous chapter, sick, hungry and unwashed children were by no means unusual in the town. Yet, as even those extreme cases sometimes showed, parents did try to do their best for their children. Historians of the working class have seen by this time the emergence of a more 'humane' family life, with husbands and wives spending more time together on a day-to-day basis and their relationship, and that with their children, becoming more 'companionable'.[20] The caring aspect of family life is captured for us when tragedy overtook one family in March 1912. This was that of Charles and Hannah Vast of Oatlands. At the time, two of their children were suffering from whooping cough and it was whilst Hannah went upstairs to attend to one who was coughing that the cradle of the youngest, Marjory, which was in front of the fire in the parlour, set alight. To keep draughts from the child, paper had been packed around the cradle but this had ignited when a newspaper put in front of the dead fire to draw it had fallen. Charles, who was having his breakfast in the kitchen, realized what was happening, called out and attempted to put out the fire. Hannah rushed downstairs, picked up the child and with the help of a neighbour attended to its burns but she died a few days later, having been sent home from hospital as she also was found to be suffering from whooping cough. She was also said to be a delicate child, suffering from the bronchial pneumonia which hastened her death from the shock brought on from burns.[21]

At the 1911 census the family had been recorded as living in a four-room house on Cromwell Road. They are an example of a multiple family household comprising no fewer than thirteen individuals: Charles and Hannah and their four children, including then five-month-old Marjory, his widowed mother, a brother and sister and another married sister, who, however, is recorded under her maiden name, plus two young nieces and a nephew. Other than the conjugal family norm, families displayed considerable variety and the experience of children was therefore similarly diverse. Although three quarters were with their mother and father and at least one other sibling, 3 per cent lived with a widowed parent and more than one in ten in a household with other relatives. Since remarriage was common at this time, with nationally 9 per cent of widowed men and 7 per cent of women doing so, many children now lived with a new mother or father.[22] The census returns do not always make this clear, as some householders seem to have found difficulty with the fertility question. One couple, for example, recorded six children born to their marriage but then went on to list four of them as the husband's stepchildren. There were also some cases where the housekeeper's children were with her but, as we saw, these were cases where she was likely to be in a relationship with her nominal employer. The census also records a small number of adopted children and those described as 'nurse' children, usually taken to mean that they were fostered.

There were also large numbers of children at this time living in an institution, although this was not the situation solely of those of the working-class, as those hundreds of boys and girls boarding at private schools showed. In 1911 seventy-five boys and girls lived at the Northern Police Orphanage off Otley Road. They mostly attended school locally

55. Northern Police Orphanage at Otley- and Harlow Moor Roads. Opened in 1898 in a former private school it was later closed, finally demolished in 1976 and housing built on the site. Note the uniforms. (Author's postcard)

but a few older girls were 'training in housework' and Joseph Lowe, aged sixteen, was recorded as having tuberculosis. (55) The Primitive Methodist Orphan Homes off Pannal Ash Road accommodated forty-two boys and girls between the ages of five and thirteen. There were also thirty children at Dr Barnardo's Home for Crippled Children on Tewit Well Road, who came from all over the country to be treated for hip disease, spinal problems, rickets and paralysis. The workhouse now accommodated only a small number, just ten in 1901, as where possible they were now boarded out with families or lived in 'cottage' homes and from 1913 could no longer be maintained in a general workhouse.[23] We get a glimpse of their lives from the 1914 case of Ethel and Wilfrid Williamson, aged thirteen and twelve, who had run away to sleep rough at Starbeck, where the NSPCC's inspector had found them 'amid surroundings that were absolutely vile'. Their father was admitted to the workhouse infirmary but the mother would not go. Ethel was placed in a foster home and Wilfrid in one of the cottage homes but after a week they ran away. Although they had no complaint about their treatment, in clean surroundings, with warm clothing and good food, they just 'wanted their mother' and averred that they would rather go to prison. To this the chairman of the bench responded that 'they would have to go back whether they wanted to or not'.[24]

One final member of many working-class households was the boarder or lodger. The census authorities did seek to distinguish them, based on their degree of independence, but in practice the distinction is unclear and I counted both together. In 1901, one in five households in Harrogate took in at least one lodger, a proportion comparable to that found in studies of other towns.[25] This is, however, an underestimate. Those described as visitors probably included people who were in fact lodging with the family, but I excluded them from my count. In total in Harrogate that year over a thousand persons were in lodgings, 85 per cent of them men, most in private households but including others in lodging houses. Both the men and the women were predominantly single and young. Looking at the men, 84 per cent were single, although just over one in ten were married and 6 per cent widowed. Three quarters of them were aged under thirty-five and most of them in turn were under twenty-five. This profile was true also of the women. Many lodgers had also come some distance: a third of men and 43 per cent of women had been born outside Yorkshire. The men were divided evenly between the skilled on the one hand and the semi- and unskilled on the other. This was something of a contrast with women, over 70 per cent of whom were in occupations such as shop assistant or dressmaker. Of the latter, for example, two young women aged nineteen and eighteen, born in Sussex and Catterick respectively, boarded with a shoemaker, his wife and their young daughter in a four-roomed house in Regent Terrace.

The census of course provides us with only basic details from which we might infer more of the reality of lodging. It is misfortune again which affords us a more detailed glimpse. John Scales was a stonemason from Kiltimagh in County Mayo who arrived in Harrogate in March 1900. Ireland was the birthplace of twenty-seven lodgers in the town at the census the following year. We do not know exactly how he came to Valley Mount, but this was a street where several households took in lodgers. He explained to Mary Jane Chapman of number 8, the wife of John, a

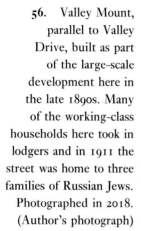

56. Valley Mount, parallel to Valley Drive, built as part of the large-scale development here in the late 1890s. Many of the working-class households here took in lodgers and in 1911 the street was home to three families of Russian Jews. Photographed in 2018. (Author's photograph)

groom, that he had been travelling all night and that although he did not suffer from bronchitis, Ireland did not agree with him. She took him his tea up to his room in the morning but he dined with the family in the evening. Three weeks later, however, he failed to come down for dinner and she found him dead in bed. A local woman who laid the body out explained to the inquest, from which we know these details, that his body was 'wasted, but clean', with a plaster on his left side, and a verdict of death from natural causes was returned.[26] (56)

Whilst most lodgers were with working-class households, there were some with a lower middle-class family and others in lodging houses, that is where the householder is specifically described as a lodging-house keeper. In 1901, 15 per cent of male lodgers were with the former and slightly more in the latter, whilst for women one in five and almost

175

a quarter were with a lower middle-class household or in lodgings. Typically, they were run by a widow or single woman but the wives of working men also sometimes catered for them.

With its central location and working-class character, Tower Street accommodated a particularly large number of lodgers. In 1901, Simeon Bolton, for example, was in business as a draper but he and his wife also provided accommodation for fourteen lodgers, of whom eleven were working men, plus one woman with her husband and two other elderly women. Next door, a sixty-four-year-old woman had three male boarders on census night. The street's public houses also offered lodgings to working men. Six were accommodated at the Belford Hotel whilst on the opposite side of the street the Coachmakers' Arms had taken in thirteen single men, all described, however, as visitors, probably indicating their transience. That they were unlikely to have been in Harrogate to take the waters is clear from the pub's subsequent history. It was deprived of its licence in 1906 but continued to be run as a common lodging house. As such, it should have been registered with the local authority. Failure to do so led to the prosecution of its proprietor George Parker. The police report of their visit on the 18 April 1910 shows that the lodging house had been created from the former pub and adjoining properties. In one were two downstairs rooms, one of which was the common room, in which on their visit were seated seven men 'of the tramp class', some eating and others cooking. Upstairs, four bedrooms contained twenty-one beds, with sixteen occupied at the time. In another house were two kitchens and a common room, wherein were twelve men mostly of 'the vagrant class' and upstairs another four bedrooms for sixteen men. According to Parker men were admitted for the one night if they looked respectable but the police evidenced that they were asked when on duty where Parker's lodging house was located and that the place was undoubtedly one of the '"padding kens" of the lowest type' in which drunken disorder was a frequent occurrence and to which they had been often called to quell disputes.

The case was dismissed on payment of costs and Parker then applied for registration, supported by character references, which was granted for a first-floor front room for single adults, married couples or children. At the census the following year, George and his wife Mary, with the help of his sister-in-law, were providing beds for twenty-three, mostly older, working men from around the country and in one case Ceylon, including labourers, men in the building trades, a rag and bone dealer and a pedlar. Two years later, Mary, now widowed, was again charged with keeping an unlicensed lodging house. Two men had approached police officers, having walked from Thirsk on their way to Bradford, and paid 6d. for a bed for the night. No women were taken in and the place was 'the abode of thieves, beggars and hawkers'. She pleaded guilty and the case was dismissed on payment of costs. Before it came to court, Mary wrote to the town's Medical Officer of Health, pleading straitened circumstances and promising faithfully that it would never happen again, adding that she did not want the contents of the letter to be known 'as people would know she was hard up'. Another lodging house of this type was registered by Francis Crolla in 1910 in Grove Place off Denmark Street. At the 1911 census it accommodated twelve men and women, six of whom were pedlars or hawkers, plus two infants.[27]

Men and women using common lodging houses were on the margins of society in Edwardian Harrogate. They were joined there by those sleeping rough and begging. They received short shrift in the town. In January 1890 Richard Donston had been found by the police asleep in a kiln at Oatlands brickworks. He explained that he was a miner who had last worked in Wales. Sentencing him to seven days with hard labour as a vagrant, magistrate Richard Ellis told him he had no business to be seeking work in this part of the country as there were no mines in Harrogate.[28] The brickyard was a favourite with rough sleepers throughout this period. In July 1908 nine men 'of the labouring class' were let off with a caution for sleeping there, as the bench was 'in a lenient mood', but another thirteen in August were sent to prison. The following year three more men were discharged on promising to leave town, as they 'were not tramps in the usual sense' but seemed to be respectable men out of employment.[29] Others coming to the attention of the police included a labourer sleeping on a seat in Prospect Place, another in an outhouse in John Street, a widow also in an outhouse at Forest Moor and Arthur Burrows, 'a coloured man' sleeping out in West Park, described by the inspector as 'a nuisance to the town' and given seven days.[30]

Like tramps, those begging might receive more lenient treatment if they could give some account of themselves. Arthur Wilson, a youth from Newcastle, had his charge of begging in West Park dismissed and was even provided with some assistance when he explained that his mother was dead, that he had been abandoned by his father and now made his living moving about the country, with a promise then of some work in Knaresborough.[31] Any suggestion of professional begging, the 'begging nuisance' as it was referred to in the local newspapers, received no sympathy. The eighteen-month career of a man, woman and two children, the latter begging from house to house while he kept watch, was brought to a close in January 1910 when the adults got three months each and the children were sent to an industrial school.[32] Children begging seems to have been a common sight, one form encouraged, it was said, by visitors who threw pennies to them from their charabancs and coaches.[33]

The domestic economy

The provision of lodgings was clearly an important source of income for many householders. It is one of many things we need to bear in mind when assessing how our working-class households made ends meet. In families generally the husband was the chief breadwinner. Few wives went out to work, although it has been argued that the census did not always record their employment, particularly part-time or casual work. Of relevance to Harrogate, it seems markedly to have under-recorded those running lodging houses or letting apartments. There were only twenty-two so described in 1901 and fifteen in 1911, figures which were dwarfed by the numbers of such establishments in directories, something found in similar research in the Lakeland resort town of Keswick.[34] With this caveat in mind, in 1901 just ninety-eight wives, or 4 per cent of the total and in 1911 ninety-four, or 3 per cent, were in paid employment. Apart from catering to lodgers or those taking apartments, the only occupations of any significance were laundry work, dressmaking or charing, plus caretaking in 1911. That wives should be at home was the contemporary ideal, one expressed by the authors of the census report itself, noting that married women were 'fortunately in this country free at all ages to devote their attention to the care of their households'. Or, as a well-known study of the family expressed it, 'a well-ordered household ...

is a woman's first duty towards the predominant partner, her husband'.[35] It was shared, it has been argued, by the women themselves. Most did not want paid employment, which would increase their workload, since they would still need to take care of their home and families, and possibly incur extra expenditure on clothing and childcare. Managing the household was the better option for them to improve their and their families' living standards through effective management of their resources, for example taking time to seek out better value shops.[36]

Since the husband was the main source of the family's income, that it should be enough to meet their needs was of paramount importance. Conversely, should it be too low or interrupted in any way, this could reduce a family to poverty. The late Victorian and Edwardian period saw great attention paid to the problem of poverty, most famously by Booth in London and Rowntree in York.[37] Rowntree provided figures for income levels below which families would be in poverty, which he divided into primary and secondary poverty. The first was where a family's total earnings were 'insufficient to obtain the minimum necessaries for the maintenance of mere physical efficiency'; the second was where that minimum would be met but for other spending, some useful but some not, by which he meant drink above all. An income of 21s. or under would place a family in poverty. Whether one between that and 30s. a week did so would depend upon individual family circumstances. We should also note a modern estimate of the minimum income necessary for a family of four or five to enjoy a diet of adequate calorific value, proteins, carbohydrates and fats was also 30s.[38] If we think back to the chapter on men at work, few fell into that lowest group, but many more were in the second, whilst comparatively few in turn earned more than 30s. a week. Among railway workers, for example, only drivers, firemen and guards did so. Railwaymen were in comparatively secure employment; in many other trades in contrast workers were subject to unemployment and underemployment. Trades unions provided some help to unemployed members and state insurance was introduced in legislation of 1911 for those in trades like building which were particularly affected. At 7s. a week for a worker's contribution of 2½d. a week, with one week's benefit payable for every five weeks' contributions up to a maximum of fifteen weeks, it was, however, limited.

179

Incomes also fell short due to the impact of old age, sickness or disability. That of old age was mitigated by the introduction of a non-contributory old age pension in 1909 but this was just 5s. a week, payable at age seventy to anyone with an income of less than 8s. a week from other sources. That amount was reduced on a sliding scale up to 12s. a week, above which nothing was payable. Those not deserving, to use the contemporary phrase, or who had been in prison, or received assistance from the Poor Law within the previous two years, or who drank or were workshy got nothing. The effect of sickness might also be mitigated by payments through commercial insurance companies, friendly societies or trades unions until the introduction of the state insurance scheme, administered through those bodies, which required contributions from both employers and workers. Whilst unemployment insurance was confined to certain trades, sickness insurance covered all manual workers. The insured worker would receive medical treatment, which however did not extend to other members of the family, and sick pay of 10s. a week for men and 7s. 6d. for women for the first twenty-six weeks, backed by medical, maternity and sanatorium care. Although the non-contributory pensions were welcomed, national insurance was not popular. It was compulsory for all workers earning less than £160 a year and cost men 4d. a week and women 3d. Although Lloyd George, the scheme's architect, characterized it as 'ninepence for fourpence', since employers paid 3d and the state not quite 2d, the low paid found that in effect their wages had been cut and the fact that all paid the same contributions regardless of income meant that the poorest workers lost the highest proportion of their earnings.[39]

Whilst recognizing the crucial importance of the main wage, Rowntree also took account of the total family income, including that of the wife if she worked, of working children and of payments by lodgers. Infants or children at school conversely were dependents, as were elderly or infirm relatives living with the family. Those influences make it extremely difficult to make overall estimates of living standards and illustrate the very varied circumstances of individual families and of families at different points in their life cycle, a point emphasized by, for example, Roberts in her study of working-class living standards in Barrow and Lancaster.[40] Some examples from Starbeck in 1911, which were replicated throughout the town's working-class districts, illustrate this. On Victoria Terrace, Arthur Castle, aged thirty-five, was a railway porter, which depending upon whether he was a platform or goods porter would pay him a little over 23s. on average weekly. This was to support him, his wife Mary and their six-year-old daughter, which he would have been able to do, providing illness, for example, did not keep him off work. James Lumley was a stone breaker for the Corporation, for which he could earn 23 to 24s. a week. His two eldest sons were errand boys, which would add another 10s. at the most to the family's income, but that consisted of James, Sarah and seven children, three of whom were at school and two aged just three and five months. Although having a total income of over 30s., this family of nine would just be making ends meet. John Eshelby was a sewer labourer but out of work. The reason is not noted but at aged sixty-seven it may have been due to illness or infirmity of some kind. The only support for him and his wife and a fifteen-year-old still at school was the bricklayer's labourer's wage of another older son. As this would have been about 25s. a week if he was fully employed, this family would clearly have been struggling financially. Similarly placed was the family of Robert Lancaster, a signalman, whom we met in Chapter 4. He would earn just under 30s. a week but of he and his wife's four children, the eldest son was disabled, the second son a hotel worker not then in work and the two youngest still at school. He might have turned for help at times to his brother who lived next door, who as an engine driver would earn over 47s. a week, which was supplemented by payments from a boarder, who was a fireman, to support himself, his wife and their mentally handicapped daughter. Help from friends and neighbours might also be forthcoming, although like that from family, it is impossible to know how common this was. In 1911, Mary Handcock, a sixty-seven-year-old widow with both children dead living alone in Devonshire Place, was an invalid confined to bed and 'kept by friends' according to her census return.

Family circumstances were clearly varied but before we assess living standards, we need to look at expenditure. Rent was an important weekly outgoing. It was the norm for working-class families and as we saw was mostly between 4 and 6s. a week, representing therefore a significant proportion of a family's income.[41] Food took an even greater share. On an income below 30s. a week, two-thirds was spent on food, according to the Board of Trade's 1908 survey.[42] As with rent, the lower the income the greater the proportion that was spent on it. There were other necessities. Homes had to be heated, with coal costing from 9½d. to 1s. a hundredweight, lighted and cleaned. Clothing might be home-made or second hand, like the dress for which a Starbeck woman paid 4s. from a shop in Bower Road in 1904.[43] Local shops like this also offered credit to their customers. Resort to the pawnbroker was also common in some towns and cities but Harrogate lacked them, with just the two branches of one firm in Commercial and Oxford Streets listed in a directory for 1912. We should note again finally that this was a period of rising prices, with one estimate putting the increase in the cost of living at 17.6 per cent over the period 1896 to 1913.[44]

Other expenditure also went, as we saw, to offset the financial consequences of illness and unemployment but another significant cost for families was that of a funeral, not uncommonly for a child. Enormous importance was attached to the provision of a respectable funeral, to which the horror attached to the idea of a pauper's burial attests. In addition to all those expenses, there was some saving. The Post Office Savings Bank had been established in 1861 expressly to promote working-class thrift. The total number of savers did increase enormously from two-and-a-half million in 1870 to eleven in 1914 and did include the working class. Most accounts, however, were of low value, with a small number of transactions on average and with the high annual rate of account closure suggesting that accounts were used rather for short-term accumulation to spend rather than long-term saving.[45]

The historian of working-class saving and spending from whom those details were taken could conclude that 'many, perhaps most, manual workers could expect at some time in their lives to face acute financial crisis'.[46] Those contemporary surveys of Booth and Rowntree had both found high levels of poverty: nearly a third of all Londoners and over 40 per cent of the wage-earning population of York lived in primary and secondary poverty. Another survey at the end of the period, which took account of inflation and looked at four different locations, found that the proportion of working-class families living in primary poverty varied between different localities but was highest in Reading at just over one in five.[47] The main cause was low wages but also important were family size and the death, sickness or infirmity of the chief earner.

Many of Harrogate's families clearly shared those difficulties, although I was not able to compile information systematically in the manner of surveys such as those. This conclusion is supported by the number of children we saw who were ill-fed and poorly clad. Another piece of evidence which supports it is the rise in the number of those opting to try for a better life overseas. Emigration picked up dramatically in the Edwardian period. Well over a million people left the United Kingdom in the seven years 1903 to 1909 plus another million in the next four. There were now two key changes from the previous period of high emigration in the 1880s. The first was the decline in the proportion leaving Ireland: in the 1880s half of emigrants had come from there, whereas in 1910 nearly 90 per cent came from Great Britain. The other was the draw for the British of Australia, New Zealand and Canada rather than the United States. Over a million left for Canada in these years, including families from Harrogate. In 1911 the Revd Guy wrote to the *Advertiser* noting the many locally who were leaving for Canada and other places and the commendatory letters he had written to the chaplain of their ship and clergy in their destinations. Three generations of the Hargreaves family were bound for Canada. Two years later, the paper was again reporting on local emigrants, including a carpenter, wheelwright and gardener and their wives. They had been met by the British Welcome League in Hamilton, 'drenched to the skin' but being unable to find anywhere to live had returned to Toronto.[48] School logbooks record the departure of children for overseas, six for example from Bilton over the period: three to Canada, two to Australia and one to California.[49]

Finally, poverty in the town is revealed in the efforts made for its relief. In addition to the day-to-day aid provided by the Poor Law authorities, there was an annual treat for the outdoor (not in the workhouse) poor. In January 1900 this was organized by the mayoress, Mrs James Myrtle for around 300 at the People's Hotel and afterwards at the Albert Hall, where children received sweets and a toy from the Christmas tree, the women got some tea and sugar and the men pipes and tobacco, whilst those unable to come were sent 2s. Leftover fruit was sent to the Home for Incurables. The concert which followed in the Saloon was preceded with all standing to sing 'God Save the Queen'. The aged poor were then taken home in carriages supplied by Mrs Myrtle.[50] At the same time, the Christmas Poor Fund was distributing oranges, apples, tea, cakes and confectionery, clothing, blankets and toys to 122 families and tea and sweets to the Police Orphanage and other institutions. As T. Graham Tarn of Lyndhurst, Park Drive, expressed it to the *Advertiser*, extolling 'the privilege of ministering to the poor', in which 'we have the joy of knowing that many hearts and homes were brightened by suitable and seasonable gifts'. Such treats continued throughout the period. That of 1914 was held at the Spa Concert Rooms for 600 men, women and children, who enjoyed a meal, concert and presents paid for from a public subscription.[51]

During two periods of economic difficulty, in 1904 to 1906 and 1908 to 1909, 'distress', as contemporaries termed it, became acute. In the first period, the building trades were, according to the *Advertiser*, 'practically at a standstill' and in one district alone over a hundred families were 'acutely suffering from the lamentable lack of employment'.[52] The first response, as it had been at a previous time of distress when in January 1891 severe weather had left six hundred men, women and children for five weeks with little or any income, was to set up a town fund. This was done after a public meeting in December 1904 at the Spa Concert Rooms, chaired by the mayor, which included the unemployed themselves. A committee of council members, Poor Law guardians, clergy and the heads of elementary schools was established and a public subscription opened. The mayor, James Chippindale, declared that it was not a meeting for finding work but that some employment had been made available on sewerage, including for masons, plasterers and other skilled artisans 'not in the habit of using a spade or shovel'. Whilst not a living wage, it was keeping them from starving. To the point made by a delegate from the Trades Council that it was the council's job to find work, for example on the miles of unpaved streets, the mayor cited necessary legal formalities and the fact that people suffering quite as much as working men would have to pay for it.[53]

The council did in 1905 apply for powers under the Unemployed Workmen Act of that year to levy a rate to fund job creation but this was turned down by the Local Government Board on the grounds that the town's circumstances did not warrant such an extreme measure. Work on the sewers continued to be offered, amid accusations from working men of inadequacy and favouritism. At the same time, families were helped from the distress fund both financially and with food and clothing.[54] In February of 1906, a Labour Bureau was opened and local businesses and residents invited to offer work to the unemployed. This was closed after just three months, as the situation had improved on the previous year, with 628 men, 73 women and 28 boys on its register. The Unemployed Relief Fund was also now wound up. Local businesses and residents found work for a little over a hundred but the sewerage remained the principal means of job creation, with 600 to 700 men working for periods of from one to eight weeks. This effort, however, continued to be dogged by accusations of favouritism, including from the Fund's secretary, and of a lack of support from council officials.[55]

Whist the unemployed themselves kept asking for work not charity, the council and other local worthies worried that help would go to the undeserving. The Labour Bureau was open to Harrogate residents only, whilst the vicar of Christ Church opined to the readers of the *Advertiser* that the Relief Fund had attracted 'the usual worthless applicants for charity'.[56] Related calls for a more scientific approach to the problem than 'hurriedly formed relief committees, and doles distributed after hastily made enquiries' and the encouragement of self help among the poor led to the formation of a local Citizens Guild of Help, whose work with regard to school meals we met in the previous chapter. During the next period of distress in 1908 to 1909 it coordinated a variety of services to the town's poor, based upon case work, and set up a register of those seeking work, applicants to which it vetted.[57] Charity continued to be given to the deserving, however, and in January 1909 Councillor and Mrs Marshall increased the number of children treated to a tea and entertainment at the Kursaal from 200 to 450 owing to the 'prevailing distress in the town'.[58]

Harrogate's working people were for the most part better housed than their counterparts in Leeds or Knaresborough and those where the household head was in reasonably well-paid and secure employment were comfortably off by the standards of the time, although that comfort was being eroded by the rise in the cost of living. But also, as for working-class people everywhere, that relative comfort might be undermined by under- and unemployment, the needs of young children, the death of the breadwinner and by sickness and old age. As one modern survey put it, 'For most people in Britain life was hard in 1914.'[59]

Notes to Chapter 6:
Family, Household and Making a Living

1   J. Knodel, 'An exercise on household composition for use in courses on historical demography', *Local Population Studies*, 23 (1979), pp. 10–23.

2   Anderson, 'Social implications', p. 28.

3   For the registers see the Bibliography.

4   Dennis, *Industrial Cities*, pp. 272–3.

5   Anderson, Social implications', pp. 32–4.

6   Benson, *Working Class*, p. 99.

7   Anderson, 'Social implications', p. 29.

8   R. Phillips, *Untying the Knot: A short history of divorce* (1991), pp. 121, 175 and 182.

9   *HA*, 9 August 1902, p. 6.

10 Summary Jurisdiction (Married Women) Act 1895.

11 Anderson, 'Social implications', pp. 30–1.

12 *HA*, 13 January, 28 April and 12 May 1900, pp. 7, 3 and 7.

13 *HA*, 23 June 1900, p. 7.

14 *HA*, 18 October 1913, p. 6.

15 J. S. Heywood, *Children in Care: The development of the service for the deprived child* (1965), p. 93.

16 G. K. Behlmer, *Child Abuse and Moral Reform in England, 1870–1908* (1982), pp. 162–83.

17 H. Ferguson, 'Cleveland in history: the abused child and child protection, 1880–1914', in R. Cooter (ed.), *In the Name of the Child: Health and welfare, 1880–1940* (1992), pp. 146–73.

18 *HA*, 10 June 1905, supp.

19 *HA*, 9 March 1912, p. 6; other cases at 23 April and 24 December 1910, pp. 6 and 5.

20 Benson, *Working Class*, pp. 102–3.

21 *HA*, 2 March 1912, p. 4.

22 Anderson, Social implications', p. 31.

23 *HA*, 25 November 1903, p. 3; Heywood, *Children in Care*, p. 119.

24 *HA*, 31 January 1914, p. 5.

25 V. Holmes, 'Accommodating the lodger: the domestic arrangements of lodgers in working-class dwellings in a Victorian provincial town', *Journal of Victorian Culture*, 19:3 (2014), pp. 314–31; S. J. Page, 'Lodging and poverty in late Victorian Leicester: a socio-geographic perspective', *Transactions of the Leicester Archaeological and Historical Society*, 68 (1994), pp. 121–44.

26 *HA*, 14 April 1900, p. 7.

27 Common Lodging Houses 1910, NYCCRO; *HA*, 7 May 1910, p. 6 and 3 May 1913, p. 7. In 2020 the Tower Street site was occupied by a Travelodge.

28   *HA*, 25 January 1890, p. 5.

29   *HA*, 18 July, supp. and 8 and 22 August 1908, p. 6; 16 January 1909, p. 3.

30   *HA*, 9 June 1900, p. 5; 12 May 1900, p. 7; 21 March 1908, p. 5; and 16 June 1900, p. 7.

31   *HA*, 16 September 1905, p. 3.

32   *HA*, 8 January 1910, p. 7.

33   *HA*, 31 August 1907, p. 3 and 13 June 1908, p. 6.

34   E. Higgs, 'Women, occupations and work in the nineteenth century census', *History Workshop Journal*, 23 (1987), pp. 59–80; J. K. Walton and P. R. McGloin, 'Holiday resorts and their visitors: some sources for the local historian', *The Local Historian*, 13:6 (1979), pp. 323–31.

35   PP 1917–18 [Cd. 8491], p. 161; Bosanquet, *The Family*, p. 280.

36   J. Bourke, 'Housewifery in working-class England, 1860–1914', *Past and Present*, 143 (1994), pp. 167–97.

37   Booth, *Life and Labour*; Rowntree, *Poverty*.

38   D. J. Oddy, 'Working-class diets in late nineteenth-century Britain', *Economic History Review*, 23:2 (1970), pp. 314–23.

39   P. Murray, *Poverty and Welfare, 1830–1914* (1999), pp. 106–15.

40   E. Roberts, 'Working-class standards of living in Barrow and Lancaster, 1890–1914', *Economic History Review*, 30:2 (1977), pp. 306–21.

41   Benson, *Working Class*, pp. 82–3.

42   PP 1908 [Cd. 3864], pp. xxiii and xxvi.

43   *HH*, 6 July 1904, p. 6.

44   R. Floud and P. Johnson, *The Cambridge Economic History of Modern Britain, Vol. 2: Economic Maturity, 1860–1939* (2004), p. 286.

45   P. Johnson, *Saving and Spending: The working-class economy in Britain, 1870–1939* (1985).

46   Johnson, *Saving and Spending*, p.3.

47   Bowley and Burnett-Hurst, *Livelihood and Poverty*, pp. 36–46.

48   Clarke, *Hope and Glory*, p. 18; *HA*, 1 April 1911, pp. 3 and 5 and 3 May 1913, p. 7.

49   For the logbook see the Bibliography.

50   *HA*, 6 January 1900, p. 2.

51   *HA*, 13 January 1900, p. 6 and 24 January 1914, p. 5.

52   *HA*, 27 January 1906, p. 2.

53   *HA*, 17 December 1904, p. 3.

54   *HA*, 27 January 1906, p. 2.

55   *HA*, 10 and 17 February 1906, pp. 7 and 6 and 12 May 1906, p. 6.

56   *HA*, 27 January 1906, p. 2.

57   *HA*, 25 May 1907, p. 6 and 2 October 1909, p. 5.

58   *HA*, 2 January 1909, p. 3.

59   Clarke, *Hope and Glory*, p. 70.

CHAPTER SEVEN

Childhood and Schooling

THIS CHAPTER is concerned with the children of Harrogate's working class, focusing on their school days. They spent around two-thirds of their childhood years in school and in the organization, content and outcomes of their education we see expressed clearly the influence of class in Edwardian England. Having briefly set out the number and proportion of children in the population, I go on to examine in detail those school days. The structure of schooling in the town is explained before I look at the curriculum, including the ways in which it differed for boys and girls, their attendance, levels of attainment and destinations on leaving school.

Working-class children

Edwardian England was full of children, although it was becoming rather less so than formerly as the birth rate fell and the population aged. In England and Wales just under a third of the population was under fourteen years of age, whilst in Harrogate, with its large retirement population, the proportion was about a quarter. There were 7,531 children in Harrogate in 1901, rising to 8,484 ten years later.[1] In the latter year, just over five thousand were the children of working-class families, 60 per cent of all the children in the town. We can get some idea of their sheer physical presence in this period by looking at the number in typical working-class streets in that year. In the fourteen households in each of Archie- and Christina Streets at New Park there were respectively thirty-nine and thirty-two children. At Starbeck the twenty-six households of Ruby Street (renamed Regent Mount) were home to sixty-two children and the twenty-nine of South Beech Avenue to seventy-one. In the Regents thirty-one children lived in twenty households on Baden Street, whilst on Regent Avenue the fifty-six households were home to over a hundred children.

The school system

It was for these children that the state education system was developed. The key date was 1870, the year of Bradford MP W. E. Forster's Education Act. Prior to that legislation, in common with the national pattern, education for Harrogate's working-class children was provided by voluntary, usually religious, bodies.[2] The Anglican National Society for the Education of the Poor in the Principles of the Established Church, founded in 1811, had in the 1830s set up schools on Skipton Road at Smithy Hill, in Church Square in High Harrogate and in Low Harrogate next to St Mary's, followed in 1865 by St Peter's in Chapel Street. A Methodist school was built in 1835, near to the small Wesleyan chapel in central Harrogate, which was soon opened to the children of all denominations. The British School, as it became known, was a member of The British and Foreign School Society, originally founded in 1808 by two Quakers and supported by Methodists. A Catholic school, St Robert's, was opened off Station Parade in 1864. In addition, there was an endowed school at Bilton for boys and girls, which had been established in the late eighteenth century by Richard Taylor, a local landowner, with a donation of a house and land.

From 1833 governments had provided increasing levels of financial support to voluntary schools. Despite this, and the undoubted spread of schooling of some kind whether provided by religious or charitable bodies or paid for by parents, many children still received little or no education. Forster's Act therefore set out that wherever existing provision was shown to be inadequate, elementary schools should be built and maintained by elected school boards and financed from an education rate. Its aim was to 'fill up the gaps', whilst continuing to rely on the voluntary sector. In introducing his legislation Forster was quite explicit that his concern was with the children of the working classes. He was equally clear about its aims. Elementary education was an essential foundation for the development of the technical skills an industrial country needed to maintain its position in an increasingly competitive world. It was also necessary to secure political stability, or as he put it, 'the good, the safe working of our constitutional system', an aim made more urgent with the grant of the vote to many working men by the Reform Act of 1867.[3]

An important issue was the religious instruction which was to be given to the children in these new schools. It was to be non-denominational, which suited the Nonconformists but not the Anglicans. In Harrogate, their hostility, together with that of those opposed to paying the new rate, led to efforts to ensure the adequacy of the existing level of church provision and thereby obviate the necessity for a school board. Over the succeeding twenty years, however, the growth of the town's permanent population, the introduction of compulsion and the raising of the leaving age increased demand beyond the schools' capacity to cope. The abolition of fees in board schools in 1891 then put the voluntary sector under pressure to do the same, which would remove an important source of the income with which it supplemented the grants from the Education Department.

In the event, they failed to raise the necessary money and accordingly the Education Department in August 1893 ordered that school boards be established for the borough of Harrogate and the Bilton-Starbeck area.[4] In neighbouring Pannal a school board had already been created in 1883, which had taken over a church school opened at Oatlands Mount in 1880. It then in 1897 opened a new school on Cromwell Road. The Bilton-Starbeck School Board took over existing church schools at New Park and Starbeck, where new schools were then built, together with the endowed school at Bilton. In Harrogate, St Mary's National School was transferred to the Harrogate School Board along with its head since 1882, James Hammond, who characteristically expressed the hope in the logbook that he would have the strength to continue faithfully to do his duty.[5] It moved to its new premises in Cold Bath Road as Western School in the spring of 1897. That same summer another new board school was opened at Grove Road, taking its pupils from the Central

Board School and the National School at Smithy Hill, whose headmaster Oliver Threapleton similarly became its first head. On the extension of the borough in 1900 the United District School Board was formed, bringing in the schools at New Park, Starbeck and Oatlands, together with those at Beckwithshaw and Pannal.[6]

The new schools were impressive buildings. By the close of the century those at Oatlands, New Park and Starbeck had respectively on their rolls nearly 200, over 300 and 564 children.[7] **(57)** Western and Grove Road were larger. On its opening, the former was authorized for over 900 children, comprising 305 infants and 620 mixed scholars, whilst the latter could accommodate 1,200 children. Western comprised two stories and a basement. In the latter were the furnace and storerooms and on the first floor were the separate entrances for infants, girls and boys and

57. The new school opened by the Bilton and Starbeck School Board in 1897 in Skipton Road. It was extended in 1911 and was photographed here as New Park School in 2018. (Author's photograph)

58. The largest of the new board schools was Grove Road, which opened in 1897, 'well-planned and admirably adapted to educational purposes', according to a school inspector. Its scale is clear from this modern photograph of 2018. (Author's photograph)

cloakrooms and lavatories. In a typical arrangement, classrooms for the infant boys and girls led off a central hall. On the first floor another hall led into three classrooms. Teachers' rooms were on a mezzanine floor. Cookery and workshop rooms faced the two playgrounds to the rear. Grove Road was similarly designed but was built on three floors, each with a central hall around which three classrooms were ranged. The infants were on one floor, the mixed classes on the two higher. There were seven teachers' rooms, two dining rooms and eight cloakrooms and lavatories. It also had woodwork and cooking blocks.[8] (58)

Within just two years of the formation of the United District School Board, however, a further Education Act in 1902 abolished the school boards. Over two-and-a-half thousand were replaced by some 350 Local Education Authorities (LEAs) from April 1904. The act also introduced support from the rates for the voluntary, predominantly Anglican, schools, which were struggling financially yet still educated over a third of the country's children. They were now brought fully within the local educational system, a move which was deeply unpopular with Nonconformists who, with the Liberal Party, bitterly but fruitlessly opposed the measure.[9]

The new Harrogate LEA was responsible for schools which by 1909 were educating 3,074 children in the senior departments and 1,485 in the infants.[10] These public elementary, or council, schools, as they were collectively termed, provided education for the town's working-class children. But they were not exclusively for them. This is clearly revealed in admission registers, which I consulted for Grove Road, Bilton (as New Park School was originally known) and Starbeck, and linked the information to the census returns to determine the father's, or mother's, occupation.[11] They show that such as shop keepers and small tradesmen sent their children to them, although they were always a minority of admissions. At Grove Road between 1899 and 1901, of seventy-nine occupations found, fifteen broadly belonged to this group, like the grocer and sub-postmaster, the coal merchant, or contractor. At Starbeck at that time, thirteen of ninety were similarly placed. At Bilton, admissions for 1911 to 1912 showed that of eighty-four occupations there were just four not in my classes III to V. Of course, we cannot know if their children were sent with any reluctance to the state school, although the objections generally of those in the lower middle class to that fate are well documented. H. G. Wells, both in his real life when he was sent to a small private 'academy', and that of his fictional hero *Kipps*, showed how shopkeeper parents wanted 'something a little "superior"' to a board school'.[12] If, however, some of Harrogate's lower middle class were content to do so, conspicuously absent were the sons and daughters of the middle class. Their education was either at home or in one of the many private schools.

The board and council schools were also local schools. This is clear from the admission registers, where the children's addresses are almost all only a short distance away. Only two had a wider catchment area. It was noted in the Western School logbook in November 1904 that during bad weather, like the recent severe snowstorm, it suffered more than most of the town's schools as 'so many of our scholars come long distances'. It took children from Harlow Hill, which is about a half-hour's walk for a small child. In 1905 residents there unsuccessfully petitioned the

59. Western School Infants.
(Courtesy Western Primary School)

60. College Road, part of a small development of workers' housing at Harlow Hill, whose children walked down to Western School on Cold Bath Road. Photographed in 2018. (Author's photograph).

Education Committee for an infants' school, arguing that the distance to Western was too great.[13] It also took from there the children of the Northern Police Orphanage and, even further away on Pannal Ash Road, the Primitive Methodist Orphanage. The other was St Robert's, which as the sole Catholic school drew its pupils from around the town, as was noted of a snowstorm in February 1912, 'only twenty-seven children living near came'. (59, 60)

The curriculum

The curriculum embodied Forster's twin aims of creating children adequately educated for the modern world and able to take their place in it as good citizens. I shall look at each in turn, before attempting to gauge with what success. The logbooks are a vital source but there are also detailed descriptions of a day at Grove Road and Western Schools in reports of 'surprise' visits which were printed in the *Advertiser* in the spring of 1900.[14] At Grove Road, as at all schools, special attention was paid at all standards to the 'three Rs' of reading, writing and arithmetic. The level for the infant classes I and II was spelled out, for example at Starbeck School in 1907. In reading the children would work on fairy tales and from the blackboard. Writing aimed at their own name, school and village (as Starbeck was typically called at this time) but also at the creation of a simple sketch and even essay composition. Arithmetic, or 'number', covered addition, subtraction, multiplication and division up to twenty. Infants also were to learn from object lessons, those at St Robert's for example in the school year 1900 to 1901 covering basic shapes like line, angles, squares, oblongs and triangles, cubes and bricks. There were also object lessons on colours, impressions through hand and taste, plants and animals. Geography was taught to all standards at Grove Road but is not mentioned in the Starbeck scheme of work for the infants. Common to both, however, were drawing, singing and needlework. Singing was universal as the logbooks often indicate. At Western, for example, songs for the lower standards proposed for 1900 comprised the 'Canadian Boat Song', 'The Children's Home', 'If I Were a Sunbeam' and 'Bonnie Scotland', whilst the hymns included 'Hark, My Soul! It is the Lord', 'I Love to Hear the Story' and 'God Save the

Queen'. At Grove Road needlework was specified for the girls, although at Starbeck was not so differentiated. There it included hemming dusters or pinafores, knitting scarves and the like and making illustrations of flowers, fruit and vegetables and 'where possible – animals'. The force of this last point is sadly illustrated from another entry in the logbook the year before: 'Found the gold-fish dead on the floor this morning.'

The gendered nature of the curriculum is evident as the children progress. At Grove Road the boys were taught woodwork, bookkeeping and shorthand whilst the girls had domestic economy and cookery. As to physical exercise, all children had dumb-bell drill but whilst the older girls had figure marching and Swedish drill (a form of gymnastics aiming towards a healthy body), the boys had military drill. Only chemistry for the older children is not specified as for boys or girls. This gendered education was directed from central government, embodied in the regulations and arrangements for grants and, it has been argued, was 'extended and increasingly formalized' between 1870 and 1914'. As the curriculum was expanded, the greater competition for space in the timetable meant that girls spent increasing periods of time in activities that separated them from boys. This was in addition to their physical separation in separate entrances and playgrounds. Put simply, the curriculum for working-class girls aimed to prepare them for their primary roles as members of society serving either in the households of others or as wives and mothers in their own. As one school inspector expressed the importance of needlework, 'Not only on account of its practical utility, but because it is a splendid training for hand and eye, and has also a great refining influence; and love for the needle encourages domesticity.'[15] It might also have a more immediate practical application. At Oatlands children once a week brought clothes into school from home to mend, whilst at St Peter's work was sold. In the week commencing the 3 November 1905, handkerchiefs cost 1*d*. each plus knickers, aprons, tea towels, glass cloths, bonnets, pinafores, aprons, caps and mittens raising a total of £3 5*s*. 4*d*.[16]

This emphasis on domestic skills was sharpened into the Edwardian period by the servant shortage but more broadly by concern over what was called national efficiency. This was engendered by the threats perceived to Britain's greatness of the increasing economic competition of the

USA and Germany and the latter's military and naval strength. This in turn linked with the contemporary racial discourse of social Darwinism, which saw the world's races and nations locked in a struggle for survival. Evidence that Britain was falling behind was seen in the poverty, disease, crime, drunkenness and violence of the country's cities and all too vividly displayed both in the poor quality of recruits to the South African, or Boer, War of 1899 to 1902 and the sobering challenge which a small republic of farmers had made to the world's most powerful empire.[17] In combating this threat, the nation's future mothers had a vital role to play. The inspector's report for Grove Road for 1912 noted especially the quality of the teaching in Hygiene and Infant Care Management and in October that year Kathleen Brady of St Robert's won a prize of 5s. for the best essay on 'Infant Care' in the lady mayoress's competition.

The education provided was not solely practical. There was an effort to develop awareness, for example of the beauties of nature. The Bilton logbook in July 1902 noted how the children were delighted to see some young swallows peeping out of the nests under the school roof. They were also taken out of school to learn about and enjoy nature, the following year collecting oak leaves and acorns. At St Robert's children went on 'country rambles' to supplement their classroom object lessons and schools made use of the Valley Gardens. Some had museums and all seem to have made at least some library provision, which might be supplemented with visits to the public library. In 1907, for example, from standards VI and VII of Grove Road the boys went on one day to look at books on geography and elementary science, the girls on another for domestic science and twentieth-century inventions. Cinema afforded a new educational opportunity: children from Grove Road were taken in May 1912 to St James's Hall to see a film of the Discovery of America.

Sport of all kinds was an important part of the curriculum. Already by the close of the nineteenth century there was a swimming gala for all the boys in elementary schools and an inter-schools football competition. There were, however, differences in the timing of the development of sport between individual schools. Both boys and girls were receiving swimming lessons at Western and Grove Road by that time, whereas at St Robert's it was not until 1913 that girls began them. Their effectiveness, however, may have been limited. At Grove Road never more than a third, and frequently much lower, of the children who attended could swim. In addition to everyday games, the annual sports day became a fixture of the school year. At Grove Road one was inaugurated in September 1912, with 240 children taking part in swimming, athletics and games.

Another important event was the annual concert and prize day. That of Oatlands School, for example, was detailed in the logbook. The infants did recitations, songs and drill with dumb bells, whilst the upper scholars did musical drill with dumb bells and wands. The girls also displayed their skipping and musical scarf drill whilst the boys performed as 'The Boy Minstrels', singing songs including 'It's Massa's Wedding Day', 'Silly Sambo', 'Four Little Curly Headed Coons' and 'Good Old Aunt Eliza'. The concert ended with the glee 'Sweetly on the Evening Air' and a comic speech entitled 'Silence is Golden'. There were ninety-six prize winners for attendance and merit and each child received a Christmas present of sweets and oranges. At Western the 'annual entertainment' moved to the Spa Concert Rooms, celebrating its twentieth year in 1904. At Grove Road, in contrast, the annual school concert was not begun until 1912, according to the memory of one former pupil. It included a pantomime – Aladdin, performed on a specially constructed stage in the upper hall with costumes, scenery and lighting all the work of the children.[18] In addition to these annual events there were occasional concerts and displays by the children. Those at Bilton took part in March 1906 in a festival to welcome spring. Dorothy Day was chosen to represent Princess Spring, dressed in yellow and green paper, wearing a crown and decorated with daffodils. 'Spring songs' were sung and the children marched around carrying flags. In October there was a Princess Autumn and a Princess Summer the following year. (61)

With prizes children were also shown the rewards of hard work and conscientiousness. In such ways as this, together with the development of character through adherence to acceptable standards of behaviour, children would become good citizens. This is evident at all schools but Hammond at Western was especially keen. In common with other schools there was a general emphasis on orderly behaviour, as he showed his visitors from the *Advertiser*. This began on entry to the school when a whistle was blown 'and in a moment the boys were steadily marching in sections, under the command of the masters and sergeants, down

61. The upper department at Bilton Council School, 1904 showing the head, Mr Mawson, and Miss Marshall. (Courtesy Terry Williams, the New Park Heritage Centre)

the playground up the steps into the wings of the central hall'. From their playground the girls entered in the same way. After the morning assembly, which consisted of a short service including the singing of the Lord's Prayer, the younger children were 'marched off' to their classes. After some more music the older children then similarly 'fell in ranks and moved off with mechanical precision'. The visitors admired this 'semi-military organisation', seeing it as essential to moving the children around the school without confusion. Hammond then dealt with the 'Late Brigade', those children who had arrived too late for prayers. Some received 'a few words of reproof' and others 'a slight punishment', although its exact nature was not specified.

Children were certainly subjected to punishments. Some heads sought to restrain its use, as did Hammond who, whilst delegating the power to individual teachers, had noted in 1895 that 'Excessive or frequent recourse to this power, will of course, argue the unfitness of the teacher to wield it.' Similarly, the recently appointed head of Grove Road, George Idle, responded in July 1912 to several complaints about Mr Smith's use of corporal punishment by requesting that he cease and in future 'send unruly cases to me'. He was prepared to use it himself, as one former pupil remembered, who received first a lecture and then two 'whacks' with the 'stick' for playing rugby in the upper school hall.[19]

Schools were required to record punishments in special books. Just one has survived for Harrogate, that of Oatlands School.[20] By far the most entries were for the single year 1901, with 123. Of these, 119 were caned and just four warned or cautioned. There was clearly a distinction between the latter two, as one child was both warned and cautioned. Most of the punishments were inflicted for bad behaviour in the classroom: talking, disobedience, as with a child 'rolling pencil on the floor purposely and breaking it', but mostly simply for unspecified 'bad order', for which the child was sent out of the classroom. The next highest was for bad or careless work, followed by problems with cleanliness. The head, Tom Wilde, inspected at the start of every day the children's hands (front and back) and shoes had to be clean and the girls' hair neat and tied back. More serious cases of fighting were comparatively rare, with only one for 'striking another boy', although the previous year three had been punished with no play for 'quarrelling in yard'. The same names recur, suggestive of a particularly troublesome child or one who too often caught the teacher's eye.

It is not clear why there should have been this large number in just the one year; Wilde was the head throughout the period. It is perhaps significant that after 1902 general classroom behaviour almost disappeared from the entries. In 1903 it occurs only once as 'laughing in singing lesson' and the following year two girls were warned for 'bad behaviour in cookery'. Truancy was now more common among the small number of entries. The suggestion is that daily classroom unruliness was dealt with informally in a way that did not merit inclusion in the punishment book and that overall, corporal punishment was used less frequently. This was the conclusion of a study which made use of the logbooks of thirty-four schools in the West Riding, Cambridgeshire and

Essex, extending down to the Second World War. It also found that boys were far more likely to be punished; fewer than one in ten were girls. The Oatlands book does not usually spell out the children's first names so it is not possible to give a similarly exact figure but where it does, they were typically boys.[21]

Other attributes of good character and behaviour, such as honesty, are also referred to and were important qualities to be encouraged. Historians have stressed this aspect of schools' work. Stephanie Olsen for example defined 'character' as 'a composite of sound emotional adjustment and a well-orientated moral compass – not just knowledge of what to do, but the fibre to do it' and held that it was at least as important as formal schooling.[22] Hammond regularly gave the children lectures on aspects of good behaviour and their content reveal what was held to constitute it. The examples are from 1901. In one address he spoke to the whole school on bird-nesting, consideration for others and true politeness. On the death of the mayor, Councillor Dr Myrtle, he spoke on those traits in his character which they all should do well to imitate and drew attention to two lessons in particular:

'Whatever thy hand findeth to do, do it with thy might.' and
'Do unto others as thou woulds't have others unto thee.'

The school closed for the day for the funeral in June, as it did again for that of the first chairman of the school board the following month, underlining the respect due from the children to prominent local men.

Dishonesty and good and bad manners were the subjects of another address, as were fireworks and litter in the school yards, sliding on the slope in the yard, loitering on the causeway outside the gates, slouching and making chalk marks both on and off the school premises. This was followed the next month by running in the school corridors, together with the need for clean hands and face, neatness of appearance and obliging manners both in and out of school. He began 1902 with a topical address on 'Avoiding the first signs of incipient Hooliganism in the streets', followed later by causing annoyance to neighbours by playing marbles in the yard and street and 'cigarette smoking and its dangers'.

Schools augmented addresses such as these with outside speakers. The threats posed by the 'demon drink' were a popular topic and the temperance movement particularly sought to influence children through the Band of Hope following its motto from Proverbs: 'Train up a child in the way he should go: and when he is old he will not depart from it.'.[23] In January 1913, the Education Committee gave permission to a lecturer from the Yorkshire Band of Hope Union to give lessons generally in school hours using the Board of Education's temperance syllabus.[24] In addition to hearing lectures, children were encouraged to engage in writing on the subject: three from Western were awarded in September 1903 prizes from the National Temperance Society for their essays on alcohol.

Charity towards others was another important trait to be encouraged. A collection of over £1 for the Indian Famine Fund was made at Oatlands in 1900. But charity was also important closer to home. Bilton, for example, which was itself not without needy children, in December 1907 sent fifty-four toys brought in by pupils to York Road Council School in a poor district of Leeds.

A final, but very prominent, part of the curriculum was the stress on national identity and patriotic feeling.[25] The royal family was venerated. Schools had closed for Queen Victoria's Diamond Jubilee in June 1897 and on her birthday in 1900 all the town's children marched to the bandstand in Victoria Avenue to sing the National Anthem in her honour. What must have made the occasion even more worthwhile, the mayor provided them with buns and lemonade and made the whole day a holiday. On her death in January 1901 Hammond recorded 'Our dear Queen Victoria ceased to live last evening at 6.30 p.m. Her memory will abide with us always.' A memorial service was held and a half-holiday granted for children to see the proclamation of Edward VII by the mayor from in front of the Spa Rooms. The children at St Peter's were given an epitome of her reign and urged to 'endeavour to do their duty as she has done hers'. When the new king had an operation in June the following year for appendicitis a Day of Intercession was observed for his recovery, towards which the children at Western, for example, were asked to pray 'day and night'. When he did recover, the school was closed for a half day for a service to celebrate. His death in turn in 1910 and the accession of his son George V led to a similar outpouring and celebration: at the request of the new king and queen schools had a week's holiday for the coronation and all children over five went to the Kursaal to see pictures of the procession.

The South African War was observed. The head at Oatlands gave a lecture in November 1899 on the Transvaal in aid of the local fund for soldiers' families. The following year a half-holiday was granted on the relief of Mafeking and Ladysmith and in the town there was a procession, with music by the Volunteer and Temperance Bands, patriotic decorations, illuminations and fireworks.[26] When the war did not immediately end, the subsequent guerrilla campaign and the British response saw three teachers from Western leaving to take up posts teaching in the concentration camps which had been set up to contain the families of Boer fighters made homeless by the army's policy of burning farms thought to be harbouring or supporting them. At least 20,000 Boer women and children died in those camps.[27] In Harrogate, in honour of the campaign, new streets in the Regents district were named Baden, Powell, Mafeking and French.

The wars of the past were also celebrated, both within the curriculum and at special events. Poetry for Western's standard IV at the beginning of the 1903 to 1904 school year included 'The Piper at Lucknow' by Henry Greenleaf Whittier, with its lines on the lifting of the siege:

> Round the silver domes of Lucknow,
> Moslem mosque and Pagan shrine,
> Breathed the air to Britons dearest,
> The air of "Auld Lang Syne".

Standard V did Shakespeare's 'Henry V Before Agincourt':

> And gentlemen in England now a-bed
> Shall think themselves accursed they were not there;

Two years later the centenary of the death of Nelson was commemorated with the school's rifle company saluting the flag and admiral's portrait and the singing of the National Anthem. The period also saw the widespread adoption of Empire Day on 24 May. This was also initiated in 1905 and, although it did not receive government support until the war, many schools took it up enthusiastically along with Trafalgar Day.[28] Grove Road the following year devoted a special lesson during their 'Citizenship' time to it and it became an annual event, with the school building decorated with flags and the children marching past invited parents and friends.

Attainments and destinations

To what extent were the aims of Forster and his successors realized? It is not an easy question to answer. School was not the only influence upon children and the young adults into which they grew. Take behaviour for example. The years after the First World War, when these children came to adulthood, were certainly ones of improvement. Heavy drinking and drunkenness, which had formerly been great scourges, declined dramatically, although it is doubtful that much of this was due to temperance lectures and Band of Hope singing. Children were, however, exposed to the idea that drinking, especially heavy drinking, was wrong. Improved living standards, alternative outlets for working-class expenditure, a range of competing leisure pursuits and the effects of the First World War, which drastically increased the price and reduced the availability of drink, meshed with a by now well-developed culture of respectability to bring changes.[29] The First World War also helped to put to rest the fear of some Edwardians that the country's working men and women were not up to the struggle between nations. They did in fact prove both able and willing to respond. As a historian of the war and the threat that drink was held to pose to its successful prosecution concluded, 'national efficiency had been tested and not found wanting to the challenges of war'.[30]

Drinking had been presented as unpatriotic but to what extent had working-class children imbibed those patriotic messages. It is hard not to conclude that the sheer amount of attention paid in schools to celebrating the country, its empire and its heroic past must have had an effect. But this was not simply indoctrination, it has been argued, rather it had a genuine appeal. As G. R. Searle concluded his discussion of nationalism and nationality, 'Most late-Victorian Englishmen, from whatever class, could derive satisfaction from the thought that they constituted a successful imperial "race" – consolation indeed for the poor and underprivileged.'[31] Other historians, however, have viewed intense patriotic feeling as more of a lower-middle- or middle-class attribute. This was the view of Henry Pelling, focusing on the South African War: 'there is no evidence of a direct continuous support for the cause of Imperialism among any sections of the working class', a view echoed by Richard Price in his study of working-class attitudes towards that conflict.[32] If working-class men and women did not necessarily respond to the more strident nationalistic voices, nevertheless most did believe that their country was right and superior and that they had to give it their support in time of war.[33] The lessons of their schooldays made some contribution to that, if it remains difficult to assess to what extent. Whatever the case, the celebrations were no doubt for the children a welcome break from more everyday lessons.

What of schools' success in teaching them those basic skills of reading, writing and numeracy. In the first place there were several obstacles to its achievement. One critical one was attendance: many children missed a lot of schooling. We have already seen how illness, disease and bad weather led to many absences and sometimes the complete closure of schools. At elections some schools became polling stations. In addition to holidays for royal and other patriotic occasions or the weddings and funerals of members of staff and local dignitaries, children were also given time off for special events. In October 1904, for example, the Education Committee allowed all schools to close for the afternoon on the visit of Buffalo Bill's Wild West Show.[34] Other events chart technological change, like the arrival in May 1900 of motor cars on the thousand-mile tour of England and Scotland or the aeroplane race of July 1911 when pilots landed on the Stray at the end of the second stage. Holidays were granted for county cricket matches or the meets of hounds, which still assembled in the town. As a Catholic school, St Robert's also had extra religious holidays for the feasts of All Saints and the Ascension and St Patrick's Day. Where a holiday was not granted, high levels of absence often resulted as children went off, for example, to the amusements accompanying the Knaresborough Statutes, to watch a circus procession or to the Agricultural Show. The annual trips of Sunday schools, or of youth groups like the Boys' Brigade, also took many away for the day either locally or to the seaside. As an exasperated Hammond noted in June 1901, 'These Sunday School trips interrupt our work from Whit to Midsummer.'

Some parents kept their children away from school. Formerly this was often to work during the season, helping at home where accommodation was offered, or fetching, carrying and taking messages for visitors. With the formation of the school board, simply not coming to school seems to have declined, although children did still work after school and at weekends. One reason for this was the board's immediate appointment of a School Attendance Officer, G. C. Appleby, in October 1893.[35] His and his successors' activities, which were detailed in the local papers, give a vivid picture of how some children received little formal education. In 1900 a plasterer was charged with neglecting to provide proper education for his daughter, who was in standard VI, between 9 March and 16 June. He claimed that it was to help her sick mother but Appleby asserted that she had told him it was because she needed her for dressmaking. In another case a widow was similarly charged regarding her nine-year-old son who in one period had made only nine attendances out of a possible fifty-eight. In both cases an attendance order was made.[36] Sometimes parents, as in the latter case, pleaded that they could not get the child to go to school but this excuse cut little ice with the court. Appleby evidenced in the case of another plasterer that the man was unable to control his boy. On the child being produced, the chairman of the bench, Thomas Watson, asked, 'Is this the little man you cannot manage?' To this the father replied that they could manage him at home but not when he was outside. He sold newspapers, went to the theatre and frequently slept out. On making the attendance order Watson warned the boy that if he could not be managed at home he would be sent where he could: 'A little bit of a shrimp like you ... to set everybody at defiance, they will put you right.'[37]

'They' were the staff at an industrial school or other institution, to which persistent non-attenders might be sent and towards whose cost parents were required to contribute. That boy's father failed to keep up the maintenance payments of Adel Reformatory School but had them reduced after pleading that there was little work in his trade, that he supported his mother and blind brother who lived with them and the fact that his wife's little confectioner's shop never made more than 13s. a week. That same year, 1904, a labourer's thirteen-year-old son, with only 34 out of 170 possible attendances, was sent until the age of sixteen to the Wellesley Training Ship on the Tyne.[38]

The parents in these cases were invariably semi- or unskilled, like labourers or charwomen, and the reasons cited for non-attendance included that the child was needed to help at home, sometimes to look after younger children, to earn some money for the family, or because they could not be controlled. A contrast was provided by the perfect attenders, whom all schools conspicuously rewarded. At Western this was literally the case as on a board in the central hall, alongside one containing the names of the school captains and an Honours Board, were recorded those of all pupils who had not missed a single attendance.[39] Between the extremes were the average, as the Attendance Officer regularly reported. In 1900 in the senior departments of both board and voluntary schools it was overall 85 per cent compared with the number on the roll and just 75 per cent at infants, well below modern levels.[40]

Class size, resources and the quality of the teaching are further considerations. There were difficulties in all three areas. Of Bilton Infants in 1904, the inspector's report noted that conditions were 'cramped', with two classes using one room and the upper standard being taught in the hall. The following year some classes were still too large and the problem was only alleviated at the end of the decade with the addition of a new building. At Grove Road in 1909 the inspector also noted large class sizes of more than seventy in two cases and seven of over sixty, of thirteen classes in total. This was even though at its opening the school had been described as 'well-planned and admirably adapted to educational purposes'. St Peter's in 1910 was teaching classes in the same room divided by a curtain and in 1912 at St Robert's some of the teaching took place on a staircase landing. The inspector who noted this also saw that there were scarcely any interesting books for the 2nd class and that no use was made of the school library. Overall, however, there was rather limited comment on resources, which perhaps suggests that they generally were at least up to expectations.

They are rather clearer on the training teachers had received, the quality of the teaching delivered and their workload. The first two were variable. At the start of the period, training was undertaken by pupil teachers apprenticed to a school, who combined daily teaching with out-of-school tuition from the head and private study. At the end of their apprenticeship trainees could sit for a Queen's scholarship to gain entry to a training college or remain in school as unqualified assistants but might study in their spare time for a certificate, an option which many took.

By 1914 nationally, of women teachers, who dominated the profession, 27 per cent had certificates but had not been to college, compared to 32 per cent who were both trained and certificated, whilst the rest were neither trained nor certificated.[41] Harrogate's schools replicated this variety. At Western in 1900, of over twenty staff, half were certificated and three more were candidates. In contrast at Oatlands, an inspector's report of 1908 noted the youth and low level of qualifications of the staff and at Bilton in 1911 the only trained teacher in the infant department was the head.

Comments on the teaching methods were similarly mixed. That same Oatlands report felt that teaching could be more stimulating, although at least, like History, subjects were 'carefully taught'. Bilton Infants was judged 'not educationally in a very efficient state', with much teaching too formal, but the report also noted the high levels of absence due to illness and the obvious signs of poverty among the children. Some schools did move towards more stimulating teaching. At Grove Road, the reorganization of the mixed department into separate juniors and seniors seems to have helped to bring about improvement. The latter department was strongly praised in 1912 for its 'fresher and more modern methods of teaching'. At other schools, change did not come until after the war. At St Robert's, a report of 1923 noted how 'a complete change has been effected in the last ten years' under the 'enlightened outlook on education of the present headmistress'.

The workload was often commented upon. Teachers at Grove Road, for example, with the large class sizes, were 'obviously overworked'. This could put stress on individuals. As the report of 1912 observed of Hammond at Western, 'although no longer young [he] is an active and vigorous man, but the strain of the work is beginning to tell on him'. He had just turned sixty, having been head since 1882, his birthday celebrated with cheers, roses and an electro-plated jug from the older scholars. He was then suffering from rheumatic gout, unable at times to write. Shortly after his next birthday he died suddenly.

Despite all these difficulties, children did receive a basic education. One can certainly see improvement overall when comparing with earlier reports. The first of St Mary's, the predecessor to Western, in 1875 had stated bluntly, 'The arithmetic is almost a complete failure, and the spelling is very defective.' In 1888, the principal teacher of the seniors at St Robert's found children 'very backward in their reading and arithmetic'. One can still find damning reports at the end of our period, as we saw at Bilton, but overall these are outweighed by more positive voices, although it must be acknowledged in the end that attainments were still limited. Grove Road in 1911 reported exam results in which more than three-quarters of the children had more than three errors in a spelling list and their handwriting lacked 'style or character'. The following year 'much progress' was recorded, especially in writing and arithmetic, but nearly half the children did not meet the required standard.

For most pupils that was the end of their education. Under the school board, Harrogate had, like many, opened a higher grade school. These aimed to give children the opportunity to take a greater variety of subjects and to progress beyond a basic elementary education. The Harrogate venture, however, was not a success. Opened in 1895, it at first occupied temporary premises before being found accommodation in 1897 at Grove Road, with which it then merged within two years. It never seems to have established a clear role for itself as a higher grade school, still at first taking infants and also experiencing difficulty attracting and retaining pupils. Offered the post of first assistant master over the boys at Grove Road at his old salary, its head declined the offer, unhappy with the decision to close the school.[42] This unhappiness was shared by a parent with the *Advertiser's* readers, describing such schools as 'the working man's universities', which had given his children their chance.[43] In fact, there was wider opposition to the development by school boards of education beyond the elementary level. Expenditure on them was challenged successfully in the courts and in the Education Act of 1902 secondary education, now made the responsibility of the new LEAs, was to be clearly demarcated from elementary schooling and accessible to children only through competitive examinations.[44]

Harrogate opened a secondary day school in 1903–4 at the site of the recently opened School of Art and Technology on Haywra Crescent, although at first numbers were limited and children also applied for West Riding County scholarships to study elsewhere. Ten were awarded in 1904, for example, to six boys and four girls.[45] Eligible pupils from St Robert's went to Catholic secondary schools in Bradford or Leeds.

The Harrogate school continued to use the County Council's exam but scholarships were now also available from the LEA and from 1910 two from the Harrogate Literary Society. Free places were also offered, as required under the regulations for secondary schools, as fees of six guineas a year were payable. They could be a problem. In 1910 one Starbeck parent wrote to the school's governors asking to remove his son as he was then unemployed and could no longer afford them, something, however, which 'they could not countenance' unless he returned to school immediately, and steps would be taken to recover the lost fees.[46] In addition, forty free scholarships were available for pupils to study at the Technical College and ten for the School of Art.[47]

Who were these scholarship children? I traced nine in the 1901 census returns. Seven came from a lower middle-class background, like Mabel Annakin from Western, whose father was a coal merchant. Just two had fathers who were skilled workers: a self-employed joiner and a coach-body painter. In addition to moving on to secondary school, children had the option to take exams in bookkeeping, commercial arithmetic, shorthand and commercial correspondence. Three boys from Western did so successfully in 1903, two of whom similarly were from lower middle-class backgrounds, but the third was William Birks, the son of a stone mason, who went on to become a ledger clerk.[48] A clerical job was viewed as an achievement for a boy. When Sydney Colbeck of Grove Road was presented in June 1901 with a framed photograph of himself for winning eight medals, six certificates and two book prizes for perfect attendance, the *Advertiser's* report concluded approvingly that he had 'secured a position as clerk in the North Eastern Railway goods yard'.[49]

Overall, few went on to secondary education. Figures for Grove Road in 1914 show that of fifty-nine boys who left school, just five did so and six of fifty-eight girls, plus two to another educational institution. This was only a slight improvement on the beginning of the period, when of 177 pupils admitted between 1899 and 1902 just six went into secondary education. Most children left school when they could. The head of Oatlands in 1902 expressed regret that 'some of the brightest of First Class scholars have left to go to work.' The minimum school leaving age was twelve but under local rules children in Harrogate could only actually leave before they were fourteen if they first obtained a labour certificate showing that they had attained an appropriate standard. Just fifteen did so among those 177 Grove Road children.

At fourteen then boys began work whilst most girls stayed at home to perform 'domestic duties', as the Grove Road statistics record, with just over a fifth going into the kind of employments we saw. For boys work usually meant becoming an errand boy or taking up an apprenticeship. Over the period the number of the former increased markedly but apprenticeship declined, from 155 recorded in 1901 to 138 ten years later, largely as a result of its collapse in the building trades from 90 to 29 and only slightly offset by the 9 boys then apprenticed as mechanics. The 'hopeless position' of the errand boy with no prospects; the breakup of the apprenticeship system; the lack of post-school training; and the general problem of adolescent indiscipline led contemporaries to talk of the 'boy labour problem'.[50] I looked at some thirty Harrogate errand boys and apprentices and traced them from 1901 forward to the census of 1911. The former were in the kind of job one might expect as joiners, gardeners or labourers for example, although three had joined the army. Only one had remained in the retail trade, as a grocer's assistant. For them therefore it sems to have been a short-lived prelude to a more permanent working life. The apprentices usually remained in their trade. The number of apprenticed girls, typically in dressmaking or millinery, rose from 22 to 28 but for most girls who worked those brief years ended on their marriage.

Notes to Chapter 7: Childhood and Schooling

1   J. Walvin, *A Child's World: A social history of English childhood, 1800–1914* (1982), p. 19; Anderson, 'Social implications', p. 47; PP 1902 [Cd. 1107], p. 186; and PP 1912–13 [Cd. 6610], p. 173.

2   What follows is based on Neesam, *Chronicle*, pp. 262–7 and Jennings, *Harrogate*, pp. 382–5 and 393–8.

3   *Hansard*, 3rd Series, vol. 199, cols 438–66 (17 February 1870).

4   *HA*, 4 May 1895, p. 5.

5   For the logbooks see the Bibliography.

6   *HA*, 6 April 1901, p. 2. There are two published histories of Harrogate elementary schools: L. Clayton, *Oatlands Infant School: A centenary celebration* (1997) and E. N. Steele, *Grove Road School, 1897–1997* (1997, unpaginated).

7   *HA*, 10 February 1905, p. 10; Clayton, *Oatlands*, p. 12

8   *HA*, 26 May and 2 June 1900, p. 5; Steele, *Grove Road*.

9   Searle, *A New England?*, pp. 329–34.

10 *HA*, 25 December 1909, p. 5.

11 For the admission registers see the Bibliography.

12 M. Sherborne, *H. G. Wells: Another kind of life* (2012), p. 30; H. G. Wells, *Kipps* (2005), p. 12.

13 Education Committee Minute Book, 1 August 1905.

14 *HA*, 12 and 19 May 1900, p. 5.

15 A. Turnbull, 'Learning her womanly work: the elementary school curriculum, 1870–1914', in F. Hunt (ed.), *Lessons for Life: The Schooling of Women and Girls, 1850–1950* (1987), pp. 83–100.

16 St. Peter's School Sales Account Book: Sales of pupils' sewing work, 1906–1946, NYCCRO.

17 G. R. Searle, *The Quest for National Efficiency: A study in British politics and political thought, 1899–1914* (1990), pp. 60–1.

18 Steele, *Grove Road*.

19 Steele, *Grove Road*.

20 Oatlands Mount Board School Punishment Book, 1900–1935.

21 P. W. Musgrave, 'Corporal punishment in some English elementary schools, 1900–1939', *Research in Education* 17 (1977), pp. 1–11.

22 S. Olsen, *Juvenile Nation: Youth, emotions and the making of the modern British citizen, 1880–1914* (2014), p. 12.

23 Jennings, *Drink*, pp. 156 and 158–9.

24 Education Committee Minute Book, 29 January 1913.

25 S. Heathorn, *For Home, Country, and Race: Constructing gender, class and Englishness in the elementary school, 1880–1914* (2000), p. 3.

26 *HA*, 26 May 1900, p. 8.

27 Searle, *A New England?*, pp. 281–2.

28   Searle, *A New England?*, p. 38.

29   Jennings, *Drink*, pp. 19–23 and 198–200.

30   R. Duncan, *Pubs and Patriots: The drink crisis in Britain during World War One* (2013), p. 226.

31   Searle, *A New England?*, pp. 7–43.

32   H. Pelling, *Popular Politics and Society in Late Victorian Britain* (1968), pp. 82–100; R. Price, *An Imperial War and the British Working Class: Working-class attitudes and reactions to the Boer War, 1899–1901* (1972).

33   C. Nicolson, 'Edwardian England and the coming of the First World War', in A. O' Day, *The Edwardian Age: Conflict and stability, 1900–1914* (1979), pp. 144–68.

34   Education Committee Minute Book, 27 October 1904.

35   *HA*, 28 October 1893, p. 7.

36   *HA*, 23 June and 20 October 1900, pp. 7 and 2.

37   *HA*, 18 October 1902, p. 5.

38   *HA*, 29 October and 14 May 1904, p. 5 and supp. The report incorrectly gives 'Idle' as the Reformatory.

39   *HA*, 12 May 1900, p. 5.

40   *HA*, 12 May 1900, p. 6; Department of Education, All Schools and Colleges in North Yorkshire, pupil absence in schools in 2017 and 2018, at www.compare-school-performance.service.gov.uk (accessed 5 February 2020).

41   P. Horn, *The Victorian & Edwardian Schoolchild* (2010), p. 151.

42   Higher Grade Board School Logbook, 1895–1899, NYCCRO.

43   *HA*, 25 November 1899, p. 5.

44   B. Simon, *Education and the Labour Movement, 1870–1920* (1965), p. 246.

45   M. Neesam, *Harrogate Grammar School: A centennial history* (2003), pp. 7–19; Education Committee Minute Book, 28 July 1904.

46   Harrogate Municipal Secondary Day School, Governors' Minute Book, 1907–1927, 18 February 1910, NYCCRO.

47   Education Committee Minute Book, 2 June 1904.

48   *HA*, 29 July 1903, p. 4.

49   *HA*, 22 June 1901, p. 5.

50   M. J. Childs, *Labour's Apprentices: Working-Class Lads in Late Victorian and Edwardian England* (1992); J. H. Whitehouse (ed.), *Problems of Boy Life* (1912), p. 3; R. A. Bray, *Boy Labour and Apprenticeship* (1912); A. Freeman, *Boy Life & Labour: The Manufacture of Inefficiency* (1914).

CHAPTER EIGHT

Play and Prayer

H ARROGATE was a resort town which catered for the health and
leisure of the middle and upper classes but how did the men,
women and children of the working class spend such spare time as
they had? It was also a town amply provided with churches and chapels
for both visitors and residents but to what extent did working people
participate in organized religion? This chapter will explore each question
in turn.

Children's play

In the previous chapter I looked at the schooling of the town's
working-class children. It makes sense therefore to begin with their
play. Much of it went unrecorded in the documents used for this study
but a glimpse of everyday childhood games is provided by the memoir
of a former pupil of Grove Road. It charts one boy's morning journey
to school from a street behind Grange Avenue. From there to Skipton
Road was a passage, or snicket, which had three iron posts with smooth
rounded tops – one set slightly in front of the other two and a bit higher.
Here the children did their morning exercises: supporting themselves
on the two lower posts whilst swinging their legs alternatively over the
higher, with the winner the one who managed it the most times. Then,
in the taw-playing (marbles) season they played 'boolings-up' along the
gutter on Skipton Road all the way to the school, whilst at other times

their route across Denmark Street led to a smooth asphalt slope down to Smithy Hill, well-suited for riding down 'little-man' on a single roller skate.[1] Opportunities for play therefore were everywhere, sometimes dangerously so. The pond at Knox quarry was a favourite with the children of New Park. Brothers Herbert and Walter Bonwell had gone there one Sunday morning in 1909 and placed a plank over the water but seven-year-old Herbert fell in, pulling into the water his younger brother who was drowned.[2]

Just as this form of play was reported because tragedy intervened, so more detail is found in the local papers when the spare-time pursuits of boys generally, although not exclusively, brought them into conflict with the town's adults and authorities. Playing games in the street often did, with football, cricket, hockey, roller skating and sledging all at various times getting the participants into trouble. In 1911, for example, four schoolboys were fined costs and cautioned for playing hockey on the highway in Back Gladstone Street, Oatlands. Two of the boys' parents, described as 'respectable' by the police superintendent, apologized to the court but did not think much harm was done in a back street.[3] Also under the Highways Act, three schoolgirls and two boys were charged with racing on, or obstructing, St Mary's Walk when roller skating. For the children it was contended that it did not constitute an offence, to which the chairman of the bench replied that it ought to, adding that he himself had had to get out of the way of boys on skates on West Park. He was obliged, however, to dismiss the case with a warning to children not to be reckless in future.[4] A warning was also issued in February the following year when it was heard that between forty and fifty children had been tobogganing down the hill from the bottom of Commercial Street to Franklin- and King's Roads.[5]

Other activities more definitely fell into the category of juvenile delinquency, which at this time was evolving, it has been argued, as a distinct category of crime and coming to be associated with a stage of life – adolescence – which replaced a child or youth's class or station in life as the perceived cause of misbehaviour.[6] For another historian, disorderly behaviour, or larking about, was an important part of an aggressive and irreverent working-class street culture constituting a form of resistance to authority.[7] However one interprets the development, it did lead to offenders appearing more frequently in court, acquiring criminal records and sometimes being institutionalized for what were often relatively minor offences, however annoying to those on the receiving end.[8] Stone-throwing, vandalism and minor thefts fell into this category, as when, for example, a schoolboy and an errand boy were fined for knocking pears off a tree with stones in the garden of Strawberry Dale Lodge and making off with them.[9] Generally, however, the Harrogate bench, sometimes at the request of the prosecutor, exercised leniency. Bonfire night often caused brushes with the law, as in 1902 when Samson Fox's agent charged a schoolboy with damaging an oak tree on his Grove House estate, a branch of which he had been surprised by the police in the act of removing. He was fined 1s. and costs, which it was hoped would be a lesson, Fox having expressed the view that he would be satisfied 'If the justice of the case would be met by any method.'[10]

Juvenile first offenders, along with others where the offence was deemed to be 'trivial', could now be placed on probation and from 1908 children's and young people's cases were heard in separate courts. In September 1909, two schoolboys aged twelve and fifteen were charged with stealing a silver watch and chain from another schoolboy at the swimming baths on Skipton Road. The older boy had offended before and was now sent to a reformatory until he was eighteen and the younger placed under a probation officer for six months.[11] Another option for offenders was birching. Twelve- and thirteen-year-old brothers from Starbeck received this punishment in May 1904 for stealing two pigeons from a cote on Wordsworth Crescent, which they had then tried to sell to a dealer. Their father requested the punishment as he had had a lot of trouble with them during their mother's recent illness. He had given them 'slight smacks' but no more as 'you have to be careful because of the law'. Sentencing the boys to six strokes of the birch rod, which was to be administered by a police officer in the father's presence, Mr Hunt opined that 'Birching never hurt anybody yet. I can vouch for that personally.' This was not a view, however, shared by the secretary of the Society for the Reform of School Discipline, who was prompted to write to the *Advertiser* pointing out the mischief of subjecting children to 'an indecent and loathsome punishment', which the majority of civilized countries had abolished. Later that same month the younger boy was back in court with three other Starbeck boys for stealing an axe to chop firewood, although his father now claimed he had been very much better since the birching. Reiterating that it had been good for him, Hunt discharged the boys with a warning, as the bench was anxious not to spoil boys' lives.[12]

A great deal of space could be taken up with youthful bad behaviour. This ranged from the boys larking about and being a nuisance in Starbeck library, even barricading the door to keep out the attendant, to the 'young hooligans' who had been observed one Sunday in the Valley Gardens monopolizing chairs at the expense of ladies desiring them and who eventually had given them up on the intervention of two gentlemen whom 'the cringing pair had neither the right nor the courage to refuse'.[13] Clearly many desired to preserve the good order and repute of the town in the face of the threat which the children of some of its inhabitants were perceived to pose to it.

Adult leisure

In Edwardian England the pub and drinking remained the most important leisure pursuits, particularly for men, although by that time both were becoming less central to working-class lives. The number of pubs nationally had peaked in 1869 and drink consumption declined from a mid-1870s high but there were still in 1900 over 100,000 licensed premises and average male beer consumption was twelve pints a week, that of women about half that figure.[14] The largest cluster of pubs in Harrogate was in the Tower Street district, which in 1900 contained the Albert and Belford Hotels and the Coachmakers' Arms, together with the Coach and Horses, Golden Lion and Muckle's Vaults at its junction with West Park. There were a number in the town centre, like Hale and Company's Vaults opposite the Royal Pump Room, the Borough Vaults in Montpellier Gardens, Ebor Hotel in Cambridge Street and Ship Inn off Chapel Street. (62, 63) Another group was at the Skipton Road/ Westmoreland Street junction, consisting of the Black Swan, Spread Eagle and Devonshire Hotels. The opening of some of them had been facilitated by the Beer Act of 1830 which, until its repeal nearly forty years later, allowed anyone to set up a public house just for the sale of beer without the requirement of a licence from the magistrates. Other

62. W. H. Hale and Company Vaults, formerly the Promenade Inn, opposite the Royal Pump Room, *c.*1890. (Courtesy the Walker-Neesam Archive)

beerhouses were the Denmark Tavern at Smithy Hill, the Star Inn at Starbeck, the West End Tavern on Otley Road and the Slip Inn on Cold Bath Road. **(64)**

Overall, however, the town's main working-class districts were served by nothing like the number of pubs to be found both in industrial cities and market towns. New Park residents had the Little Wonder at the junction of Ripon- and Skipton Roads and those of Starbeck the Harrogate Hotel and the Prince of Wales in addition to the Star. Repeated efforts to provide those at Oatlands with a public house all failed, despite supportive evidence from locals, offers to transfer the licence from the Coachmakers' Arms and claims that the lack of one had driven drinking

63. The Ship Inn, an early nineteenth-century public house off Chapel Street, photographed here decorated probably for the Queen's Golden Jubilee of 1887. It later traded as the Cock and Castle and was demolished for retail development. (Used with permission from Harrogate Library, North Yorkshire County Council.)

underground into shebeens and illegal drinking clubs. On that occasion it was also despite assurances that the proposed premises would be a hotel with separate entrances for the better class of visitor and the working class.

In addition to refusing a licence to those premises, which were at Tewit Well Road, another application for a licence at Oatlands Mount was also turned down. One, however, was granted to the Kursaal.[15] Clearly the licensing magistrates had a view of the type of premises which they considered desirable. Unsurprisingly then they took advantage of legislation in 1904 which permitted them to close pubs deemed to be no longer required, or whose premises were unsuitable, providing

64.   The Denmark Tavern, the local pub of the district. It was
demolished in the post-World War Two clearance of the area.
(Courtesy the Walker-Neesam Archive)

compensation was paid to the owner and tenant. In this way, the
Coachmakers' Arms, the Spread Eagle and the Albert Hotel were closed
in 1906, 1907 and 1910. These were all basic local pubs, with characteristic
interiors. The Coachmakers' Arms had a tap room, snug and kitchen, in
which customers also sometimes drank; the Spread Eagle had a vaults,
snug and smoke room.

The Albert, the only one of the three with a full licence, also had a
club room which accommodated a society of seventy men who met there
every Monday. In ways like this pubs acted as vital social spaces for
working men. A charge of 1903 against its landlord for selling drink to
a drunken person gives us a glimpse of its working-class male clientele,
other than the woman coming in for a small bottle of whisky and a
packet of Woodbine cigarettes, whose drunken behaviour had occasioned

the prosecution. They comprised a barber's assistant, painter, drayman, joiner and out porter. Having picked up somebody's beer, the woman had then tried to sing.[16] Whilst this may not have been welcome on this occasion, music was another entertainment on offer at pubs, although it, along with dancing, now required a licence when the Corporation adopted the relevant powers in 1898. Pubs and hotels alike were granted them, although renewal could also be refused, as it was to the Belford Hotel in 1901 after the police objected.[17] Another important function at the Albert was that from five to fifteen men went there every day for their dinners. Pubs in Tower Street, as we saw, also provided accommodation for working men and the Spread Eagle similarly let rooms to the servants of visitors at the Granby and other hotels.[18]

Just as their pubs attracted the attentions of the police, so did working-class drunkenness. Of 125 individuals prosecuted for this in Harrogate in 1900 and 139 in 1905, which were reported in the local paper, just over half were described as labourers, followed by those in the building trades, who made up just over one in ten. Not a single railwayman was reported, which may have been due to the threat of dismissal which this posed. Prosecutions of lower middle- or middle-class men were rare: only six in the former year and seven in the latter. Those prosecuted were mostly men, with just twenty-four women in 1900 and sixteen in 1905, whose occupations where given were charwoman, servant, laundress and in one case musician. Of those drunks, nearly a third in 1900 and over a fifth in 1905 were described as of no fixed abode. They attracted the particular notice of the police, as the 1903 licensing sessions for example heard: 'wayfarers', in the form of professional beggars, who then spent their donations on drink, accounted for a number of convictions.[19] In September 1909, Elizabeth Blythe, 'a Scotch harvest woman' was arrested for being drunk and disorderly when singing and dancing in the street. She explained that she had been harvesting, had come fifteen miles that day and claimed that it was impossible that she was drunk as 'the Scotch can take a lot of drink'. Drunken women such as her were often reported humorously and this remark, according to the *Advertiser*, was met with laughter. She was let go on promising to leave town.[20]

Some of those in court were clearly dependent on alcohol. One was a labourer of New Park, arrested in June 1909 for being drunk and disorderly in John Street, whose mother evidenced that although sometimes 'steady', he was 'perfectly crazed' when he gave way to drink, posed a danger to himself and others and had once attempted suicide. Inspector Jackson, for the police, similarly told the bench that he had known him for sixteen or seventeen years, that he would drink for up to six months at a time, when he was a 'perfect lunatic', with twenty-four convictions for drunkenness since 1892. He was committed to the inebriates' reformatory at Cattal, near York, under the provisions of the 1898 Inebriates Act which permitted compulsory detention, an outcome which he expressed his willingness to undergo.[21]

Over the Edwardian years, however, total proceedings and convictions for drunkenness declined in Harrogate, from around 250 annually to less than half that total in 1914, except for short-lived rises to 1908 and from 1909 to 1911.[22] Drunkenness had always been linked to prosperity historically and the period was one where the cost of living was rising and under- and unemployment were common. But they also reflect changes in working-class behaviour. Although alcohol consumption was still high, the long-term trend was downwards. Despite the recent setbacks, working-class living standards had been improving since the 1860s, showing men and women that a better life, to however limited an extent, was now possible – a more comfortably furnished home, better clothes, a wider variety of foods. Money could be spent on those things rather than on the immediate pleasures of drinking. This was linked to the important contemporary ideal of respectability, of maintaining certain standards of behaviour, which was widely held among working-class people, and of which drunkenness clearly formed no part.[23]

Moderate drinking, however, was acceptable to the majority and found expression in the foundation of working men's clubs. Although they were never allowed a pub, the men of Oatlands did establish for themselves a club. The Oatlands Mount Working Men's Club and Institute was inaugurated in November 1899 with just sixteen men but within just over a year this had risen to seventy financial and eleven honorary members. The club had a library stocked with newspapers and periodicals and its respectability is made clear by the general meeting, which noted its good discipline and the lack of complaints about members' behaviour. A cricket club was started in 1904 and in December of the following year new premises were opened in Spring Terrace, opposite the original club in Hookstone Road, with bar, smoke room, concert, billiard- and games rooms.[24] From 1902 clubs selling alcohol were required to register with the licensing magistrates. By 1910 there were twelve in the town, of which those for working men included others at Starbeck and High Harrogate and the Trades and Labour Club, although the 348 members of the largest, the Conservative Club, and those of the Catholic Club may have included them.[25]

For others, in contrast, drinking and respectability were incompatible and other clubs were run on teetotal lines. One was the New Park Institute, inaugurated in March 1901, explicitly aiming for the 'men who formerly frequented the public house'. It opened new premises with an adult school on Ripon Road in April 1906, which included a large lecture hall, billiard- and reading rooms. It was financed with money loaned interest-free by J. S. Rowntree of the York confectionery family, who lived in Harrogate. It offered cricket and football, games, bible- and first aid classes and a weekly sewing meeting for members' wives and other interested women. But it did not prosper, closing in 1914, despite Rowntree's continuing financial support, a failure which a correspondent to the *Advertiser* attributed to the expense and size of the building, the monotony of its offering (although it was licensed for music and dancing) and the lack of working-class involvement in its management.[26] Social clubs run on similar lines were established at Oatlands, Starbeck, High Harrogate and Bilton Grange, with middle-class and church support. That at Oatlands in 1903 was under the auspices of several 'ladies and gentlemen' providing rooms for reading, billiards and games and a café. The problems which could be raised by such middle-class patronage were referred to explicitly by Councillor Marshall at its opening, when he hoped that the local inhabitants would not consider that its promoters held themselves superior, as 'all men who worked were "working men"'.[27] Less self-aware perhaps was the chairman of the committee of the Bilton Grange Social Club who on the opening of its premises in November 1910 noted the 'great social work that is going on in the town, and achieving much good amongst the artisan classes'.[28]

In addition to pubs and clubs, there was now a widening range of leisure pursuits, partly based in the growth of working-class free time, as working hours declined and the Saturday half-holiday became widespread, and which offered alternative ways of spending whatever spare cash might be available. Organized sports flourished, as the local papers show in considerable detail, although it is not possible from these reports alone to gauge the extent of working-class participation or spectating and some sports, like tennis or golf, were clearly middle-class pursuits. Rugby and cricket clubs had been formed at the beginning of the 1870s, although cricket had been played earlier. At the time of the 'Great Split' in rugby in 1895 over the issue of payment of players which led to the formation of the future Rugby League, Harrogate retained its amateur status, whilst cricket had both professional and amateur players. The clubs enjoyed middle-class, and in the case of cricket, aristocratic patronage.

Association football similarly was played between teams from private schools towards the end of the century but in 1899 a Harrogate District League was formed. Starbeck had two teams, Starbeck AFC and St Andrew's. Starbeck's star player was Donald Bell, who was an assistant master at the local council school and went on play professionally. There was also a Wharfedale League, with Harrogate teams from the YMCA, St Mark's, West Park and New Park. Local histories provide limited detail on the backgrounds of players or supporters, although the location of some teams does suggest a more working-class following.[29] This is certainly the conclusion of a general history of the game, that by 1914 playing and watching had become a widespread activity among working men and boys, 'one of those things which working men did'.[30]

In addition to those three major sports, there were clubs for bowling, cycling, curling, angling, shooting, lacrosse and cross-country running, although once again it is not always possible to determine the extent of working-class participation. Certainly, proletarian Starbeck did have a bowling club. Cycling was predominantly a middle- and lower middle-class pursuit but the cost of a bicycle was within the reach of better-off working men and women through hire purchase.[31] Swimming was possible at the Corporation baths at Starbeck and Skipton Road, although some preferred a free and unsupervised alternative, like the large numbers of men and boys reported bathing in the Oak Beck above the electricity works in the summer of 1911.[32] There were roller skating rinks on Dragon Road and Myrtle Road, although the former, which had opened in May 1909, was within a year running at a loss, blaming a decline of interest in the pastime.[33]

Accompanying enthusiasm for sport was an equal fondness for gambling on the horses or football, which flourished from the later nineteenth century, facilitated by the use of the electric telegraph for the provision of results and the development of a sporting press. Both nationally and in Harrogate it attracted opposition, a National Anti-Gambling League being formed in 1890 and the borough bench dealing with many cases throughout the Edwardian period.[34] Street bookmaking was variously carried on in Station Parade or around the station itself, in the Market Place, Cambridge Street, School Court and Devonshire Place or in the yards of pubs like the Golden Lion at the end of Tower Street. In one case at least more permanent premises were used, by Joseph Gibson, a hairdresser in Oxford Street. The watching police that June of 1908 witnessed 148 visits on one day and 169 another, almost all men, before entering in plain clothes and placing bets themselves. A total of 553 betting slips were found from three days, in amounts ranging from 6d. to £8.[35] In addition to such organized betting, informal gambling also flourished, as by the two newsvendors and a waiter playing 'banker' on top of an upturned dustbin at the back of the Central Arcade or the workmen playing pitch and toss in the fields between the County football ground and Dragon Junction, all in May 1911.[36]

Other 'hobbies' such as gardening, which did not attract opposition, were also popular. They provided individual satisfactions but competition was also important, shown, for example, in the popularity of shows for cage birds, cats and dogs, although unfortunately there are no details of local members.[37] Hobbies like these would require some financial outlay, which would put them beyond the reach of the poorest. This was true also of music-making, which enjoyed huge popularity. Contemporaries referred to the brass band as the 'working man's orchestra' and in the words of a modern study of popular music represented 'one of the most remarkable working-class cultural achievements in European history'.[38] There were several local bands, like the Starbeck Brass Band, Harrogate Borough and Harrogate Temperance Bands and a Salvation Army Band, performing at events in the town and on the Stray or in the Valley

Gardens. The first annual general meeting of the Starbeck Band in October 1905, which attracted a 'large company', heard an inventory including twenty-three instruments and drums and twenty-one uniforms and noted a payment from the Amalgamated Society of Railway Servants for 'services on Sunday'. Similarly, in March 1911 the Independent Labour Party was given permission to use the bandstand in Bogs Field the following August, subject to making 'satisfactory arrangements' with the Borough and Temperance Bands.[39] Music in public open spaces and in the streets was accessible to the town's working people and enjoyed by them, as we saw with the pierrots and organ grinders. Making music at home was also popular, with the ownership of pianos, for example, becoming common amongst better-off working families.[40]

Some of the musical entertainment was clearly aimed at the visitors to the spa, like the mid-morning recitals by the Municipal Orchestra in the Winter Gardens for drinkers at the Pump Room. Evening recitals at the Kursaal were attended in full evening dress, 'not a working man's place', as we heard earlier.[41] The Empire Music Hall offered more popular entertainment, as in August 1913 for example, with 'Harrogate's favourite comedians Karr and Kooney' and the Cairo Duo, among other acts on the bill. In fact, light music dominated at the Kursaal and the Opera House similarly was offering that August *The Dancing Mistress*, a 'charming musical comedy'.[42] To the music hall was added the cinema in these years. St James's Hall was used to show films, a programme for example for May 1907 included *Son's Revenge, Married in Haste, I've Lost My Eyeglass* and *Dog Detective*, with two performances daily at 3 and 8 p.m. So too was the Kursaal and by 1913 the Picture House in Cambridge Street was showing *The Orphan*, 'a beautiful story full of interest' and *The Suspect*, 'a stirring picture of a capture of a band of robbers' in its programme. The cost was 1s. in the circle and 6d. in the pit, with children under twelve half price.[43] The cinema was especially attractive to women and children; the latter on Saturday afternoons made up a large proportion of total attendees in a survey of those in Leeds that year.[44] Some Harrogate children resorted to theft to make it possible. Two schoolboys in February 1913 used the proceeds of several to go to the 'pictures' and an eleven-year-old girl from Oatlands, 'out of control' according to the newspaper headline, stole from a neighbour, went down to Leeds and visited a picture house there. She was returned home by the police and later sent to St Mary's Home at Leeds.[45]

Popular with children and adults alike were the visiting events, some of which were noted in the previous chapter. One of the most spectacular was Buffalo Bill's Wild West Show and Congress of Rough Riders of the World, whose 800 members, including 100 'American Indians' and 500 horses required three trains to bring them in October 1904 on 'Positively Its Last Visit to Great Britain'. To see attractions including the Battle of the Little Big Horn cost between 1s. and 4s., with children half price except in the cheapest seats.[46] Those prices would have been beyond the incomes of many of Harrogate's working-class families but the parade itself, like many amusements, was free. So also were the informal leisure pursuits which women, particularly married women with limited time and means, might enjoy, such as doorstep gossip, socializing with friends and family, or visiting other houses.[47] The world of leisure was gendered as much as it was divided by class, women's enjoyment of it more limited than that of men or their children.

Prayer

Organized religion also flourished in the late Victorian and Edwardian years. Harrogate had a wide range of churches and chapels which between them offered not only worship and the celebration of life's rituals of baptism, marriage and death, but also social and indeed leisure pursuits. Although some of this was more clearly aimed at middle-class visitors and residents, there was considerable effort made to meet the religious needs of the town's working-class and particularly of their children.

Between 1850 and the First World War, the Anglicans constructed a further seven churches to add to Christ Church at High- and St Mary's at Low Harrogate. The centre of the town was served by St Peter's from 1870–71, whilst outer districts were provided with St John's at Bilton in 1857, All Saints at Harlow Hill in 1871 and St Andrew's at Starbeck in 1888 (rebuilt in 1909–10). To these were added St Luke's on Walker Road in 1898, St Mark's on Leeds Road in 1904 and St Wilfrid's on Duchy Road from 1908. Nonconformity had an even greater presence in the town. In the central area imposing new buildings were erected in 1862

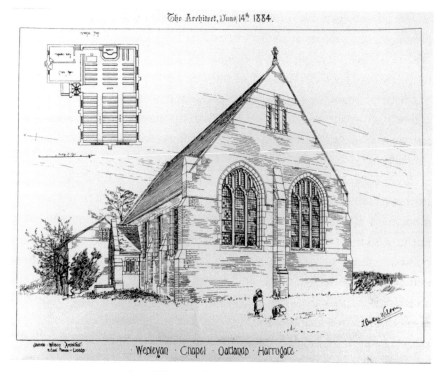

The Architect, June 14th 1884.

Wesleyan · Chapel · Oatlands · Harrogate ·

65. The new Wesleyan Chapel at Oatlands. (Reproduced from The Architect, 14 June 1884.)

by the Wesleyans in Chapel Street and the Congregationalists on West Park, the United Methodists in 1865 on Station Parade, the Primitive Methodists at Mount Parade in 1872, the Baptists on Victoria Avenue in 1883 and, also there, the Presbyterians St Paul's in 1885. There were in addition in more purely residential areas Trinity Wesleyan at West Park in 1879, from which an offshoot was a chapel at Oatlands, **(65)** a new Methodist Chapel on Skipton Road, known as the Bar Chapel, in 1889, Grove Road Methodist in 1896 and in 1900 a new Primitive Methodist Chapel on Dragon Parade. Starbeck had both Primitive and Wesleyan Methodist Chapels and New Park a Wesleyan Chapel. The Victoria Park Methodists established a chapel in 1903 at Harlow Hill and the Congregationalists a church at Bilton Grange three years later. Finally, the Quakers had built a meeting house in Chapel Street in 1854, the Roman Catholics a permanent church of St Robert's in 1873, and a Salvation Army Citadel was opened in Chapel Street in 1899

Taken together, they represented a massive investment in religious provision, providing accommodation for thousands of worshippers. Wesley Chapel had seating for nearly 1,000 and, to take just a few further examples from those most recently built, the new St Andrew's at Starbeck had space for 650, the Dragon Parade chapel seating for around 550, whilst among smaller premises the Bar Chapel provided seating for 220 on the ground floor plus 44 in a gallery and that at Harlow Hill similarly for around 200 people.[48] **(66, 67)**

The question is to what extent was this accommodation taken up by the town's working-class citizens. Looking first at the Church of England, other than St Andrew's and to some extent St Luke's, the churches were not in working-class districts. Their registers of marriages and baptisms do show, however, that the town's working-class used them for those rituals at least. But the Church certainly did reach out to them, as the location of the Starbeck church shows. Similarly, St John's at Bilton had opened a Mission Church and Sunday School at New Park in 1884 and Christ Church had also opened a Mission Hall at Smithy Hill in 1883, which was taken over from 1898 by St Luke's. St Peter's opened another mission room in Tower Street and Christ Church again built one in 1909 for the population of the Regents district in Grove Park Terrace.[49]

66.   Early nineteenth-century workers' cottages in Skipton Road, with Bar Chapel to right. Photographed in 2018. (Author's photograph)

67.   Bar Chapel, Skipton Road, opened in 1889; here in a modern photograph of 2018. (Courtesy Bilton Area Methodist Church)

Nonconformity also drew its strength from Harrogate's middle and lower middle classes. Prominent members at various times of Victoria Park United Methodists included one of its founders, three-times mayor Richard Ellis, who donated the site on which the church was built, fellow aldermen and councillors and a Lord Mayor of Leeds, Joseph Hepworth of the ready-made clothing business, who lived then in Harrogate. The lists of officials and members of the Congregational Church on West Park show that most of their addresses were in middle-class streets. The occupations of the trustees for Grove Road Methodist were almost all middle- or lower middle class. Those of Oatlands Wesleyan Methodists similarly included several gentlemen, a bank manager and two insurance brokers but there were also a brickmaker's foreman, gardener and painter.[50]

Nonconformity did also reach out to the working class. The 'migratory' congregation of Wesley Chapel was due to the number of visitors but also to the 'young people in situations who move on'. The Pastor of West Park Congregational Church, addressing the congregation in 1911, called their attention to the young people and 'the Poor of our town' and the need to 'engage in a serious and strenuous effort to attract the non-Church goers among them'. Grove Road made an impressive effort through its Brotherhood to reach out to working men, their wives and sisters. Established in 1904, by March 1906 over 600 men were then enrolled from the immediate working-class streets, not a few of whom, it was said, had never been in a church since they married. It ran a Holiday Fund and a Sick and Needy Fund, which had sent one member to a convalescent home at Southport for three weeks. That July the Brotherhood held a gathering on the Stray, following a procession from Grove Road which with members and the wider public made up a congregation of at least 1,500 people. There was another Brotherhood at Starbeck, holding, for example, an open meeting with talks and a singing recital at the school in February 1910.[51]

Another initiative was the nondenominational Harrogate Town Mission. Celebrating its 32nd anniversary in 1905 the Revd Kirkup noted how they had in their midst 'the drink curse, the gambling fever, and in addition they had a great mass of religious indifference'. As its name suggests it carried out missionary work to people's homes and at outdoor meetings as well as at its mission, first in Tower Street and, from 1889, on Mayfield Grove, 'in the centre of an industrial population'. It also reached out to specific groups of workers: to cabmen, bath-chairmen and out porters with a tea and 'entertainment' in 1903; or in 1913 providing on Wednesday, their free evening, an extra meeting to servant girls who had converted.[52] The Railway Mission at Starbeck, part of an international movement, had been started by the Honourable Mrs Jones in the waiting room at the station in 1886 and then used other temporary premises until the opening of a new mission in Forest Avenue in 1910.[53] Reaching out to the young were the YMCA and the YWCA. At the latter's annual meeting in 1905 it was noted that 124 visitors had used its accommodation, including in the summer 'a number of weary working girls … in sore need of rest and bracing air' and that there were nineteen boarders 'engaged in business during the day'. During the summer season they had been busy contacting girls and young women new to the town and introducing then to 'helpful companions'. They had also visited those whose work prevented them from attending classes, sought to rescue 'unwary ones from perilous positions' and made special efforts 'to reach the girls who stroll about on Sunday evening' on the Stray front.[54]

The YWCA also had a junior branch for girls under sixteen and it was towards children that the churches collectively made their greatest effort. Most of the town's children must have attended Sunday school. All churches ran them. St Luke's, for example, offered Sunday schools for infants and for junior and senior boys and girls, plus a Sunday School bible class, young men and youths' bible classes, a 'children of the congregation class' and a choir.[55] Similarly Trinity Wesleyan ran several classes for nearly a hundred children each week, as well as offering a juvenile missionary association and a junior branch of the Girls' League.[56] The schools offered not only religious instruction, which could be conveyed in story and song, but a variety of entertainments like lantern slides and concerts and the special attraction of the annual trip: 120 going to Bridlington from the Congregational Church in 1901 or 142 from Trinity in June 1906 by train to Ripon and then by motor bus to Fountains Abbey, in typical outings.

Closely linked to the Sunday schools was the Band of Hope, which sought to encourage children along the path of abstinence from alcoholic drink. Most, if not all, churches seemed to have had a branch. Oatlands Methodist had 'a particularly active one', according to its history.[57] A surviving admission book to that of Trinity Wesleyan Church shows children coming from a wide area on the west side of the town, often from the same street and brothers and sisters together, like the Fearnside, Fairley, Wilkes and Holgate siblings, all living in West Cliffe Terrace when joining in 1899.[58] In April 1903 the conference of the Yorkshire Band of Hope Union was held in Harrogate, as part of which the Harrogate Temperance Union gave an entertainment to 400 children at the Friendly Societies' Hall. This included 'a grand cinematograph exhibition' with photographs of war heroes, statesmen and the King and Queen plus some comic views. A representative of the District Band of Hope also gave the children a talk on how many leading doctors, nurses and ministers were abstainers and urged them 'to stick to their pledge'. The same plea was made by Councillor Abbott to children of the Harrogate Town Mission Band of Hope, confessing to them that he had tried both drink and temperance and he was quite convinced that the latter was safest and in the long run paid the best. The singing which followed included a solo rendition of 'No Mother at Home' by Miss Silk.[59]

Sport and recreation were also increasingly part of church life, as we saw with football teams. The Young Men's Club at the Congregational Church, formed in 1911, could enjoy cricket, boxing and self-defence as well as chess, draughts, dominoes and a reading circle. The Baptist Church had cricket and recreation clubs. Some also set up branches of the youth organizations which had been initiated in the later nineteenth century in the context of those anxieties about the nation's future and the emergence of a perceived problem of adolescence.[60] Both Christ Church and St Luke's, for example, had companies of the Church Lads' Brigade, which with the battalions and regiments into which they were formed indicates its more militarized aspect than the nonconformist-based Boys' Brigades, whose founder insisted upon adherence to the movement's religious aims. The largest of the three was the scout movement. Baden Powell's avowed purpose in forming it was 'to train [the] boys to be more efficient and characterful citizens', through a combination of public-school manliness and woodcraft naturalism. Its UK membership in 1913 of over 150,000 was more than that of the other two organizations combined and several troops were set up in Harrogate, including one at St Luke's Mission Room. Although the establishment of a troop there does suggest a desire to bring into the movement working-class boys, their historian has characterized its appeal as rather to the lower middle-class, with some of the upper working class, rather than to the whole working class.[61]

Measured by buildings, accommodation for worshippers and activity, there would seem to be little obvious evidence in this period of a decline of religious observance. Nevertheless, the signs are there, most obviously the 'great mass of religious indifference' perceived by the Revd Kirkup. Similarly, the Pastor of West Park Congregational, voicing the need to reach out to non-church goers among the poor, had done so after noting that the church was 'not so strong numerically as we should be'. Surviving details of membership show that the accommodation offered was never wholly taken up. That of the Wesley Chapel was about 300 in this period but the chapel itself could seat nearly 1,000, although of course more than members would have worshipped, especially during the season. Some experienced financial difficulty, like Oatlands Methodist Church, due to the inadequacy of the regular collections from ordinary working-class people. The Baptist Church had to issue several special appeals to members in order to end the year free of debt.[62] Although two new Anglican churches were built after 1900 and another two rebuilt, in the case of St Mary's on a new site, and a second Catholic church of St Aelred opened at Starbeck, there was little Nonconformist development. Whilst the Methodist Chapel at Harlow Hill survived, when a Wesleyan Mission Room was set up at Stonefall Park, it proved to be a short-lived venture. Established in 1903 in a developing district, it was abandoned two years later, having remained in temporary premises. As the committee noted, they had felt it impossible to continue with their work there, observing that 'the many who go nowhere ... will not go to a cottage room for services'.[63] As the evidence from Oatlands and other chapels and missions show, working-class people did worship, particularly in a Nonconformist chapel, but, as S. J. D. Green also concluded in his detailed study of three West Riding communities, the greater part of them did not engage with organized religion.[64]

The greatest effort and their biggest impact were on children. Most in this way had some connection with a church or chapel. As Green noted of Sunday schools, 'very few can have passed through life without some exposure to the ways and word of Christian witness'. Yet he also felt that as a result of this experience only a fraction of them became regular worshippers.[65] Similarly, the Band of Hope provided entertainment for children but produced relatively few lifelong abstainers, although they had at least been exposed to the ideal of a life without drink and to the view that drink was a problem.[66] A similar failure to recruit new members met social, sporting and recreational efforts, in that they tended either to confirm the existing loyalties of those whose social life was centred on church or chapel or, like Sunday school, to produce no lasting commitment.[67] They were also competing with that world of organized secular leisure surveyed above.

In the end one cannot fail to be impressed by the scale of religious provision in late Victorian and Edwardian Harrogate and the amount and range of activities they pursued. They may not have involved most working-class people beyond childhood, other than at baptisms, weddings and funerals, but they were an important presence in the life of the town, of which all would have been aware.

Notes to Chapter 8: Play and Prayer

1   Steele, *Grove Road.*

2   *HA*, 23 October 1909, p. 5.

3   *HA*, 20 May 1911, p. 6.

4   *HA*, 3 June 1911, p. 6.

5   *HA*, 10 February 1912, p. 6.

6   J. R. Gillis, 'The evolution of juvenile delinquency in England, 1890–1914', *Past and Present*, 67 (1975), pp. 96–126.

7   S. Humphries, *Hooligans or Rebels? An oral history of working-class childhood and youth, 1889–1939* (1981), pp. 121–49.

8   B. Godfrey *et al.*, *Young Criminal Lives: Life courses and life chances from 1850* (2017), pp. 64–6.

9   *HA*, 21 September 1901, p. 2.

10 *HA*, 15 November 1902, supp.

11 *HA*, 11 September 1909, p. 6.

12 *HA*, 7 and 14 May, p. 5 and 28 May 1904, p. 3.

13 *HA*, 26 March 1904, p. 3 and 28 May 1910, p. 2.

14 Jennings, *Drink*, pp. 19–20 and 48–9.

15 *HA*, 24 August 1901, p. 7 and 11 February 1903, pp. 4–5.

16 *HA*, 2 September 1903, p. 4.

17 *HA*, 8 January 1898, p. 7 and 24 August 1901, p. 7.

18 *HA*, 10 March and 2 June 1906, pp. 5 and 6; 9 February and 9 March 1907, p. 6; 1 June 1907, p. 2; and 12 March 1910, p. 6.

19 *HH*, 11 February 1903, pp. 4–5.

20 *HA*, 4 September 1909, p. 6; P. Jennings, 'Policing drunkenness in England and Wales from the late eighteenth century to the First World War', *The Social History of Alcohol and Drugs*, 26:1 (2012), pp. 69–92.

21 *HA*, 5 June 1909, p. 6; Jennings, *Drink*, pp. 164–5.

22 Based on figures given to the licensing, or Brewster, sessions as they were called. Strictly speaking these were for offences against the intoxicating liquor laws generally but most would be for drunkenness.

23 Jennings, *Drink*, pp. 20–1 and 134

24 *HA*, 19 January 1901, p. 4; 21 January 1903, p. 6; and 21 January and 16 December 1905, pp. 2 and 5.

25 *HA*, 12 February 1910, p. 6.

26 *HA*, 21 January 1903, p. 4; 7 April 1906, p. 4; and 21 February 1914, p. 5.

27 *HA*, 29 April 1903, p. 4.

28 *HA*, 12 November 1910, p. 4; Centenary History of Bilton Social Club, 1910–2010 (2009).

29 P. Harrison, *The History of Harrogate Town Football Club: Highlights from a bygone era* (2004), pp. 11–12 and *The Official History of Harrogate Town Football Club* (2010), p. 7; B. Forshaw, *A History of Harrogate Rugby Club, 1871–2011* (2011); G. L. Greaves, *Over the Summers Again: A history of Harrogate cricket club* (1976); Abbott, *Spirit of Starbeck*, p. 88.

30 T. Mason, *Association Football & English Society, 1863–1915* (1980), p. 222.

31 D. Rubinstein, 'Cycling in the 1890s', *Victorian Studies*, 21:1 (1977), pp. 47–71.

32 Borough of Harrogate Lighting Committee Minutes, 31 July 1911.

33 *HA*, 15 May 1909, p. 7 and 16 July 1910, p. 6.

34 M. Clapson, *'A Bit of a Flutter': Popular gambling and English society c. 1823–1961* (1992), pp. 27–31.

35 *HA*, 7 July 1908, p. 6.

36 *HA*, 6 and 20 May 1911, p. 6

37 R. McKibbin, 'Work and Hobbies in Britain, 1880–1950' in J. Winter (ed.) *The Working Class in Modern British History: Essays in honour of Henry Pelling* (1983), pp. 139–66; *HA*, 15 July, 12 and 19 August 1905, p. 5.

38 Russell, *Popular Music*, pp. 162–98.

39 Stray etc., Committee Minutes, 30 March and 27 July 1908 and 27 March 1911; *HA*, 21 October 1905, p. 5.

40 Russell, *Popular Music*, pp. 139–40.

41 Neesam, *Music*, p. 60.

42 *HA*, 9 August 1913, p. 8.

43 *HA*, 18 May 1907, p. 3 and 9 August 1913, p. 8.

44 *Yorkshire Observer*, 9 December 1913.

45 *HA*, 22 February 1913, p. 6 and 12 and 26 July 1913, pp. 3 and 6.

46 *HA*, 8 October 1904, p. 6.

47 C. Langhamer, *Women's Leisure in England, 1920–60* (2000), pp. 171–2.

48 H. S. Kitchen and T. E. Dawson, *Wesley Chapel Harrogate, 1862–1962* (1962); C. C. Greenwood, *The Story of St Andrew's Church, Starbeck, 1910–1935* (1935); A. L. Wigley, *Dragon Parade Methodist Church, 1900–1950: Souvenir handbook of the Jubilee celebrations* (1950); Anon, *The Bar Methodist Church Harrogate, Jubilee Handbook, 1889–1939* (1939); Anon, *Harlow Hill Methodist Church, 1903–1978: 75th Anniversary* (1978).

49 Barnes, *Bilton with Harrogate*, p. 65; Canon Guy, *A Memento of 23 Years Work in Christ Church, Harrogate, 1904–1926* (1926).

50 T. Sunderland, *United Methodist Church Victorian Park Harrogate: Jubilee, 1865–1913* (1913); Harrogate Congregational Church, Manuals, 1902–1912; Anon, *'Fifty years': The handbook of the Jubilee celebrations of the Grove Road Methodist Church 1946* (1946); Oatlands Wesleyan Methodist Chapel Trustees Minutes, 1883–1949, 17 May 1906, NYCCRO.

51 *HA*, 31 March and 7 July 1906, pp. 3 and 5; and 5 February 1910, p. 3.

52 Anon, *Harrogate Town Mission Mayfield Grove Jubilee Souvenir, 1872–1922* (1922); Anon, *Evangelical Free Church Harrogate Centenary, 1872–1972* (1922); *HA*, 7 October 1905, p. 6.

53 Anon, *Starbeck Mission (formerly Railway Mission) Forest Avenue, 1886–1986 Centenary* (1986); *HA*, 15 April 1905, p. 2.

54 *HA*, 25 March 1905, p. 2.

55 *HA*, 27 January 1912, p. 2.

56 Anon, *Trinity Wesleyan Church Harrogate Jubilee, 1879–1929* (1929).

57 A. Kellett, *The Oatlands Story, 1883–1983: A brief history of Oatlands Methodist Church* (1983).

58 Wesleyan-Methodist Band of Hope Admission Book, 1899–1910, NYCCRO.

59 *HA*, 1 April 1903, p. 4 and 18 November 1905, p. 6.

60 J. Springhall, *Youth, Empire and Society: British Youth Movements, 1883–1940* (1977), pp. 13–18.

61 Springhall, *Youth, passim*; *HA*, 4 June 1910, p. 6.

62 *The Oatlands Story*; Harrogate Baptist Church: Minute Books of Committee Meetings and Church Meetings, 1876–1928, 1906, 1908 and 1910, NYCCRO.

63 Stonefall Park Wesleyan Mission Room Minute Book, NYCCRO.

64 S. J. D. Green, *Religion in the Age of Decline: Organisation and experience in industrial Yorkshire, 1870–1920* (1996), pp. 201–3.

65 Green, *Religion*, pp. 211–12.

66 Jennings, *Drink*, p. 159.

67 H. McLeod, *Religion and Society in England, 1850–1914* (1996), pp. 89–90.

Conclusion

T HE WORKING CLASS of Edwardian Harrogate may have been invisible to visitors and not a few residents but the elegant spa town they all enjoyed depended upon their labour. Its composition naturally reflected the town's interlinked economy of health and leisure resort, residential hub and retail centre. Crucial to it was service of one kind or another: in private houses, schools and institutions; in hotels and boarding houses; in laundry work; in the parks, gardens and spa facilities; and in the great variety of shops. Crucial also was its contribution to the town's infrastructure: in the building trades; in transport of all kinds; in services like gas, electricity and water; in delivering the post; and keeping the streets free of those who threatened its elegance and desirability.

This employment profile brought with it certain key characteristics. First was the importance of women in the workforce, above all as providers of services. Second was the impact of seasonality. The resort's 'season' meant that for many, despite efforts to extend its duration, work was available for only a few months of the year. This applied equally to the seasonality of the weather which governed the work of builders, gardeners or those in the clothing trades. More broadly, the town was inevitably part of the wider economy. Whilst the resort continued to prosper from those with the wealth and time to enjoy it, its building workers who suffered the general downturn in their trade and all working people who felt the impact of a rising cost of living experienced more difficult times. A further characteristic was the high proportion of incomers to the town.

This was true of the middle-class retirees and commuting businessmen but it was true also of its working class. This might have implied that the working class was relatively rootless, except that they quickly seem to have settled and a far higher number of their children were born there, attended school and continued to live and work in the town.

Those employments brought with them differences of status among workers. Domestic servants suffered the scorn of some of their fellow workers as 'skivvies'; a shop assistant in a smart James Street establishment might see herself both above her and her fellow assistant in a corner shop; or the skilled carpenter or engine driver might hold himself superior to the builder's labourer or porter at the station. Those working men whose wives let part of the family home to visitors as apartments might similarly see themselves as in business, if in a small way. And many more might look down on the reputedly rough folk who lived in Tower- or Denmark Streets and still more on the beggars and the homeless who made their way to the town. There were other divisions, as when English hotel workers resented the presence of Europeans or, more commonly, between men and women in their family relationships or over the inequalities of their pay and conditions in the same employments.

All those differences have been acknowledged in this study but it has been asserted that in the end their common experiences mattered more and that together they did indeed constitute a working-class community. They lived in the same neighbourhoods, as I showed of Denmark Street that was held to be such a low locality but which in fact was home to a range of working families. Starbeck railwaymen or gas workers at New Park were located close to their work, but those neighbourhoods too were home to a variety of workers. Those working lives may have differed, not least in levels of pay, but in the end this mattered less than the common threats of under- and unemployment, the costs of raising a young family, sickness, old age and death. Working lives also shared the fact that they were hard, whether on a building site or an engine footplate, in the damp and heat of a commercial laundry, or through the long and busy hours serving in home, school or shop.

Their family lives too displayed shared features. They married mostly within the working class and at a younger age than middle-class couples. They went on to have more children than those couples, albeit fewer than their parents and grandparents had done. Although the conjugal family was the norm, the single parent was common, whether widowed or deserted into that situation. Many households also included other relatives and commonly a lodger and sometimes relatives lived close by. They also shared leisure pursuits and a general absence, except as children, from places of worship other than to be baptised, married or buried. In the schooling of their children above all was their working-class position clear. It was in state schools, providing for the great majority an education geared for girls towards the outcomes of eventual home and family and for boys of manual labour. Only for a tiny minority was a selective route offered through secondary education to white-collar employment, typically as a clerk or teacher.

If the town depended upon them, so too from August 1914 did the country. Pre-war patriotism was intensified in schools, as the logbooks show. The evils of the Hun were highlighted by the presence of the children of Belgian refugees taken in by some schools and by relief efforts for them. The armed forces were extolled. St Robert's children, typically, on Trafalgar Day 1915 were given extra lessons on 'How we got command of the sea'. Troops were viewed on the Stray; some schools, like Grove Road or Western, were temporarily taken over to cater for them; pupils, like those of Western, entertained wounded soldiers; money was raised for tanks; and in February 1917 all the town's children went to the Kursaal, soon to be renamed the Royal Hall, to see a government film of *The Battle of the Ancre and Advance of the Tanks*. For girls, the pre-war emphasis on the skills and duties of motherhood was redoubled: 'Baby week' in July 1917 saw those at Grove Road, for example, given oral and practical lessons in the proper treatment of babies and reminded of its 'great necessity' for the 'national interest'.

Many of their former boys went off to fight. From Western, for example, forty-eight died. In total, there are 879 listed as killed on the town's Cenotaph. Private Francis Yates of Oatlands was one of them. We saw him rise from programme boy to assistant stage manager at the Kursaal. He also played the cello and bells, touring with the Municipal Orchestra, and was a footballer, cricketer and athlete. He was killed on the Western Front aged twenty-three on the morning of 28 September 1915, hit in the head by a bullet and never regaining consciousness. This

241

was according to 'his old chum Cliff', in a letter published that October in the *Claro Times*. Another was Alfred Dalby, also of Oatlands, who was just fifteen when he was blown up at Thiepval in February 1916. He had been an apprentice at cabinet maker Slater and Company on West Park.[1]

Some of those Europeans who had come to the town to work also found themselves caught up in the war's fallout. The men of the Schwarz family, who through the Edwardian period had entertained visitors and residents alike, now found themselves taken from their Valley Road home under police- then military guard into internment, eventually at a huge camp on the Isle of Man. Otto, with failing eyesight, was later transferred to Holland, pending return to Germany in August of 1918.[2]

After the war, life in Harrogate in many ways picked up where it had left off. Throughout the inter-war years it was still the leading spa in the country, adapting to changed circumstances by aiming for more, rather than necessarily richer, visitors. Its facilities continued to be extended. The Valley Gardens was provided with a bowling green, tennis courts and a mini-golf course and an elegant colonnade from the entrance opposite the Royal Pump Room to a Sun Pavilion. The Royal Baths were extended in the summer of 1939, with a state-of-the-art treatment block, a Roman 'Fountain' Court and a 'Lounge Hall' fitted out in contemporary 'ocean liner' style. The year before, the borough boundary had been extended once again to take in much of Pannal, old Bilton and outer Starbeck. This partly reflected the resumption of large-scale residential development. Much of this was of private housing, as for example along Leeds Road or between East Parade and High Harrogate. But there were also several developments of public housing, beginning with the St Andrew's estate off Knaresborough Road and later at sites including on Ripon Road and at Bilton Grange.[3] Housing clearance schemes were instituted by the council for Tower Street and Smithy Hill, although in the event were delayed by the outbreak of another war.

When Arthur Mee published *The King's England* at the close of this period, the volume on the West Riding could still write that its fame had 'come through its waters' and laud it as 'Yorkshire's most beautiful town', with 'fine houses and shops and public buildings'. At its heart was the 'magnificent common' of the Stray, 'a perfect setting for the dignified buildings and palatial hotels'.[4] Like works of its kind generally, it did not mention the town's working class, but as this book has sought to demonstrate they were as much a part of it as the visitors and well-to-do residents and their lives have been worth recording.

Notes to Conclusion

1   J. Sheehan, *Harrogate Terriers: The 1/5th Battalion West Yorkshire Regiment in the Great War* (2017), pp. 44 and 119–20; World War One exhibition at St Wilfrid's Church (viewed December 2018).

2   Schwarz, *Waves Roar*, pp. 140–69.

3   Neesam, *History*, pp. 79–90.

4   Mee, A., (ed.), *The King's England: Yorkshire West Riding* (1941), pp. 163–67.

Bibliography

Manuscript Sources

Harrogate Library
Census of the Borough of Harrogate 1901 RG13/4052–5, enumeration
districts 7–30.

Hull History Centre
Port of Hull Society's Sailors' Orphan Homes:
Girls Admissions Register 1863–1916, C DSSF/1/5/2/1.
Mixed Leaving Register 1874–1900, C DSSF/1/6/3/1.

North Yorkshire County Council Record Office, Northallerton
Bar Chapel Registers of Baptisms 1883–1912 and 1912–1969, R/M/ HRG
III 1/1–2.
Bilton Council School Infant Department Admission Register 1907–1939,
S/HRG/1/2/1.
Bilton and Starbeck Board School (New Park Infant Department) Logbook
1897–1911, S/HRG 1/1/1.
Borough of Harrogate Reports of Medical Officer of Health 1907 and
Medical Officer of Health and Sanitary Inspector 1908, DC/HRG/III 36/1.
Borough of Harrogate Shop Hours Act 1904, DC/HRG/III/63/8.
Common Lodging Houses 1910, DC/HRG/III/103/12.
Denmark Street Change of Name to Chatsworth Road 1935, DC/HRG/
III/114/6.
Dragon Parade Methodist Register of Baptisms 1875–1966, R/M/HRG III 2/1.
Grove Road Wesleyan Methodist Baptisms 1893–1917, R/M/HRG III 6/1.
Harrogate Borough Council Education Committee Minute Book 1904–1921,
DC/HRG/II 1/15/11.
Harrogate Higher Grade Board School Logbook 1895–1899, S/HRG 5/1/1.

Harrogate Baptist Church: Minute Books of Committee Meetings and Church Meetings 1876–1928, 1906, 1908 and 1910, R/1/HRG/1–4.

Harrogate Municipal Secondary School Governors' Minute Books 1907–1927, S/HRG 8/1/1.

New Park Mission Rooms Register of Baptisms 1907–1971, R/M/HRG III 4/1.

Oatlands Wesleyan Methodist Chapel Trustees Minutes 1883–1949, R/M/HRG II 8/1/1.

St Peter's School Logbook Mixed and Infants 1870–1896, S/HRG/9/1/1.

——, Logbook Infant School 1892–1923, S/HRG/9/1/2.

——, Logbook Mixed School 1896–1938, S/HRG/9/1/3.

——, Sales Account Book: Sales of pupils' sewing work 1906–1946, S/HRG 9/2.

Skipton Road Individual Property Reports 1949, DC/HRG/III/208/8.

Starbeck Wesleyan Methodist Baptisms 1882–1946, R/M/HRG III 5/1.

J. Turner Taylor, Town Clerk of Harrogate Borough Council, Letter to the Local Government Board 10 April 1907, DC/HRG/III/36/1.

Tower Street and Belford Square Clearance Area, DC/HRG/III/209/3.

Victoria Park Methodist Free Church Register of Baptisms 1892–1913, R/M/HRG III 7/2.

Wesleyan Methodist Band of Hope Admission Book 1899–1910, R/M/HRG II 11/5/12.

West Yorkshire Archive Service, Leeds

Leeds Ladies' Association for the Care and Protection of Friendless Girls: Records of Girls in Service 1889–1940, WYL 416/15.

Minute Books 1898–1915, WYL 416/2–4.

Christ Church Harrogate Register of Baptisms 1894–1902 and 1902–1913, RDP 32/1/9–10.

——, Registers of Marriages 1896–1905 and 1906–1918, RDP 32/2/5–6.

St Luke Harrogate Register of Baptisms 1897–1905, RDP 33/1/1.

——, Register of Marriages 1901–1919, RDP 33/2/2.

St Mark Harrogate Register of Baptisms 1893–1916, RDP 34/1/1.

——, Registers of Marriages 1900–1908 and 1908–1915, RDP 34/2/1–2.

St Peter's Harrogate Registers of Marriages 1890–1911 and 1911- 1923, RDP 36/2/2–3.

Harrogate Borough Council

Deeds to Properties in Tower Street, Harrogate.

Churches

Harlow Hill Free Methodist Church Baptisms Register 1903-present.

St Wilfrid's Harrogate Register of Baptisms 1902–1967.

——, Register of Marriages 1907–1920.

Trinity Wesleyan Chapel Harrogate Register of Baptisms 1880–1973.

——, Register of Marriages 1880–1924.

Wesleyan Methodist Chapel Harrogate Register of Baptisms 1883–1913.

——, Register of Marriages 1913–1919.

Schools

Grove Road Community Primary School:

Grove Road Board School Mixed Department Logbook 1897–1918.

Grove Road Council School Mixed Department Admission Register 1899–1913.

Oatlands Infant School:

Oatlands Mount Church of England School Logbook 1880–1893.

Oatlands Mount School Infants Logbook 1893–1903.

Oatlands Mount Board School Logbook 1897–1965.

——, Punishment Book 1900–1935.

St Robert's Catholic Primary School:

St Robert's Mixed School Logbook 1888–1916.

St Robert's Infants Logbook 1899–1923.

Starbeck Primary Academy:

Albert Avenue School Starbeck Infants Logbook 1894–1916.

——, Infants Admission Register 1894–1901.

——, Infants Admission Register 1901–1912.

Western Primary School:

Low Harrogate St Mary's National School Logbook 1872–1896.

Western Board School Logbook 1896–1901.

Western Board School and Western Council School Infants Logbook 1897–1918.

——, Logbook 1901–1921.

www.ancestry.co.uk

Census of the Borough of Harrogate 1911, RG14 489/2, enumeration
 districts 1–24.

Printed Sources

Official publications

*Report of Dr J. Spencer Lowe to the Local Government Board on the Sanitary
 Circumstances and Administration of the Three Sanitary Districts within the
 Knaresborough Registration District* (London: HMSO, 1908).

General Register Office, Census 1951: Classification of Occupations (London: HMSO, 1956).

Wages of Domestic Servants. Board of Trade (Labour Department) Report by Miss Collet on the Money wages of Indoor Domestic Servants; PP 1899 [C.– 9346] XCII.1.

Report on the Standard Time Rate of Wages in the United Kingdom in 1900 with Comparative Tables; PP 1900 [Cd. 317] LXXXII.335.

Annual Report of the chief Inspector of Factories and Workshops for the Year 1900; PP 1901 [Cd. 668] X.1.

Census of England and Wales 1901, Area, houses and population, also population classified by ages, condition as to marriage, occupations, birthplaces and infirmities, County of York; PP 1902 [Cd. 1107] CXXI.639.

Census of England and Wales 1901, General Report with Appendices; PP 1904 [Cd. 2174] CVII.

Report of an Enquiry by the Board of Trade into Working Class Rents, Housing and Retail Prices, together with the Standard Rates of Wages Prevailing in Certain Occupations in the Principal Industrial Towns of the United Kingdom; PP 1908 [Cd. 3864] CVII.

Census of England and Wales 1911, Area, families or separate occupiers, and population, Vol. 1: Administrative areas, Counties, urban and rural districts etc.; PP 1912–13 [Cd. 6258] CXI.1.

Census of England and Wales 1911, Families or separate occupiers, and population, Vol. VI: Buildings of various kinds; PP 1912–13 [Cd. 6577] CXIII.1.

Census of England and Wales 1911, Vol. VII: Ages and condition as to marriage in administrative counties, urban and rural districts, and registration counties and districts; PP 1912–13 [Cd. 6610] CXIII.379.

Census of England and Wales 1911, Vol. VIII: Tenements in administrative counties and urban and rural districts; PP 1913 [Cd. 6910] LXXVII.1.

Census of England and Wales 1911, Vol. IX: Birthplaces of persons enumerated in administrative counties, county boroughs etc. and ages and occupations of foreigners; PP 1913 [Cd. 7017] LXXVIII.1.

Census of England and Wales 1911, Vol. X: Occupations and Industries, Part 1; PP 1913 [Cd. 7018] LXXVIII.321.

Census of England and Wales 1911, General Report with Appendices; PP 1917–18 [Cd. 8491] XXXV.483.

Department of Education, all Schools and Colleges in North Yorkshire, pupil absence in schools in 2017 and 2018 at www.compare-school-performance.service.gov.uk.

Hansard, 3rd Series, vol. 199, cols 438–66 (17 February 1870).

Newspapers and periodicals

Gentleman's Journal and Gentlewoman's Court Review.

Harrogate Advertiser.
Harrogate Herald.
Leeds and Yorkshire Mercury.
Yorkshire Evening Post.
Yorkshire Observer.

Directories

Ackrill's Harrogate Directory 1867 and 1873 (Harrogate, 1867 and 1873).
*Robinson's Harrogate, Knaresborough, Ripon, Pateley Bridge & District
Directory 1900 and 1902* (Leeds, 1900 and 1902).
Robinson's Harrogate, Knaresborough and District Directory 1911 (Leeds, 1910).
*Robinson's Harrogate, Knaresborough, Wetherby and District Directory 1912
and 1914* (Leeds, 1911 and 1913).

Other printed sources and novels

Borough of Harrogate Committee Minutes, 5 vols 1907–1916 (Harrogate).
Female Servants Home Society: Annual Reports 1890–1901 (Leeds, 1901).
Harrogate Corporation Act 1893
Harrogate Congregational Church Manuals 1902–1912 (Harrogate).
Leeds Industrial School for Girls and Boys Refuge: Annual Reports
1860–1886 and 1887–1909 (Leeds).
Moore, G., *Esther Waters* (Oxford: Oxford University Press, 2012, first pub.
1894).
Thomson, A. A., *The Exquisite Burden* (Harrogate: Manor Place Press, 2003,
first pub. 1935).
Tressell, R., *The Ragged Trousered Philanthropists* (London: Penguin, 2004,
first pub. 1914).
Wells, H. G., *Kipps* (London: Penguin, 2005, first pub. 1905).

Secondary Sources

Contemporary works

Anon., *Downward Paths: An inquiry into the causes which contribute to the
making of the prostitute* (London: G. Bell and Sons, 1916).
A Servant, *The Conditions of Domestic Service By A Servant: A book for
masters, mistresses and servants* (London, 1894).
Barnett, M. G., *Young Delinquents: A study of reformatory and industrial
schools* (London: Methuen, 1913).
Beeton, I., *The Book of Household Management* (London, Ward, Lock,

Bowden & Co, 1891, first pub. 1861).

Booth, C., *Life and Labour of the People in London* (London: Macmillan, 1902).

Bosanquet, H., *The Family* (London: Macmillan, 1906).

Bowley, A. L. and Burnett-Hurst, A. R., *Livelihood and Poverty: A study of the economic conditions of working-class households in Northampton, Warrington, Stanley and Reading* (London: G. Bell and Sons, 1915).

Bray, R. A., *Boy Labour and Apprenticeship* (London: Constable & Co, 1912).

Butler, C. V., *Social Conditions in Oxford* (London: Sidgwick & Jackson, 1912).

———, *Domestic Service: An enquiry by the Women's Industrial Council* (London: G. Bell and Sons, 1916).

Cadbury, E., et al., *Women's Work and Wages: A phase of life in an industrial city* (London: T. Fisher Unwin, 1906).

Cloete, J. G., 'The Boy and his Work', in Urwick, E. J. (ed.), *Studies of Boy Life in Our Cities* (London: J. M. Dent, 1904), pp. 102–38.

Dearle, N. B., *Problems of Unemployment in the London Building Trades* (London: J. M. Dent, 1908).

Drake, B., 'The West End tailoring trade' and 'The waiter', in Webb, S. and Freeman, A. (eds), *Seasonal Trades* (London: Constable, 1912), pp. 70–91 and 92–106.

Freeman, A., *Boy Life & Labour: The manufacture of inefficiency* (London: P. S. King & Son, 1914).

Hallsworth, J. and Davies, R. J., *The Working Life of Shop Assistants: A study of conditions of labour in the distributive trades* (Manchester: The National Labour Press, 1910).

Jebb, E., *Cambridge: A brief study in social questions* (Cambridge: Macmillan & Bowes, 1906).

Layton, W. T., 'Changes in the wages of domestic servants during fifty years', *Journal of the Royal Statistical Society*, 71 (1908), pp. 515–24.

Papworth. L. W., 'Charwomen', in Black, C. (ed.), *Married Women's Work: Being the report of an enquiry undertaken by the Women's Industrial Council* (London: G. Bell and Sons, 1915), pp. 105–13.

Popplewell, F., 'The gas industry' in Webb and Freeman, *Seasonal Trades*, pp. 148–209.

Poynte, J. S., 'Seasonal trades', in Webb and Freeman, *Seasonal Trades*, pp. 1–69.

Rowntree, B. S., *Poverty: A study of town life* (London: Macmillan, 1903, first pub. 1901).

Webb, A. D., 'The building trade', in Webb and Freeman, *Seasonal Trades*, pp. 312–93.

Wells, H. G., *Experiment in Autobiography: Discoveries and conclusions of a very ordinary brain (since 1866)* (London: Gollancz, 1934).

Whitehouse, J. H., 'The reform of elementary education', in Whitehouse (ed.), *Problems of Boy Life* (London: P. S. King & Son, 1912), pp. 2–16.

Local works

Abbott, S. G., *Starbeck: A journey through the past* (Starbeck: author, n. d.).

- *The Spirit of Starbeck* (Ashbourne: Landmark, 2003).

Anon., *1887 to 1908 21 Years of Progress: The Harrogate & District Co-operative Society, Ltd* (Harrogate, 1908).

——, *A Short History of Bilton Grange United Reform Church 1928–1978* (Harrogate, 1978).

——, *Evangelical Free Church Harrogate Centenary 1872–1972* (Harrogate, 1972).

——, *'Fifty Years': The handbook of the Jubilee celebrations of the Grove Road Methodist Church Harrogate October 1946* (Harrogate, 1946).

——, *Harlow Hill Methodist Church 1903–1978: 75th anniversary* (Harrogate, 1978).

——, *Harrogate Town Mission Mayfield Grove Jubilee Souvenir 1872–1922* (Harrogate, 1922).

——, *Primitive Methodist Church Harrogate Circuit Starbeck Jubilee Souvenir 1878–1928: Bazaar handbook* (Harrogate, 1928).

——, *Starbeck Mission (formerly Railway Mission) Forest Avenue 1886–1986* (Harrogate, 1986).

——, *The Bar Methodist Church Harrogate: Jubilee handbook 1889–1939* (Harrogate, 1939).

——, *The Quaker Meetings of Knaresborough and Harrogate* (Harrogate, 1984).

——, *Trinity Wesleyan Church Harrogate Jubilee 1879–1929* (Harrogate, 1929).

Beaver, P., *A Pedlar's Legacy: The origins and history of Empire Stores 1831–1981* (London: Henry Melland, 1981).

Broadbank, P., *Twentieth Century Housing Development in Harrogate; A study of development in the town* (Harrogate: author, 2003).

Carpenter, D., *Ilkley: The Victorian Era* (Otley: Smith Settle, 1986).

Chapman, M. and B. *The Pierrots of the Yorkshire Coast* (Beverley: Hutton Press, 1988).

Clayton, L., *Oatlands Infant School: A centenary celebration* (Harrogate, 1997).

Deane, E., *Spadacrene Anglica or the English Spa Fountain* (London: Simpkin, Marshall, Hamilton, Kent, 1922, first pub. 1626).

East, G. C., *The Constables of Claro: A history of policing in Harrogate and District* (Harrogate: author, 1996).

Forshaw, B., *A History of Harrogate Rugby Club 1871–2011* (Harrogate: Harrogate RUFC, 2011).

Grainge, W., *The History and Topography of Harrogate and the Forest of Knaresborough* (Guiseley: M. T. D. Rigg, 1988, first pub. 1871).

Greaves, G. L., *Over the Summers Again: A history of Harrogate Cricket Club* (Harrogate: Harrogate Cricket Club, 1976).

Greenwood, C. G., *The Story of St Andrew's Church, Starbeck 1910–1935* (Harrogate, 1935).

Grizzard, N., 'Demographic: the Jewish population of Leeds – how many Jews?', in Fraser, D., *Leeds and its Jewish Community: A history* (Manchester: Manchester University Press, 2019).

Guy, Canon, *A Memento of 23 Years Work in Christ Church Harrogate 1904–1926* (Harrogate, 1926).

Hallows, M. P. F. and Smith, D. H., *Harrogate Gas Works: Its railways and other transport systems* (Narrow Gauge Railway Society, 1995).

Harrison, P., *The History of Harrogate Town Football Club: Highlights from a bygone era* (Ripon: Phil/Car, 2004).

——, *The Official History of Harrogate Town Football Club* (Ripon: Phil/Car, 2010).

Jennings, B. (ed.), *A History of Harrogate & Knaresborough* (Huddersfield: Advertiser Press, 1970).

Kellett, A., *The Oatlands Story 1883–1983: A brief history of Oatlands Methodist Church* (Harrogate, 1983).

Kitchen, H. S. and Dawson, T. E., *Wesley Chapel Harrogate 1862–1962* (Harrogate, 1962).

Leach, T. M., *'Twopenny Single to Starbeck': Early public transport in the Harrogate area* (Keighley: West Yorkshire Information Service, 2000).

Livshin, R. D., *The History of the Harrogate Jewish Community* (Leeds: Leeds University Press, 1995).

Mee. A., (ed.), *The King's England: Yorkshire West Riding* (London: Hodder and Stoughton, 1941).

Neesam, M., *Exclusively Harrogate* (Otley: Smith Settle, 1989).

——, *The Archive Photograph Series: Harrogate* (Stroud: Chalford, 1995).

——, *Hotel Majestic* (Paramount Hotels, 2000).

——, *History & Guide: Harrogate: A history of the English spa from earliest times to the present* (Stroud: Tempus, 2001).

——, *Harrogate Grammar School: A centennial history* (Harrogate: Manor Place Press, 2003).

——, *Harrogate Great Chronicle, 1332–1841* (Lancaster: Carnegie, 2005).

——, *Ogden Harrogate: 120 years – a history of a family business* (Harrogate: Manor Place Press, 2013).

——, *Music Over the Waters* (Harrogate: Manor Place Press, 2017).

——, *Harrogate in 50 Buildings* (Stroud: Amberley, 2018).

——, *A-Z of Harrogate: Places – people - history* (Stroud: Amberley, 2019).

Neesam, M., et al., *Kursaal: A history of Harrogate's Royal Hall* (Harrogate: Harrogate International Centre, 2008).

Patmore, J. A., *An Atlas of Harrogate* (Harrogate: Corporation of Harrogate, 1963).

Rogers, J., *The Railways of Harrogate and District* (North Eastern Railway Association, 2000).

Schwarz, D. K., *The Waves Roar: A Kapelmeister's journey* (author, 2011).

Sheehan, J., *Harrogate Terriers: The 1/5th Territorial Battalion West Yorkshire Regiment in the Great War* (Barnsley: Pen and Sword, 2017).

Smith, A., *Harrogate Baptist Church Centenary 1880–1980* (Harrogate, 1980).

Steele, E. N., *Grove Road School 1897–1997* (Harrogate, 1997).

Sunderland, T., *United Methodist Church Victoria Park Harrogate Jubilee 1865–1915* (Harrogate, 1915).

Taylor, M. H (ed.), *Alice's Story: This was my childhood* (Ripon: Ripon Civic Society, 1991).

Thrower, G., 'Centenary History of Bilton Social Club 1910–2010' (unpublished typescript, 2009 at Bilton Historical Society).

Walker, H. H., *History of Harrogate under the Improvement Commissioners 1841–1884* (Harrogate: Manor Place Press, 1986).

Wigley, A. L., *Dragon Parade Methodist Church 1900–1950: Souvenir handbook of the Jubilee celebrations* (Harrogate, 1950).

Williams, T., *A Pictorial History of New Park Harrogate* (Chorley: Countryside Publications, 1984).

Younge, M., (ed.), *Echoes From Ripon's Past* (Ripon: Ripon Local Studies Research Centre, 2004).

General works

Anderson, M., 'The social implications of demographic change', in Thompson, F. M. L., *The Cambridge Social History of Britain, Vol. 2: People and their environment* (Cambridge: Cambridge University Press, 1990), pp. 1–70.

Armstrong, W. A., 'The use of information about occupation', in Wrigley, E. A., *Nineteenth-century Society: Essays in the use of quantitative methods for the study of social data* (Cambridge: Cambridge University Press, 1972), pp. 191–310.

August, A., *The British Working Class 1832–1940* (Harlow: Pearson Education, 2007).

Bagwell, P. S., *The Railwaymen: The history of the National Union of Railwaymen* (London: George Allen & Unwin, 1963).

Behlmer, G. K., *Child Abuse and Moral Reform in England, 1870–1908* (Stanford: Stanford University Press, 1982).

Benson, J., *The Penny Capitalists: A study of nineteenth-century working-class entrepreneurs* (Dublin: Gill and Macmillan, 1983).

——, *The Working Class in Britain 1850–1939* (London: I. B. Tauris, 2003, first pub. 1989).

——, *The Rise of Consumer Society in Britain 1880–1980* (London: Longman, 1994).

Best, G., *Mid-Victorian Britain* (London: Fontana, 1979).

Blackbourn, D., 'Fashionable spa towns in nineteenth-century Europe', in Anderson, S. C. and Tabb, B. H. (eds), *Water, Leisure and Culture: European historical perspectives* (Oxford: Berg, 2002), pp. 9–21.

Bourke, J., *Working-Class Cultures in Britain 1890–1960: Gender, class and ethnicity* (London: Routledge, 1994).

——, 'Housewifery in working-class England 1860–1914', *Past and Present*, 143 (1994), pp. 167–97.

Briggs, A., *Victorian Cities* (Harmondsworth: Penguin, 1968).

Canadine, D., *Class in Britain* (London: Penguin, 2000).

Chase, M., 'Twentieth-century labour histories', in Dyer, C., *et al* (eds), *New Directions in Local History Since Hoskins* (Hatfield: University of Hertfordshire Press, 2011), pp. 54–65.

Childs, M. J., *Labour's Apprentices: Working-class lads in late Victorian and Edwardian England* (London: Hambledon Press, 1992).

Clapson, M., *'A Bit of a Flutter': Popular gambling and English society c. 1823–1961* (Manchester: Manchester University Press, 1992).

Clark, A., *The Struggle for the Breeches: Gender and the making of the British working class* (London: Rivers Oram Press, 1995).

Clarke, P., *Hope and Glory: Britain 1900–2000* (London: Penguin, 1997).

Crossick, G. 'The emergence of the lower middle class in Britain: a discussion', in Crossick (ed.), *The Lower Middle Class in Britain 1870–1914* (London: Croom Helm, 1977), pp. 11–60.

Crow, G., *What Are Community Studies?* (London: Bloomsbury Academic, 2018).

Davis, G., '"The scum of Bath": The Victorian poor', in Stapleton, B. (ed.), *Conflict and Community in Southern England: Essays in the social history of rural and urban labour from medieval to modern times* (Stroud: Alan Sutton, 1992), pp. 183–98.

——, *Bath as Spa and Bath as slum: The social history of a Victorian city* (Lewiston NY: Edwin Mellen Press, 2009).

Delap, L., *Knowing Their Place: Domestic service in twentieth-century Britain* (Oxford: Oxford University Press, 2011).

Dennis, R., *English Industrial Cities of the Nineteenth Century: A social geography* (Cambridge: Cambridge University Press, 1984).

——, and Daniels, S., 'Community and the social geography of Victorian cities', in Drake, M. (ed.), *Time, Family and Community: Perspectives on family and community history* (Oxford: Blackwell, 1994), pp. 201–24.

Duncan, R., *Pubs and Patriots: The drink crisis in Britain during World War One* (Liverpool: Liverpool University Press, 2013).

Dwork, D., *War is Good for Babies and Other Young Children: A history of the infant and child welfare movement in England 1898–1918* (London: Tavistock, 1987).

Ebery, M. G. and Preston, B. T., *Domestic Service in Late Victorian and Edwardian England 1871–1914* (Reading: Department of Geography, University of Reading, 1976).

Ferguson, H., 'Cleveland in history: the abused child and child protection, 1880–1914', in Cooter, R. (ed.), *In the name of the Child: Health and welfare, 1880–1940* (London: Routledge, 1992), pp. 146–73.

Floud, R. and Johnson, P., *The Cambridge Economic History of Modern Britain, Vol. II: Economic maturity 1860–1939* (Cambridge: Cambridge University Press, 2004).

Gillis, J. R., 'The evolution of juvenile delinquency in England 1890–1914', *Past and Present*, 67 (1975), pp. 96–126.

——, 'Servants, sexual relations, and the risks of illegitimacy in London, 1801–1900', *Feminist Studies*, 5:1 (1979), pp. 142–73.

Godfrey, B., et al., *Young Criminal Lives: Life courses and life chances from 1850* (Oxford: Oxford University Press, 2017).

Goreau, A., 'Introduction' to Brontë, A, *Agnes Grey* (London: Penguin, 1988, first pub. 1847), pp. 7–47.

Gray, R., *The Aristocracy of Labour in Nineteenth-century Britain c. 1850–1914* (London: Macmillan, 1981).

Green, S. J. D., *Religion in the Age of Decline: Organisation and experience in industrial Yorkshire 1870–1920* (Cambridge: Cambridge University Press, 1996).

Harris, J., *Private Lives, Public Spirit: Britain 1870–1914* (London: Penguin, 1994).

Heathorn, S., *For Home, Country and Race: Constructing gender, class and Englishness in the elementary school, 1880–1914* (London: University of Toronto Press, 2000).

Heywood, J. S., *Children in Care: The development of the service for the deprived child* (London: Routledge & Kegan Paul, rev. 2nd ed. 1965).

Higgs, E., 'Domestic servants and households in Victorian England', *Social History*, 8:2 (1983), pp. 201–10.

——, 'Domestic servants and household production', in John, A. V. (ed.), *Unequal Opportunities: Women's employment in England 1800–1918* (Oxford: Basil Blackwell, 1986), pp. 125–50.

——, Women, occupations and work in the nineteenth century', *History Workshop Journal*, 23 (1987), pp. 59–80.

——, *Making sense of the Census Revisited: A handbook for historical researchers* (London: National Archives, 2005).

Hobsbawm, E. J., *Labouring Men: Studies in the history of labour* (London: Weidenfeld and Nicolson, 1968).

——, *Worlds of Labour: Further studies in the history of labour* (London: Weidenfeld and Nicolson, 1984).

Hoggart, R., *The Uses of Literacy* (Harmondsworth: Penguin, 1958).

Holcombe, L., *Victorian Ladies at Work: Middle-class working women in England and Wales 1850–1914* (Newton Abbot: David & Charles, 1973).

Holmes, V., 'Accommodating the lodger: the domestic arrangements of lodgers in working-class dwellings in a Victorian provincial town', *Journal of Victorian Culture*, 19:3 (2014), pp. 314–31.

Hopkins, E., *A Social History of the English Working Class 1815–1945* (London: Longman, 1979).

Horn, P., *Labouring Life in the Victorian Countryside* (Gloucester: Alan Sutton, 1987, first pub. 1976).

——, *The Victorian and Edwardian Schoolchild* (Stroud: Amberley, 2010, first pub. 1989).

Hosgood, C. P., ''The "pigmies of commerce" and the working-class community: small shopkeepers in England, 1870–1914', in Benson, J. and Shaw, G. (eds), *The Retailing Industry, Vol. 2: The coming of the mass market 1800–1945* (London: I. B. Tauris, 1999), pp. 393–413.

——, '"Mercantile monasteries": shops, shop assistants and shop life in late-Victorian and Edwardian Britain', *Journal of British Studies*, 38:3 (1999), pp. 322–52.

Humphries, S., *Hooligans or Rebels? An Oral History of Working-Class Childhood and Youth 1889–1939* (Oxford: Basil Blackwell, 1981).

Irving, R. J., *The North Eastern Railway Company 1870–1914: An economic history* (Leicester: Leicester University Press, 1976).

James, L., *The Middle Class: A history* (London: Abacus, 2008).

Jefferys, J. B., *Retail Trading in Britain 1850–1950* (Cambridge: Cambridge University Press, 1954).

Jennings, P., *The Public House in Bradford, 1770–1970* (Keele: Keele University Press, 1995).

——, *The Local: A History of the English Pub* (Stroud: The History Press, rev. 3rd ed. 2021, first pub. 2007).

——, 'Policing drunkenness in England and Wales from the late eighteenth century to the First World War', *The Social History of Alcohol and Drugs*, 26:1 (2012), pp. 69–92.

——, *A History of Drink and the English 1500–2000* (Abingdon: Routledge, 2016).

Johnson, P., *Saving and Spending: The working-class economy in Britain 1870–1939* (Oxford: Clarendon Press, 1985).

——, 'Conspicuous consumption and working-class culture in late-Victorian and Edwardian Britain', *Transactions of the Royal Historical Society*, 38 (1988), pp. 27–42.

Jones, G. Stedman., *Languages of Class: Studies in English working-class history 1832–1982* (Cambridge: Cambridge University Press, 1983).

——, *Outcast London: A study in the relationship between classes in Victorian Society* (London: Penguin, 2nd rev. ed. 1984, first pub. 1971).

Joyce, P., *Visions of the People: Industrial England and the question of class 1848–1914* (Cambridge: Cambridge University Press, 1991).

——, *Democratic Subjects: The self and the social in nineteenth century England* (Cambridge: Cambridge University Press, 1994).

Knodel, J., 'An exercise on household composition for use in courses on historical demography', *Local Population Studies*, 23 (1979), pp. 10–23.

Langhamer, C., *Women's Leisure in England 1920–1960* (Manchester: Manchester University Press, 2000).

Laybourn, K., 'The new philanthropy of the Edwardian age: the Guild of Help and the Halifax Citizens' Guild, 1905–1918', *Transactions of the Halifax Antiquarian Society*, 23 (2015), pp. 73–94.

Lewis, S., '"A resort of the common people in great troops" – Llandrindod Wells Spa and its workers in the late nineteenth an early twentieth centuries', *The Transactions of the Radnorshire Society*, 76 (2006), pp. 144–67.

McBride, T. M., *The Domestic Revolution: The Modernisation of household service in England and France 1820–1920* (London: Croom Helm, 1976).

McKibbin, R., 'Work and Hobbies in Britain, 1880–1950', in Winter, J. (ed.), *The Working Class in Modern British History: Essays in honour of Henry Pelling* (Cambridge: Cambridge University Press, 1983), pp. 139–66.

——, 'The franchise factor in the rise of the Labour Party', in McKibbin, *The Ideologies of Class: Social relations in Britain 1880–1950* (Oxford: Clarendon Press, 1990), pp. 66–100.

McLeod, H., *Religion and Society in England, 1850–1914* (Houndmills: Macmillan, 1996).

Malcolmson, P., *English Laundresses: A social history 1850–1930* (Urbana: University of Illinois Press, 1986).

Mason, T., *Association Football & English Society 1863–1915* (Brighton: Harvester Press, 1980).

Miles, A., *Social Mobility in Nineteenth- and Early Twentieth-Century England* (Houndmills: Macmillan, 1999).

Morris, C., (ed.), *The Journeys of Celia Fiennes* (London: Cresset Press, 1947).

Murray, P., *Poverty and Welfare 1830–1914* (London: Hodder & Stoughton, 1999).

Musgrave, P. W., 'Corporal punishment in some English elementary schools, 1900–1939', *Research in Education*, 17 (1977), pp. 1–11.

Nicolson, C., 'Edwardian England and the coming of the First World War', in O'Day, A. (ed.), *The Edwardian Age: Conflict and stability 1900–1914* (London: Macmillan, 1979).

Oddy, D. J., 'Working-class diets in late-nineteenth century Britain', *Economic History Review*, 23:2 (1970), pp. 314–23.

Olsen, S., *Juvenile Nation: Youth, emotions and the making of the modern British citizen, 1880–1914* (London: Bloomsbury, 2014).

Page, S. J., 'Lodging and poverty in late Victorian Leicester: a socio-geo-graphic perspective', *Transactions of the Leicestershire Archaeological and Historical Society*, 68 (1994), pp. 121–44.

Panayi, P., 'Sausages, waiters and bakers: German migrants and cultural transfer to Britain, c. 1850–1914', in Manz, S., *et al* (eds), *Migration and Transfer from Germany to Britain 1660–1914* (Munich: K. G. Saur, 2007).

Pelling, H., *Popular Politics and Society in Late Victorian Britain* (London: Macmillan, 1968).

——, *A History of British Trade Unionism* (Harmondsworth: Penguin, 2nd ed. 1971).

Peterson, M. J., 'The Victorian governess: status incongruence in family and society', *Victorian Studies*, 14:1 (1970), pp. 7–26.

Phillips, R., *Untying the Knot: A short history of divorce* (Cambridge: Cambridge University Press, 1991).

Pooley, S., 'Domestic servants and their urban employers: a case study of Lancaster, 1880–1914', *Economic History Review*, 62:2 (2009), pp. 405–29.

Postgate, R. W., *The Builders' History* (London: Labour Publishing, 1923).

Price, R., *An Imperial War and the British Working Class: Working-Class Attitudes and reactions to the Boer War 1899–1902* (London: Routledge & Kegan Paul, 1972).

——, *Masters, Unions and Men: Work control in building and the rise of labour 1830–1914* (Cambridge: Cambridge University Press, 1980).

Prochaska, F., 'Female philanthropy and domestic service in Victorian England', *Bulletin of the Institute of Historical Research*, 54:129 (1981), pp. 79–85.

Rappaport, E. D., *Shopping for Pleasure: Women in the making of London's West End* (Princeton: Princeton University Press, 2000).

Read, D., *England 1868–1914* (London: Longman, 1979).

Reid, A. J., *Social Classes and Social Relations in Britain, 1850–1914* (Basingstoke: Macmillan, 1992).

Roberts, E., 'Working-Class Standards of Living in Barrow and Lancaster, 1890–1914', *Economic History Review*, 30:2 (1977), pp. 306–21.

——, *A Woman's Place: An oral history of working-class women 1890–1940* (Oxford: Basil Blackwell, 1984).

Roberts, R., *The Classic Slum: Salford life in the first quarter of the century* (Harmondsworth: Penguin, 1973, first pub. 1971).

Ross, E., '"Not the sort that would sit on the doorstep": respectability in pre-World War 1 London neighbourhoods', *International Labor and Working Class History*, 27 (1985), pp. 39–59.

Rowbotham, S., 'Search and subject, threading circumstance', in Rowbotham, *Dreams and Dilemmas: Collected writings* (London: Virago, 1983), pp. 166–89.

Rubinstein, D., 'Cycling in the 1890s', *Victorian Studies*, 21:1 (1977), pp. 47–71.

Russell, D., *Popular Music in England 1840–1914: A social history* (Manchester: Manchester University Press, 1987).

Savage, M. and Miles, A., *The Remaking of the British Working Class 1840–1940* (London: Routledge, 1994).

Searle, G. R., *The Quest for National Efficiency; A study in British politics and political thought, 1899–1914* (London: Ashfield Press, 1990, first pub. 1971).

——, *A New England? Peace and War 1886–1914* (Oxford: Clarendon Press, 2004).

Sherborne, M., *H. G. Wells: Another kind of life* (London: Peter Owen, 2012).

Simon, B., *Education and the Labour Movement 1870–1920* (London: Laurence & Wishart, 1965).

Springhall, J., *Youth, Empire and Society: British youth movements, 1880–1940* (London: Croom Helm, 1977).

Szreter, S. R. S., 'The genesis of the Registrar-General's social classification of occupations', *British Journal of Sociology*, 35:4 (1984), pp. 522–46.

Thompson, F. M. L., *The Rise of Respectable Society: A social history of Victorian Britain 1830–1900* (London: Fontana, 1988).

Thompson, P., *The Edwardians: The remaking of British society* (London: Weidenfeld and Nicolson, 1975).

Turnbull, A., 'Learning her womanly work: the elementary school curriculum, 1870–1914', in Hunt, F., (ed.), *Lessons for Life: The Schooling of Girls and Women 1850–1950* (Oxford: Basil Blackwell, 1987), pp. 83–100.

Waller, P. J., *Town, City and Nation: England 1850–1914* (Oxford: Oxford University Press, 1983).

Walton, J., *The Blackpool Landlady* (Manchester: Manchester University Press, 1978).

——, and McGloin, P. R., 'Holiday resorts and their visitors: some sources for the local historian', *The Local Historian*, 13:6 (1979), pp. 323–31.

——, and Walvin, J., 'Introduction' in Walton and Walvin (eds), *Leisure in Britain 1780–1939* (Manchester: Manchester University Press, 1983).

Walvin, J., *A Child's World: A social history of English childhood 1800–1914* (Harmondsworth: Penguin, 1982).

Whitaker, W. B., *Victorian and Edwardian Shop Workers: The struggle to obtain better conditions and a half-holiday* (Newton Abbot: David & Charles, 1973).

Wilcox, P., 'Marriage, mobility and domestic service in Victorian Cambridge', *Local Population Studies*, 29 (1982), pp. 19–34.

Williams, A., *A Detested Occupation? A history of domestic servants in North Wales 1800–1930* (Llanrwst: Gwasg Carreg Gwalch, 2016).

Williams, R., *Keywords: A vocabulary of culture and society* (London: Fontana, 1983).

Index